Christian

an Introdu
Western Tradition

Christian History:
an Introduction to the
Western Tradition

Diarmaid MacCulloch

 EPWORTH

To W. C. Sellar and R. J. Yeatman
who wrote a much better history textbook than this one

British Library Cataloguing in Publication data

A catalogue record for this book is available
from the British Library

978 0 7162 0624 8

First published in 1987 by Epworth Press as
Groundwork of Christian History.
Published by Epworth in 2006
Second impression 2010

Printed and bound in Great Britain by
CPI Antony Rowe, Chippenham, Wiltshire

Contents

Preface

So many debts lie behind the writing of this book that I will only single out a few for particular mention. I am indebted to the late Professor Sir Geoffrey Elton for giving me my training in historical research, to the Editorial Committee of Epworth Press for stimulating me to write this book, to Mr Sean Gill for reading and commenting on part of the text, to the late Mrs Ann Warden for constant secretarial help, and now to Dr Natalie Watson for her expert assistance in renewing this text. As with every teacher who turns to writing, I am chiefly grateful to all those whom I have taught: who with their questions, with their enthusiasm and their boredom have taught me to look at problems afresh, and to look beyond my own priorities and interests.

St Cross College, Oxford,   Diarmaid MacCulloch
August 2006

Chapter One

Introduction: What is Christian History?

History is one of those unfortunate subjects which suffers from the way in which it is taught at school. This is probably less true today than it was a few generations back, but however well schools deal with history there will always be a problem. Like mathematics, it is a subject which demands a large amount of factual input before it begins to make any sense or before it can begin to be used in an exciting way: if maths is built on 'times tables', history also has basic building blocks like the dates of the Kings and Queens of England. This book contains some of these building blocks – dates and a narrative of events – yet it also tries to set in motion the questions which historians ask of these events: not just when and how something happened, but why it happened, and what its consequences were. It is when we ask these questions that history can cease to be a dull grind of facts, and become something to enjoy and explore. The ancient Greeks created a goddess called Clio to look after historians, who ought to remember that she started her career as a goddess of song. Woe betide them if they forget that they are supposed to entertain and delight as well as to instruct.

Is history any use? What is the point of spending time reading a book like this? Putting it crudely, it is to stop you going mad. Those who have no history are always on the verge of insanity. When individual people lose their memory, they find it a very distressing experience; history is like a collective memory, the recollections of a nation, of a culture, or of the entire world. When a nation forgets its history, or worse still, invents a history to take the place of the facts, the consequences are tragic. The proof o that can be seen by looking at what happened in Nazi Germany half a century ago; there Hitler began rebuilding a whole society on lies about the past, filling the past with demons, of which the worst were the Jews. Under the influence of these lies, ordinary, decent human beings became accomplices in some of the most horrific crimes which humanity has ever committed. There are plenty of other examples, perhaps the most chilling coming from the world of fiction. In the novel *1984*, George Orwell created a world where those in power could never be defeated or removed because they were always right; they were always right because they constantly rewrote the past to show that they were always right. They removed the possibility of change from the world by removing the consciousness from people's minds that change could take place.

I hope that I can rest my case! However, we might go on to ask if there is any use in making a particular exploration of Christian history. After all, there are some ways in which a historian can never be of any use to religious faith. Jacob Neusner, a historian of Judaism and early Christianity, recently asked 'what "critical historical" facts can ever testify to the truth or falsity of salvation, holiness, joy and love?' There is no answer to that; but there are ways in which history can play a vital role for the Christian faith. I hope that it does not sound too flippant if I describe Christianity as a personality cult: for at the heart of the Christian message is an individual person, an aspect of the God who was, is, and ever shall be, yet who is at the same time a human being set in historic time. The Christian faith necessarily involves a meeting with this person, although Christians have talked about this meeting in a huge variety of ways. All such meetings, the earliest of which are recorded in the canon of the Christian scripture, represent single fragments of the experience of a whole community with a memory over time: the church. The church symbolizes this ever-repeated meeting in its central act: the Lord's Supper.

Christian faith is thus a great series of ever-changing meetings with an unchanging personality: a series which collectively forms the tradition of the church which in turn regulates its faith. The tradition has a past and a future. In the most solemn statement of this tradition prepared after three and a half centuries' reflection, the Nicene Creed, there is embedded a historical statement, placed there with what can only be termed calculated effrontery:

'He suffered under Pontius Pilate.' Amid statements of eternal truth, we are pulled rudely into the human world: not in the time of *any* provincial governor, but under Pontius Pilate, at a given moment in the sequence of time.

So Christian faith is profoundly historic, in a way that is not found in great world religions outside the family of Judaism, Christianity and Islam. The Christian faith therefore has a special relationship with historians, but what is the relationship to be? In the experience of the West, four main attitudes to the writing of history have been common, and I will consider each of them in turn. I will term them the 'imperialistic Christian' view, the 'sectarian Christian' view, the 'Liberal Western' tradition, and the Marxist interpretation.

Imperialistic Christian history

On this view, which has been the most common during the church's existence, history explicitly reveals God's purpose, which is working towards his ultimate triumph. The Christian historian's job is to witness to the unfolding of this purpose in history and to relate it to the community of the faithful. The world is the property of the church – hence my terming the attitude 'imperialistic'. This approach was inherited by Christianity from ancient Israel, whose sacred books consist of an account of world history uniquely centred on the experience of an insignificant semitic people who played very little part in the calculations of the important states in the ancient world. Great kingdoms which were neighbours of this people but nevertheless did little for good or evil in the career of Israel were liable to be virtually ignored; thus it took the efforts of nineteenth- and twentieth-century archaeologists to discover that the Hittites, far from being an insignificant neighbour of the Israelites, worthy of a casual mention in a list of lesser breeds, had in fact been the masters of one of the greatest empires in the ancient world.

The early Christians found this way of looking at history con- genial, particularly as their expectations of an imminent end to the world faded and their interest in worldly affairs grew correspond- ingly greater. If this world did concern Christians after all, it was up to the church to assess the world's history as the people of the old dispensation had done. Here was to be found the revelation of God. This impulse was much strengthened by the wholly unexpected change in the church's fortunes which resulted from the Emperor Constantine's alliance with Christianity in the fourth century. For Christian historians, Constantine's action was clearly a direct sign from God of the working out of his purpose, a moment to which all previous history had been moving, and it should influence the way in which history should be narrated. The Roman Empire was now the positive instrument of God, not merely his passive instrument for disciplining the wicked.

However, this view was to be cruelly disappointed by the collapse of the Western Roman Empire during the fifth century. This disaster, and in particular the sack of the ancient Imperial capital by barbarians in 410, prompted Augustine of Hippo, one of the greatest minds of the ancient world and a bishop of the Christian church, to write a weighty book called *The City of God* which is an extended meditation on the purposes of God in history. I deal with Augustine's career and this book in Chapter Eight, but we need to note now that this was the most subtle exposition of the imperialistic Christian method which the early church produced; its influence was immense. By dividing the whole of human history into a cosmic struggle between the earthly city (under the control of selfishness and Satan) and the city of God, Augustine was subordinating history to theology; the pursuit of historic facts was subjected to the purposes of the church, which was increasingly claiming the dominant role in Western culture. During the Middle Ages, this ecclesiastical imperialism affected the whole historical process, to the extent that the English monk, Bede, greatest of all medieval historians, popularized a way of organizing chronology which we now take for granted: the dating of events by the birth of Christ, the Year of Our Lord *(Anno Domini)*.

In their intoxication at the central place of the church in European affairs, medieval churchmen forgot the caution and subtlety of Augustine's historical outlook in *The City of God*: they constructed schemes which would explain all history. Most influential was that of Joachim of Fiore (see Chapter Nine below), who divided world history into three ages, and predicted that the year 1260 would be a great turning-point. The passing of the year 1260 without notable incident did not dampen people's enthusiasm for Joachim-like schemes of history; indeed, one of the most potent sources of self-confidence for English Protestantism in its earliest generations after the sixteenth-century Reformation was a similar scheme mapped out by John Foxe in his *Acts and Monuments* ('Foxe's Book of Martyrs'). His scheme, neatly divided up into units of three hundred years, set out the decline of Western Christianity into popish blindness and its triumphant resurrection in his own time, a new age of victory for Protestantism conveniently opening up on the death of the Catholic Queen Mary of England, and the accession of Queen Elizabeth. It was naturally a popular scheme with Elizabeth's government, and it gave Englishmen a good sense of their own importance in God's plans! Although Western history-writing began to take a different direction at this time, similar schemes to that of Foxe, with similar purposes, emerged in nineteenth-century America, organizing history into a series of 'dispensations' which were about to be completed by the Second Coming of Christ.

'Sectarian Christian' history

An important strain in Christianity, influenced by the thought of the Greek philosopher Plato and the Christian deviations known as Gnosticism, rejects the world and its works, and hence takes little interest in its history; what point is there in learning about the affairs of the world when it is a worthless place? On this view, history is reduced to an exposition of how the Christian community came into being, and how it remained faithful (or not, as the case may be) to its doctrinal standards. This is the sectarian view of history; in contrast to the post-Constantine Christian view of history that seeks to absorb the world into the affairs and concerns of the church, it tries to exclude worldly influences from an understanding of the church's development.

A trace of this attitude remained in the curriculum of the theological college which appointed me a tutor some years ago. The job advertisement was for a Tutor in Church History; almost from the moment of my appointment, I began biting the hand which was about to feed me by emphasizing that I did not believe in Church History. My colleagues were not appointed to teach Church Philosophy or Church Sociology or Church Psychology of Education; I did not see it as my role to provide instruction solely in the development of solafidianism or in the evolution of liturgical colours. Such instruction would ignore the fact that the church, particularly the Western church, is inextricably bound up from the beginning with the development of the secular culture round it. I hope that this will become obvious as you read this book. It is worth my stating from the outset that I see the most important dates in the history of the church (apart from the coming in flesh of God in Christ) as events outside 'church history'. They are not the Council of Chalcedon in 451 or the sixteenth-century Reformation, but successively the establishment of democracy in classical Athens (fifth century BC), the various political struggles involving Constantine in the 310s AD, the Industrial Revolution of the eighteenth century, and the French Revolution of 1789. I would be interested to see whether you agree with me after reading *Groundwork of Christian History*! However, if I reject both imperialistic and sectarian Christian history as models for historical writing, what is left?

Liberal Western history

The tradition of historical enquiry which has become general in the non-Marxist West is not that of imperialistic Christian writing. It lacks a sense of ultimate direction; it has no dogmatic scheme; it is concerned not to illustrate divine purpose, but to provide explanation, to comfort humankind in its perplexities by exploring the causes of the apparently baffling events which surround us. Its origins were with the ancient Greeks, and with two great historians, Herodotos and Thucydides, whose work is described in Chapter Two. Their tradition was replaced by the concerns of Christian history already described, after the Roman Empire was Christianized; however, the revival of classical learning with the last great Renaissance (see Chapter Ten below) brought a revival of interest in the writing of history on these classical lines, a history which could regard itself as 'scientific' in the increasingly restricted meaning of the word. No longer were theological considerations to dominate historical enquiry.

In the eighteenth century, the church lost its place at the centre of intellectual life, both in the Catholic and the Protestant world. It was not surprising that the 'imperialistic' Christian view of history should give ground to this scientific approach, although it did bequeath to it an idea of direction in history. This was an optimistic society, and it transformed the idea of a guiding hand of

God into the notion of a 'progress' continually at work improving the lives of human beings. Even for historians who retained a religious faith, this picture of human events stripped of the sacred was very attractive. The concern now became to get behind the web of legend to find out what had actually happened, by the intense study of every available document from the past. The political upheavals caused by the 1789 French Revolution and its consequences suddenly made available vast quantities of documents previously jealously guarded by governments and great families, so historians now had the opportunity to put their plans into action.

The achievements of nineteenth-century historians with this sort of aim were colossal. The greatest of them, the Prussian Leopold von Ranke, produced works which run to fifty-four volumes in the collected edition. For Ranke, this immense labour had a definite purpose, which became clearer as his beloved Germany came out of its early nineteenth-century political confusion and united into an Empire in 1871. The actions of individuals and institutions throughout history had all been directed towards the formation of nation-states like post-1871 Germany; in particular, the history of Europe was now moving steadily to a point where a Protestant Germany would lead its destiny. In Britain, the Cambridge historian Sir John Seeley held a similar view of the British Empire as the focus for his researches. The whole tendency of nineteenth-century historical research in this country has been characterized by the great historian Sir Herbert Butterfield as 'Whig' (the name of the dominant political party in eighteenth-century England): in other words, the story of British history was seen as a matter of explaining this country's inevitable progress to liberal parliamentary government, with all that stood in the way of this aim being a turning from the right road.

So liberal historical writing, under the influence of a secularized version of Christian imperialistic history, gained a sense of purpose and direction in the nineteenth century. However, this sense of purpose was frequently not explicit. So often the sheer burden of detailed and accurate research in the pre-xerox world prevented liberal historians from raising their sights beyond their own research area. In the twentieth century, this often became an escape from the problem of finding a convincing goal for the historical process. The political disasters of the twentieth century, the destruction of Germany, the failure of parliamentary government through much of Europe, the disintegration of the British Empire, all provided good reasons for abandoning the search for a unifying theme in the movement of history. Westerners had been rudely reminded of the brutality of many civilized people in times of stress. The typical attitude of the liberal historian came to be a guarded secular agnosticism, expressed in the rather battered optimism of Dr E.H.Carr in the last words of his book *What is History?*: 'I shall look out on a world in tumult and a world in travail, and shall answer in the well-worn words of a great scientist: "And yet – it moves".'

Marxist history

During the nineteenth century another development of the Judaeo-Christian imperialist tradition was produced, in direct opposition to the liberal tradition: the Marxist view of history. Although Karl Marx lost any notion of religious faith, his deep grounding in both Jewish and Christian culture made him produce a schematic view of history. Like many of the variants of Christianity, Marxism sees all historical process converging on a foretold end: the classless society in this case. It divides history into a series of periods; yet all this is constructed on a strictly materialist basis, with class interest, economic motivation and control of the means of production as motors of historical change rather than the Trinity or the will of God.

Marxist historical writing has been of great benefit to historians. It has drawn their attention to the importance of economic and social structures in human life, and thus it throws fresh light on the institutions which human society has constructed. No historian of the past can afford to ignore such insights in looking at the past, and the way in which the narrative of this book has been shaped owes much to the legacy of Marxism. Yet Marx was a man of his time, a nineteenth-century figure believing in the inevitability of progress and seeing the passage of history as rather like the scheme of evolution which Charles Darwin had systematized in biology; it is significant that Marx wanted to dedicate *Das Kapital* to Darwin (the offer was refused). Marx took his understanding of English history, drawn from his friend Friedrich Engels, as the basis for a scheme which made predictions about the future. Few of these predictions have been fulfilled. The rigidity of the strict Marxist picture of history will no doubt in time make it look as dated as the theories of Joachim of Fiore.

Which method?

It will probably be obvious that of the four methods described so far, I am trying to adopt the liberal Western approach to history in writing this book. The ideal lying behind the method is a commitment to teasing out facts and retelling them in a coherent and neutral way. It has to be said at the outset that this worthy aim is impossible to achieve, for two main reasons: no one is objective, and it is never completely certain what a 'fact' is in history.

First, objectivity. As a member of the Christian community, I can never claim complete freedom from bias when I look at its past. Within the Christian community, I have allegiances to particular sorts of Christianity which have been particularly precious to me. With a training as a historian, I can use my professional skills to tell the story as I would like it to be heard. This is not so much a matter of lying, inventing false facts in the manner of Hitler's Germany or of the State in Orwell's *1984*; it is much more a business of selecting, quietly ignoring some facts and putting the spotlight on others. Every historian, however conscientious, will end up doing this, for a whole variety of reasons of which religious commitment is only one possibility. That is why to assess what a historical event was really like, you must read as many different acounts of it as possible, so that you can raise objections to one version of the story. The historian's motto should be 'Yes, but . . .'; historians should always be ready to qualify and alter what they are saying. This often makes for a dull and complex story rather than one which is exciting and straightforward, but the complex story may also have its own beauty because it is more like the truth.

But how like the truth can it be? The basic problem with any piece of historical writing is in deciding what a historical fact is, and on what evidence it can be based. Over the last three hundred years or so, we have come to accept that the most authentic facts are those which can be proved by experimental demonstration: an attitude already displayed by the Apostle Thomas when he was first told of the resurrection of Christ. 'Facts are facts'. However, as soon as we begin looking at history, it becomes evident that there are many degrees of fact, dependent on the amount of evidence available to prove them, the degree of bias which is built into the evidence in the first place, and the possibility or impossibility of there being any evidence at all. For instance, the most pure and trustworthy sort of historical fact is represented by the statement that 'the Battle of Hastings was fought in 1066'. There is plenty of evidence to support this statement; all sorts of events which can be dated interlock with the date of the battle and fix it with a reasonable degree of certainty. More importantly, it is unlikely to be to anyone's advantage to falsify the date of the Battle of Hastings. Whatever one thinks of the causes or of the outcome of the battle, the date is going to be fairly uncontroversial.

However, let us take another historical statement and see whether we can treat it in the same way: suppose that I, as a professional historian, say that 'the Protestant Reformers of the sixteenth century were the scum of the earth'. There are certainly historical statements embedded inside this: there is a date, and a reference to a group of people who with a fair degree of certainty are known to have existed. It might even be possible to bring a fair amount of evidence to justify the rest of the statement: a disagreeable character here, a shabby action there. But even so, I think that anyone hearing the remark might be forgiven for thinking that there was a fair degree of bias involved in the way it was constructed; and they might also think it worthwhile gathering evidence which contradicted it. They might also feel inclined to cast doubt on the value of any other historical statement which I made!

Here, therefore, we have two quite distinct points on the spectrum of historical truth; although these instances may look quite straightforward, there are many more examples which may be less easy to assess. Moreover, there are statements which look like historical facts which can never be such because they are incapable of proof; they are beyond evidence. The Christian doctrine of the virgin birth of Jesus (to be more accurate, the virgin conception) is one of these; it is more or less impossible in the twentieth century to observe every stage of the biological processes which lie behind the phenomenon of conception, and at the beginning of the Christian era it would have been out of the question to do so. The raising of Christ from the dead is another such instance. Here the historian can never be of use; with regard to the resurrection, all a historian can do is to point to the effect that it had on other people. So the statement in the Nicene Creed that 'on the third day he rose from the dead' is not at all the same sort of historical statement as 'he suffered under Pontius Pilate', even though the two clauses look much the same.

In effect, the liberal Western approach to history presents an impossible dream when it tries to give a complete picture of events in history without bias or distortion. If there are ultimate patterns in history, the limits of our minds and perceptions mean that we can never make out their shapes. However, there is no more reason for the historian to give up the struggle to see the patterns than there is for the Christian to give up faith. To write history is an act of faith, and it is an act which can never see complete results; so it can never end.

There are particular limitations on this book which must be realized from the outset. It is a history of Western Christianity: the tradition which stemmed from the church of the Roman Empire to drift apart from the Eastern Orthodox world in the early Middle Ages, the church of Roman Catholicism and Protestantism. In doing so, it says nothing about Orthodoxy, and the ancient Churches of the East and Africa beyond Orthodoxy, and if the reader wants to gain a full picture of the riches of Christian experience, the Eastern Christian experience demands to be explored. I make no further apology for this yawning gap in the story, nor for a further feature of the book which may strike home after a few chapters. Once during my time teaching in Wesley College, after four terms taking a particular class through the history of the church in the ancient world and the Middle Ages, one of my students asked in despair 'But where is the good news in all this?' It was a fair question, to which I could best reply that all the story was good news. The history of Christianity is frequently sordid and depressing, and very frequently, apparently sacred events turn out to have very secular causes. Christians will remain beginners in their faith if they do not face up to this. The miracle of the church's story is that after all its mistakes, bewildering transformations and entanglements in human bitterness, it is still there.

How to use this book

One or two technical pieces of advice may help the reader. To give you some shape to the narrative at each point, and to keep as many dates as possible out of the text, each chapter is preceded by a table of dates relevant to its narrative. There is a full index of names and events, and also in an effort to keep dates out of the text, it is in the index that you will find the dates of birth and of death of the various personalities mentioned.

Finally, this book will have failed in its purpose if it is the last work of history that you read. After the *Conclusion* you will find some suggestions for further reading.

Part I

The Building of a Culture

Chronology for Chapter Two

BC

c. 1400	Mycenean civilization flourishes
c. 1200	Mycenean civilization destroyed
(*c.* 1055-1015	David the King of the Jews)
c. 800	Beginning of Greek Archaic period
753	Traditional date of foundation of Rome
(587/6	First Jewish Temple destroyed by Nebuchadnezzar)
c. 580	Solon legislates for Athens
546	Death of Thales of Miletos
510	Tyrants overthrown and democracy established, Athens
509	Monarchy overthrown in Rome
490	First Punic War between Rome and Carthage begins
479	Final defeat of Persians by Greek alliance
468	First public triumph for a play by Sophocles
c. 465	Herodotos begins career writing and researching history
431	Peloponnesian War begins
c. 427	First play of Aristophanes performed
409	Plato begins to hear Socrates
404	Peloponnesian War ends in Athenian defeat
399	Socrates forced to commit suicide
c. 364	Aristotle begins studies with Plato
338	Battle of Chaeronea: Alexander defeats Greek coalition
332	Alexander founds Alexandria in Egypt
323	Alexander dies on campaign
188	Roman victory against Antiochus III sealed with peace treaty
147	Third Punic War ends with total destruction of Carthage by Rome
90	Civil War breaks out in Rome
44	Julius Caesar assassinated
31	Octavian's victory over Anthony and Cleopatra at Actium
30	Egypt becomes Roman province
27	Octavian becomes *Imperator* and takes name 'Augustus'
c. 6	Jesus Christ born

AD

14	Death of Augustus: he is accepted among the gods

Chapter Two

The Greek and Roman Roots

It may seem strange to begin a survey of Christian history not in the lands of the Bible, but in a world which knew little and cared less about the Jews: the world of ancient Greece. However, there is good reason for this. Although the life of Jesus Christ seems to have been lived in an entirely Jewish setting, his followers were immediately faced with an ancient and sophisticated culture which filled the minds of anyone who was anyone from Boulogne to Beirut, which had lapped the Himalayas and which would soon spread as far as the remote and backward British Isles: a culture spearheaded by Roman armies, but shaped amid the mountains and islands of Greece. As the church developed, it could not help but be shaped by Greek thought, in the way it organized itself, in the way it talked about moral problems, even in the way in which it tried to form ideas about the man Jesus who was also God.

The attitudes and the thought of the Greeks survived the collapse of the Roman Empire which carried them through Europe, and they did so because the Christian church used them in its own battle for survival. The combination of Greek, Roman and Jewish ideas which lies at the heart of Western European civilization has been one of the most successful cultures in human history; no part of the world today remains unaffected by it, even in settings which have vigorously rejected the West and everything that it stands for. And it is always worth remembering that only where Western civilization has been able to wipe out its rivals has Christianity known massive success. Christian culture and the Graeco-Roman values which it adopted conquered the Americas, smashed the empires of the Aztecs and the Incas and made sure that the

New World would be a Christian world, but in the Old World, Christianity has made little impact on Islam, on Hinduism or Buddhism, or on the immensely old and self-confident culture centred on China. Perhaps this lack of success is because Christians still express their faith in thought-forms which were bequeathed them by the Greeks and the Romans, and which do not address the ways of thought and the main interests of the world's other great faiths. So ancient Greece matters to us.

Early Greece (c. 2200 BC to c. 800 BC)

People speaking an early form of Greek drifted into the Greek peninsula before the beginning of the second millennium BC. By 1400 BC, these peoples had developed their own highly complex and wealthy culture centred on cities and palace-fortresses like Mycenae: hence the name of the Mycenean culture. It was short-lived: in only a couple of centuries, archaeology shows us that its settlements were quite suddenly destroyed. A Dark Age followed, but not an age of complete stagnation. It was during this period that the Greeks started using iron, when previously their technology had been based on the use of bronze; and it was also at this time that the great foundation documents of Greek culture, the Iliad and the Odyssey, came into being.

These two works of literature were as central to the Greek's image of himself as the Hebrew scripture is to a Jew. Like the earlier part of the Bible, they were composed in a society which knew nothing of the use of writing, and they represent only a fragment of a much greater oral tradition; for ease of remembrance, they are composed in verse. We know nothing definite of their author, who was early given the name Homer, but the two works show that his aim was to portray that lost world of the Myceneans. That world was so remote from his own that he got it wrong in many ways – for instance, he had no idea that the Myceneans had not used iron tools. But it was the future woven from his stories of the past which mattered; these books gave the Greeks a common vision of the past which kept them secure in a single culture for centuries. They needed some such cultural bond, because they had little else to keep them together. Not until the twentieth century have the Greeks had a single land called Greece which is home to most of them. In the ancient world some of them lived in what is now Greece, but many more lived in settlements scattered thinly along the coast of the whole Mediterranean, and eventually there would be cities which thought of themselves as Greek as far away as northern India. Their world was bewilderingly diverse. The word which embraced all these scattered peoples was '*Hellas*', which was not the name of a country like France, but an identity, more like our word 'Christendom'. Everyone else was spoken of a part of the *barbaroi*, because to a Greek all foreign languages sounded as meaningless as a baby crooning 'Ba, ba, ba'.

The ancient Israelites were one of the few other ancient peoples to preserve this sort of cultural unity without any political structure, but at least they could look back in later centuries to a united kingdom which they had once enjoyed, and they looked forward to a time when God would let them rebuild this kingdom once more. The Greeks neither looked to such a past state, nor wanted to see one built in the future. It was enough for them that they could share a common literature, and that they could come together in certain other great shared institutions, like the ceremonies around the oracle of Apollo at Delphi, or the games held in honour of their chief god Zeus on Mount Olympus. Perhaps it was this which gave them their cultural strength, but also part of the energy and creativity which made them so exceptional can be seen in the ways in which Homer's works treat the gods.

If you read the Iliad or the Odyssey, you will probably be struck by the triviality which Homer's gods seem to display. They have tantrums; they take sides in a human war; they get a mortal man to judge a beauty contest among them. You might say that this is not very flattering to the gods, but the reverse side of that is that it is very flattering to humankind: if the gods are a little like us, then we are a little like them. The achievements of Classical Greek civilization were founded on a massive confidence in human ability to make progress, and we see this idea already in the work of Homer. Humankind is not a helpless plaything of divine forces.

Archaic Greece (*c.* 800 BC to 500 BC)

The Greece which emerged from the Dark Ages was very different from the Mycenean world. Its settlements were now organized not round great palaces of noblemen but around temples, which henceforth were the normal architectural focus of a Greek city. These temples were houses of the gods, not places for congregations to gather, like most Christian churches; they were places where sacrifices were offered or rituals performed according to a great variety of local custom, and the priests who performed these duties were rarely seen as any more sacred than any other official of the state, like a tax-gatherer or a soldier. Nor was there any theology as traditional Christians would understand it, just a collection of myths which often bewildered later Greeks who tried to make sense or a logical system out of them. Here was something which would be significant for the future intellectual freedom of the great Greek thinkers; if there was no developed notion of a sacred caste of priests or of fixed theology, there could be little idea of heresy and restraints on belief. Only one great Greek philosopher, Socrates, ever suffered death for his beliefs, and his case seems to have been mixed up with the confused politics of his day. Equally important for the future of Greek thought was the form of writing which they borrowed from their seafaring neighbours the Phoenicians when they began to write things down once more: the ancestor of our own script, the alphabet. Most ancient scripts were based on the idea that a written symbol should represent an object or a concept: at its simplest, that an apple should be represented by the picture of an apple, for instance. The alphabet takes the principle that a sound is represented by a single constant symbol whatever the word in which it is found. Only comparatively few symbols need be employed – twenty-six in our alphabet, generally twenty-two in the Greek – compared with the hundreds or even thousands in 'pictogrammic' scripts; it is thus much easier to commit abstract ideas to writing, and it would be in the world of abstract ideas that many of the Greeks' contributions to the West's development would come.

Another characteristic of Greek society which was already obvious in the Archaic period was the very fragmented political organization which the Greeks preferred; with no central state, there were hundreds of tiny independent communities, perhaps fifteen hundred in the end. Perhaps the geography of Greece encouraged this, with its mountains, isolated valleys and islands, but the Greeks did not change when they started founding colonies in very different regions like Sicily, with its great open plains. They seem to have felt that small was beautiful. Their life was organized round the *polis*. This is a word often translated into English as 'city', but it is a much richer and warmer word than that, as difficult to translate fully into another language as our word 'home'. The *polis* was the place where people lived and the place which gave them their identity, and it was also the people themselves: the *polis* of Athens, for example, was the city round the hill called the Acropolis, but also its countryside beyond, and all the citizens who were the Athenian people. Long after Greek city-states had been conquered by the Roman Empire, people in the ancient world would see the *polis* as the natural way to live, and the early church picked up this idea. Even the Greek word for the church (a word which Latin-speakers subsequently took from the Greek) was *ekklesia*, which was simply borrowed by Christians; previously the word had been used to describe the assembly of citizens who met to decide the affairs of the *polis*. Think how many different meanings you can give to our word 'church', and you will begin to have some idea of how important the *polis* was to the Greeks.

However, it took a long time for the Greeks to reach the stage in the organization of the *polis* which they commonly regarded as perfect. Most of their states in the Archaic period were ruled by groups of noblemen, but all over the Greek world at various times, these aristocratic groups faced crises in their government. Their little states were faced by discontent and civil war as the population rose and made more demands on the precious and limited areas of fertile land between the mountains; constant challenges to their power were sometimes headed off by sending the ambitious and energetic off to found colonies elsewhere, as far away as Spain and the south of France. Nevertheless, many aristocratic regimes were in the end overthrown, and replaced by the rule of a single strong man. He was commonly styled a *tyrannos*; although this is the origin of our word 'tyrant', it did not have the overtones of disapproval which we have given it, and it simply meant someone who ruled without traditional authority. But this was very important; if the *tyrannos* could not appeal to the past, or to divine permission, in the normal fashion of an ancient king, how would he exercise power?

The answer in states all over Greece was that the community itself, having allowed the *tyrannos* to seize power to end conflict, would make up laws to govern the state. Often a semi-legendary figure was remembered as the lawmaker – Lycurgus in Sparta, Solon in Athens – but it was still an ordinary human being who was seen as making law. To us this idea is so familiar that we will find it hard to see how revolutionary it was in Archaic Greece. There had been lawgivers before: Moses, for instance, or the Babylonian king Hammurabi, but such men had always claimed that it was not they who made the laws but God, or divine power which worked through them. But now an ordinary man or collection of men was deciding law – that Greek self-confidence again – and within the state it was the law and not the *tyrannos* who was supreme.

In practice, of course, many *tyrannoi* disapproved of this notion, and like the aristocratic cliques before them, they abused their power. The next stage in the Greek pilgrimage through political life came as many of the *tyrannoi* were overthrown, and were replaced by a form of government in which every man who was a citizen could have a say in policy (notice how that word relates to the affairs of the *polis*). Democracy, the rule of the people, was born. The whole process is most commonly remembered for the state of the Athenians: here a tyranny which had lasted for half a century was overthrown after a trivial quarrel over a love-affair, and after two years of civil war, a democracy was established in 510 BC. Greece was entering its classical period.

Classical Greece (fifth and fourth centuries BC)

We must be careful to realize that the democracies of classical Greece were not like ours. The citizen of a Greek *polis* enjoyed his freedom to make decisions because of two great unfreedoms: for women and for slaves. After the Archaic Age, women played little part in Greek public and cultural life; the important emotional and intellectual relationships were between men. Similarly, for Greek males to have the leisure to gather in the market-place crowd (the *ekklesia*) to make life and death decisions for their fellow-citizens meant that someone else did the work: that meant a large body of slaves. Add to this the fact that no Greek who was not born a citizen of a particular *polis* could have a say in how it was run, even if he lived there, and you will see that ancient Greek 'rule of the people' excluded a large majority of the people.

Perhaps that might not seem so strange to us as the fact that there was no delegation in Greek democracy: no elected MPs, no

Prime Minister or Cabinet to take the work of decision-making off the ordinary man's shoulders. The buck stopped with the *ekklesia*; anyone might be chosen to do the state service, right up to the command of an army or a fleet of ships. It would terrify us now, but when no one in history had done it before, it must have been more terrifying still. This is perhaps why Greek civilization was so astonishingly creative in the two centuries after the coming of democracy; they were forced into thinking and creating ways of coping with a responsibility which might send anyone mad. One way was to act out the situations which confront all of us in our everyday life, both happy and sad. It was the Greeks who formed the idea of theatre out of the ceremonies of their religious life. In this very beginning of drama they produced works which explored the depths of human tragedy in ways which have never been surpassed. At the same time, Aristophanes could produce comedies which poked outrageous fun at the very Athenian audiences who watched them: and the Athenians loved it. They knew that they had to laugh at themselves if they were to remain sane. As we shall see, the effort of sanity and balance was in the end too much even for the Athenians.

Another way in which Greeks could explore ways of controlling their world was to gain experience by studying the past; they began taking history seriously. The impulse seems to have started in those Greek cities which were scattered along the coast of Asia Minor (what is now Turkey), and which were under the rule of the non-Greek Persian Empire; these Greeks were forced to come into contact with their barbarian neighbours, and they developed much more curiosity than mainland Greeks about these people who shaped their lives. They began gathering data about them. The crucial stage came when the Persian Empire started coming into conflict with the states of mainland Greece, which it saw as encouraging its own Greek subjects to rebel. Full-scale war broke out between the two cultures, ending in the defeat of Persia by a Greek coalition led by Athens: Greek democracy and the culture which went with it were saved. One Greek from Asia Minor, Herodotos of Halikarnassos, decided that he would not only combine what he could find out about non-Greek nations with a personal visits to them, but that he would also make the climax of his work an account of these Persian wars, the greatest clash between Greek and non-Greek in history. It was a very bave undertaking: the Persian wars had been over for more than a generation, and no one had ever before tried to gather memories and documents together to tell a connected story about the past. In this, we owe Herodotos so much that for all his faults, his unreliability and untidiness, it would be unjust to pick up the gibe made about him by some ancient authors that he was the Father of Lies rather than the Father of History.

Herodotos's work in history was taken further by Thucydides, a leading Athenian whose career in his city's affairs had been ruined by the Peloponnesian War. This had been as great a disaster for Athenian confidence and self-respect as the Persian Wars had been a triumph. The Persian Wars had left Athens at the head of a victorious coalition of states, the Delian League. Success was too much for the Athenians, who yielded to the temptation of using their leading role to turn the League into an empire for themselves. Although the wealth and power which this gave them was the background to some of their most brilliant achievements in art, they also attracted jealousy and resentment, particularly from the rival *polis* of Sparta. Sparta was a very different state from Athens; a small minority of its people ruled a conquered and cowed population through military force, keeping themselves in a state of permanent armed readiness. Now, however, the Athenians' selfish behaviour helped Sparta to intervene against Athens as the defender of Greek liberties, and after a bitter twenty-seven years of war, Sparta and its allies left Athenian power totally shattered.

Among the victims of this disgrace was Thucydides, who was forced into exile after being involved in defeat. In his enforced leisure he pondered why such a catastrophe had come to him and his fellow-Athenians, and he decided to write an account of what had happened. His startlingly original idea was to look for deep underlying causes for such a terrible series of events: not the whims and fancies of a single personality as Herodotos might have seen it, but the collective corruption of an entire society. It was the pride and decline in political morality of the Athenians which had brought them down. Thucydides saw that vital historical lesson that groups of people behave differently and have different motivations from individual human beings, and that often they behave much worse than individuals. He saw his task as the production of history which was a work of art, as cool, balanced and perfectly-structured as a Greek temple, and although his work has come down to us unfinished, he remains the greatest historian that the ancient world produced: an example to all those who have written history ever since.

The analytical artistry of Thucydides brings us to a further Greek gift to the future: the development of philosophy. The Greeks were exploring their experience in drama and in trying to recover important events in the past; in philosophy, they began to reflect on meaning and questions of morality and choice outside mythological stories about the gods, to find universal answers which would not necessarily involve telling a story. The first great figures came from the same part of Asia Minor as Herodotos, although they lived about a century before him, men like Thales of Miletos. The first questions which interested them were to do with the origin of the world and of humankind. To begin with, therefore, the preoccupations of philosophy were in areas which we might consider more the province of disciplines like physics and geology; it was difficult to separate out philosophical investigation from scientific investigation, and this remained true throughout ancient times and into the world of the fifteenth- and sixteenth-century Renaissance. A little fossil of this universal embrace of philosophy (which, after all, simply means 'love of knowledge') survives in the custom which British and American universities have borrowed from the German tradition of calling successful post-graduate researchers Doctors of Philosophy, regardless of whether they study Julius Caesar or nuclear physics.

The greatest achievements of Greek philosophy came in the Athens of the late fifth and early fourth centuries, with a succession of contributions made by Socrates, Plato and Aristotle. Socrates himself never wrote anything, and most of what we know about him comes from the writings of his pupil Plato; we can never be sure that the words which Plato puts in the mouth of Socrates represent his views in detail. However, this hardly matters. With the writings of Plato we have one of the foundations of the West's ways of thinking, and it is the height of impertinence for me to try and make any summary of his work in a few lines. Writing usually in the form of dialogues between friends, Plato reflected on the problems with which we are faced by the idea of immortality, of pleasure, of political organization: of the whole range of human existence.

Of particular importance for the thinking of the Christian

church would be Plato's ideas about the nature of the supreme God: being perfect, such a God would be indivisible, since perfection involves unity, and passionless, since passions involve change from one mood to another, and changeable things cannot be perfect. Such a God would have difficulty in creating the sort of changeable, imperfect, messy world in which we live; difficulty, indeed, in having any meaningful contact with it. Even if what we see is just a pale reflection of ideal 'Forms' which represent a truer and higher version of reality from the one which we can readily know, those Forms themselves could only have been created by one other than the God who is the Supreme Soul – perhaps an image of the Supreme Soul, an image which Plato describes in his dialogue the *Timaeus* as a craftsman (*demiourgos*, from which the English word Demiurge). The soul of the individual should do its best to find its way back to the Forms which lie behind the world of our clouded senses; 'goodness of soul' is the chief purpose for all of us, for goodness is the characteristic of the Supreme Soul who is God. These Platonic notions of the nature of God will tug at our sleeves when we come to consider how the early Christians formed their views about God.

Plato's pupil Aristotle was led in a very different direction in his quest for truth. Whereas Plato had sought for reality in abstract ideals, feeling for instance that an ultimate ideal Form of a tree was more real than any individual tree, Aristotle sought for reality in inidividual objects. For him, therefore, the way to knowledge was to search out as much information and opinion about the objects and forms which exist to and which can be described by our senses. The difference can be seen by comparing the approaches of the two men to government; whereas Plato described an ideal state (and a very different one from his native Athens) in his dialogue the *Republic*, Aristotle organized a research team to gather data on as many different governments in the ordinary world as possible, and to produce potted descriptions of them – only one remains, rediscovered only a century ago, and as luck would have it, it is the description of the constitution of Athens. But Aristotle applied the same technique in all branches of knowledge, from subjects like biology and natural history to theories of literature and rhetoric (the art of public speaking and debate); his work is like a gigantic filing system, and it survives to us not in the polished dialogue form of Plato but as the lecture notes taken down by his pupils and assistants.

Would any modern lecturer remain celebrated down the centuries if all we had of him was his pupils' lecture notes? It is a tribute to Aristotle's greatness and originality that for some two thousand years after his death, he would set the way in which the West shaped its thoughts about how the physical world, arts and ethics could be organized. The church began by being suspicious about him, preferring the other-worldliness which was the basis of Plato's thought, but there was no other scheme for understanding the organization of the world in which we live which was remotely as comprehensive as Aristotle's. When Christians were faced with making theological comments on natural subjects like biology or the animal kingdom, they turned to Aristotle, just as Christian theologians today may turn to modern science to give them information about matters in which they are not technically expert. The result was, for instance, that two millennia after the death of this pagan philosopher, two monks in a monastery somewhere in northern Europe might consider an argument settled if one of them could say 'Well, Aristotle says ... '. If you begin looking at the story of Christians thinking about their faith and the world, right down to the seventeenth century you will hear a ghostly debate going on between Plato and Aristotle, two Greeks who had never heard the name of Jesus Christ.

Few philosophers abandoned belief in the ancient family of gods of Greece; atheism was a very rare and shocking thing in the ancient world. However, in their different ways, Aristotle and Plato had found new means of talking about the nature of God: a contrast to the myths which were the foundation of the rituals of everyday religion. Philosophical language and religious practice tended to go their own ways. There were no great names in Greek philosophy after Plato and Aristotle; indeed, in all fields, the outburst of creativity in classical Greece surprises us not merely by its intensity, but by the shortness of its life. Where were the later playwrights to equal names like Aeschylus and Sophocles, historians to equal Thucydides? Classical Greece, which had been so damaged in the exhausting struggles of the Peloponnesian War, lost its independence in 338 BC, and a new phase of Greek culture began.

The Hellenistic Age (from 338 BC)

To the north of mainland Greece was the non-Greek kingdom of
Macedon. Its king Philip II launched a war of conquest south
which in 338 resulted in a close-run but decisive victory for him
over combined Greek forces at Chaeronea. Philip's son Alexander
launched an astonishing set of conquests eastward, completely
defeating and annexing the Greeks' ancient enemy the Persian
Empire, together with the kingdom of Egypt, all before his death
at the ridiculously early age of thirty-two. Although his empire
then broke up, its parts were taken over by his generals, who
manoeuvred and fought with each other until they had established
themselves in kingdoms whose collective borders touched the
Adriatic in the west, the Himalayas in the east and the upper
reaches of the Nile in the south. These kingdoms they ruled like
the absolute rulers whom Alexander had defeated, semi-divine
monarchs with armies and tax-collecting bureaucracies; yet in
these very un-Greek settings they founded new cities or refounded
old ones as imitations of the classical Greek *polis*, complete with
temples in Greek style and theatres where Greek drama was
performed. The greatest Greek city of all became Alexandria, the
Egyptian city which was founded by and named after Alexander
himself, with a famous university and the most splendid library in
the ancient world, a symbol of Greek culture in an alien Egyptian
setting.

For all that we call this world Hellenistic because of its Greekness,
it was very different from the Greece which had gone before; the
heart of Classical Greece had been democracy, and here were
states which were undisguised dictatorships, with rulers who had
taken on the divine trappings which the Greeks had long ago
rejected. Never again would the Greek *polis* enjoy the true
independence which was its ideal, and the new Greek cities which
littered the eastern Mediterranean from Hellenistic times for
nearly a thousand years remained little élite colonies, as if a
Surrey village were to be dumped down in the British India
of Queen Victoria. What independence they had was just to
administer themselves and to come up with taxes for their royal
masters. We can hardly escape the feeling that there was a sense of
sham about Greek culture in this world, and it may be because of
this that the exuberant creativity of classical Greece came to an

end. A strain of pessimism began to run through culture, encouraged by Plato's pessimism about everyday things, his sense of their unreality and worthlessness.

If philosophy could no longer hope to alter the policies of cities through influencing the thought of the people in the market place, it might as well concentrate on the inward life of the individual which no mighty absolute monarch could tamper with; so philosophy became concerned with the cultivation of the self. Exploration of practical skills became despised, since the practical world was of little account to the true idealist; so the remarkable advances which classical Greece had seen in the understanding of technology, medicine or geography had no follow-up; the steam-engine, for instance, invented in Alexandria, remained a toy, and the ancient world failed to make the breakthrough in energy sources which came in eighteenth-century England. Abundant slave labour blunted the need for technological advance.

This was the world which surrounded the Jewish society into which Jesus was born; however, by then, it had been taken over politically by the armies of a western power: Rome.

Rome and the coming of the Roman Empire

At much the same time as the characteristic forms of society in archaic Greece were emerging, a small settlement was founded in the centre of the Italian peninsula; the Romans traditionally took the equivalent of our date 753 BC as the foundation date of their city, and this is probably not far wrong. Rome started life as a city-state with a king, rather like a *polis* in Archaic Greece, but the monarchy was overthrown in 509, and the Romans thereafter had such a pathological fear of the idea of kingship that they never had a king again until the Middle Ages. There followed a generation of conflict between an aristocracy (the patricians) and the people (plebeians), just as in Greece. However, the result of this war was the opposite to the general result in Greek city-states: the aristocracy won, and the constitution of the Republic which they developed influenced Roman forms of government down to the end of the Empire. The plebeians lost whatever power they had possessed under the monarchy; there were still popular assemblies, but their powers were completely unreal. Real power lay in the hands of the consuls, two officers chosen annually from among the patricians, and with the Senate, an assembly of patricians; even here, the junior senators had little say in the running of affairs. The people only had influence on policy through the popularly elected tribunes of the people, who were peculiarly honoured and sacrosanct during their year of office. They looked after the legal rights of the people, and even in the later Republic when popular rights had dwindled still further, they still vetoed legislation proposed by the Senate.

This stark contrast with the situation in the advanced Greek city-states probably developed because Rome had a continual yearning to expand: a state which was more or less permanently engaged in warfare either to maintain or to expand its frontiers could not afford the luxury of real democracy. But why was Rome's expansion so remarkably successful? Plenty of other states produced dramatic expansion, but they mostly survived for no more than a few generations or a couple of centuries at most; the western part of Rome's empire survived for twelve hundred years, and in its eastern form it had a further thousand years of life after that. What was the secret of this extraordinary success?

The key probably lies in another contrast with Greece: the fact that the Romans had no sense of racial exclusiveness. They gave away Roman citizenship to deserving foreigners; occasionally whole areas would be granted citizenship. Where this peculiar idea came from is not clear; it must have happened during the struggle for power between the patricians and the plebeians after the fall of the kings. In any case, the effect was to give an ever-widening circle of people a vested interest in the survival of Rome; think of that little Jewish tentmaker from Tarsus, far away from Rome in Asia Minor, who could proudly say that he was a Roman citizen, and who knew what advantages it brought.

There is no need to go into the history of the Roman Republic in detail; on the whole it was a story of steady expansion. Rome started taking an interest in Greece during the second century BC, but her eventual conquest of Greece and the Near East beyond ruled by the Seleucid dynasty was the result of a series of unplanned events: relations between Rome and the Seleucid king Antiochus III (192-188 BC) gradually deteriorated until the two sides lurched into war. Now Rome was the master of Greece, and during the first century BC the Romans would take over the entire Mediterranean basin with their final conquest of the Ptolemaic monarchy of Hellenistic Egypt. The cliché about this conquest of the Greek world, no less true for being a cliché, is that Greece conquered Rome as much as Rome conquered Greece. The Romans became fascinated by Greek culture and by the riches of Greek philosophy, which complemented their own highly developed skills in military affairs, administration and matters of law. It would be a Graeco-Roman combination of culture which would dominate the world into which Jesus Christ was born; Greek would be as much an international language for the Roman Empire as Latin, and it would be the main language which Christians spoke for the church's first century and more of existence. But before Christ was born, there had been a great upheaval in the political structure of the Roman state, which would transform it permanently. The Roman Republic fell into deep internal trouble.

It is surprising that trouble had been postponed for so long, but increasing poverty, hunger for land and an accumulated sense of injustice among the bulk of the Roman people led to fighting between a popular party and the aristocracy by 100 BC. Seventy years of misery and intermittent civil war followed for the Republic, ending with the defeat of one party boss by another when Octavian beat Mark Anthony and his ally the Ptolemaic queen of Egypt Cleopatra, at the naval battle of Actium. Octavian, the adopted heir of the assassinated general and dictator Julius Caesar, achieved supreme power within the Roman state in a bewildering series of highly unscrupulous manoeuvres; his job now was to hang on to his power and to bring peace back to the shattered state.

Octavian succeeded brilliantly in retaining supreme power by meticulously adhering to all the old forms of the Republican constitution; the Senate and the two annual consuls continued to function for centuries. Behind this facade, he carried out a revolution in government. His own position was given the harmless-sounding title of First Citizen (*princeps*), for he was careful to avoid the hated title of King. He renamed himself Augustus, and to show his good intentions he took the office of Tribune, the only figure in the old constitution who still commanded any affection among the people. He was given the title of Commander – *imperator* – the first of the Roman Emperors. Ordinary people raised few objections to his new position; they were fed up with the Republic, which had done nothing for seventy years except produce misery and civil war. As far as they were concerned, the old forms had been a sham anyway, so what did it matter if Augustus carried on the pretence? For most people, the important thing was that Augustus brought them peace and prosperity, paying particular attention to beautifying Rome, and extending the bounds of the Empire to give it greater security.

All this was deeply depressing for the battered remains of the old Roman upper classes. They were no more taken in by the Emperor's Republican window-dressing than anyone else. They had done well out of the old Republic, and they had the sense to see that they could continue to do well out of Augustus's regime, but it was bitterly humiliating for them and their traditions. Worst of all for them was the increasing reverence paid to Augustus; after his death, his successors declared him a god, and subsequent emperors saw the usefulness of this; the consecration of a predecessor as divine could give the living emperor prestige and legitimacy as well as glorify the dead. Nearly all Augustus's successors assumed the role of a god in their lifetimes. Upper-class Romans resented worshipping a man who had once been a colleague. A note of regret for the past, a note of defeat, of merely grudging respect for the Empire, runs through the work of an early Imperial historian like Tacitus, and as long as the western part of the Roman Empire lasted, this regret was never wholly to leave the old aristocracy – or the newly rich who were anxious to take on aristocratic manners and attitudes.

Naturally this attitude affected the traditional gods of Rome (a pantheon rather like that of the Greeks), for the gods were bound up with that golden and dead past. Increasingly their worship became formal at least among people with power and influence – rather like Anglican army Church Parade at its worst – part of the Roman heritage, but lacking emotion, passion or compelling power. Just as in the Hellenistic world, with its prevailing pessimism among the thoughtful and religiously sensitive, there was something of a spiritual vacuum by the first century AD. Many religions were waiting to step into the breach: fertility cults galore from the east, or religions like Persian Mithraism which spoke of life as a great struggle between life and darkness, good and evil. But among the contenders, few people noticed or took seriously an eccentric little sect on the fringes of the Jewish synagogues.

Chronology for Chapter Three

BC

587/6	First Jewish Temple destroyed Babylonian exile of the Jews begins
c. 460	Return to Jerusalem by Ezra's group
301	Judaea assigned to Ptolemy of Egypt
c. 285	Septuagint version of scriptures compiled in Alexandria
167	Campaign against Jewish life by Antiochus IV
152	Hasmonean monarchy established among the Jews
63	Pompey conquers all Palestine for Romans
40	Herod the Great made King of Judaea by Roman Senate
c. 6	Birth of Jesus Christ
4	Herod dies; his kingdom is divided

AD

c. 30	Crucifixion of Jesus
39	Philo of Alexandria in Jewish embassy to Roman Emperor
44	James 'the Great' beheaded by Herod Agrippa
46	First missionary journey of Paul
48	Council of Christians at Jerusalem
62	James the brother of the Lord put to death by Sanhedrin
66–74	First Jewish Revolt against Rome: fails
c. 75	Romans strictly enforce tax on Jews
132–5	Second Jewish revolt against Rome: fails

Chapter Three

The Jews and the Gentile Mission (to AD 100)

To find the origins of the Christian church, we have to focus down on the birth of Jesus Christ in one small and troublesome client state of the Roman Empire, Palestine. There were several kingdoms like this owing allegiance to Rome in the early decades of the Empire, but none of the others can have contained a people so proud of its identity and convinced of its God-given destiny in the world as the Jewish subjects of King Herod the Great. This was not because the Jews of Palestine were particularly fond of Herod; most of them regarded him as an outsider and a betrayer of ancient national traditions, and they looked beyond his frontiers to fellow-Jews who through the long history of their race, had formed communities scattered throughout the Near East and the Mediterranean basin.

The history of the Jewish people during the biblical period is dealt with elsewhere in this series (see *Groundwork of Biblical Studies*, 1979, Chapter Ten), so we need not repeat that outline in detail; what we need to appreciate is that it was a constant struggle for the Jewish people to retain their sense of a common Jewish identity and their special relationship with the supreme God, in the face of odds which seemed overwhelming. Their kingdom had split up and then been overwhelmed by the Babylonian Empire; yet obstinately some of the race who thought of themselves as Israelites had returned to their homeland in Palestine. Here they no longer had prophets like Isaiah or Jeremiah to guide them, but this only strengthened their determination to remain faithful to their ancient identity. If there were no prophets, they could still find this identity in the laws and stories which they found in their sacred writings: what Christians call the Old Testament. So uniquely in the ancient world, their religion became focussed on a series of written documents – even more profoundly than the Greeks, with their sense of unity through a common heritage in the works of Homer.

In the troubled centuries after the return from Babylon, the Jews were faced with the constant prospect of more powerful cultures absorbing them and ending their sense of being different; this became particularly true after Alexander the Great of Macedon had burst into the eastern Mediterranean and his successors had established Hellenistic kingdoms. Hellenistic rule first by the Ptolemies of Egypt and then by the Seleucids of Syria meant that the Jews had to face the Greek culture which we have already examined. It was always an uneasy relationship, and it would remain so when Christianity had to decide whether or not to throw off all its links with Judaism and become a Greek religion. However, long before that, the conflict between a Jewish identity and the Greek world around it exploded into open violence when the Seleucid king Antiochus IV (who boastfully called himself *Epiphanes* or 'Manifestation') tried to force Greek ways on the Jews and to attack the religious life centred on the Jewish Temple in Jerusalem. From 167 BC the Jews began a revolt against Antiochus, initially under the leadership of Judas Maccabeus; this succeeded in winning them independence under native rulers known as the Hasmoneans, high priests and descendants of the heroes of the war of independence.

It was this Hasmonean dynasty which first established official contacts between the Jews and the Romans. At this stage Rome was far away and relations would remain friendly for about a century, until the Romans invaded Palestine as part of their mopping-up operations around the conquest of their real prize, the Seleucid Empire. Complicated political manoeuvres followed which resulted in the final destruction of the Hasmoneans and their replacement by a Roman puppet king, an outsider from the territory to the south of Judaea which the Romans called Idumaea (Edom): Herod, somewhat inappropriately nicknamed the Great. More complications followed his death, because the extensive territories which the Romans had allowed him to build up were divided up between his sons. During the first century AD the Romans experimented with a mixture of indirect rule through various members of the Herodian family and direct rule of parts of Palestine through a Roman official (Pontius Pilate being one of these), but eventually by the second century all this heartland of Jewish tradition was brought under the Roman Emperor's direct control. A series of Jewish revolts (particularly in AD 66-74 and 132-5) tried to repeat the success of Judas Maccabeus, but they only resulted in the Romans completely smashing Jewish political organization in its homeland.

Long before this, however, both the misfortunes of the Jews and their restless energy had resulted in them spreading much further than Palestine; they left behind communities in the territories round Babylon which would be very important centres of Jewish life for a thousand years and more. In seaports all round the Mediterranean there were Jewish communities looking for their round of worship to their local synagogues, and looking beyond them to the life of the Jerusalem Temple; from the first century BC there was an increasingly flourishing community in Rome itself, concentrated in the downtown area over the River Tiber near to where the Basilica of St Peter now stands. But one of the greatest and most significant Jewish communities was in the great seaport of Egypt, Alexandria. There may have been a million Jews in the city by the time of Christ, and they were only kept from dominating city politics by the exclusive practices of their religion. Naturally for such a wealthy and prosperous community, it was a great temptation to take on the ways of the world around them, and that was a Greek world.

At least a century before hatred of all things Greek would push Judas Maccabeus and his fellows into open rebellion, the Jews of Alexandria were commonly speaking Greek instead of Hebrew, to the extent that they were forced to translate their sacred books into Greek to make sure that they did not lose touch with the meaning. The name that has been given to this collection of translations (together with some books in Greek which they added themselves) was an indication of how proud Greek-speaking Jews were of their achievement; it became known as the Septuagint, from the Latin word for seventy, in allusion to the seventy-two translators whom legend said had produced it in seventy-two days, and who were themselves an image of the seventy elders who had been with Moses on the sacred mountain in the wilderness.

The thought of such Hellenized Jews was very influenced by the reaction of Greeks to the contents of the Septuagint: interest in and respect for such ancient writings, but also considerable puzzlement that a God who was supposed to be so powerful could do strange things like walk in the garden of Eden or indulge in arguments with earthly men like Lot or Jonah. Many Jews came to feel that such things, and such unscientific absurdities as the creation stories of Genesis, must be stories which concealed deeper layers of truth. Many Greeks had already applied this idea of allegorical meaning to their own untidy collection of myths about the gods and even to the writings of Homer; and it became naturalized among Alexandrian Jews with the biblical commentaries of Jesus Christ's contemporary, Philo. When a Christian community eventually became established alongside the Jewish community in Alexandria, it would be much influenced by Philo's allegorical method.

Jewish life in the time of Christ thus presented a picture of such rich complexity that we might wonder how one sort of Jew could recognize a different sort of Jew as worshipping the same God. The extent of the problem becomes apparent if we consider that scholars are certain that for centuries before the first century AD, Judaism had not one but three differing versions of the Hebrew scriptures. Within Palestinian life, besides the supporters of the upstart Herod and his family, there were at least four identities for Judaism: Sadducees, Pharisees, Essenes and Zealots, let alone many lesser sects. Each saw itself as the most authentic expression of the message: perhaps one way to understand the difference between them is to realize that they all took a different stance to the outside world and all the temptations away from Jewish tradition that it represented.

The Sadducees provided the élite which ran the Temple; they had done well out of successive regimes both Jewish and non-Jewish, and they continued to do well when the Romans were in charge. It was therefore not surprising that they were the most flexible of our four groups in relation to outsiders; for them, it was enough to keep the basic commands of the Law in the scriptures and not add to them the complex additional regulations which governed the everyday life of the Pharisees and which made Pharisee life obviously distinct from the world of non-Jews around them. For the Essenes, however, even the distinctiveness which the Pharisees maintained was not enough to keep them from pollution by the world of semi-colonial Roman Palestine. The Essenes got right outside ordinary society by setting up their own separate communities, usually well away from others, with their own literature and their own traditions of persecution by other Jews. The Zealots held a militant version of the same theme; for them, the only solution to the humiliation of Roman rule over the Jewish homeland was to take up the old traditions of violence, and it was they who gave the impetus to the disastrous revolts which shattered Jewish life in Palestine by the second century AD.

When the Christian sect appeared on the scene announcing its crucified leader as Messiah and God, it was therefore fitting into a religious world which was used to one section of Judaism claiming that it had the real answer to the problem of Jewish identity. The Christians were unusual in that their Messiah was not a victorious military figure, but a man who followed a minority tradition in Jewish literature, a leader who suffered and was humiliated for the people, like the Suffering Servant described by the second of the prophets whose work is found in the Book of Isaiah. They were also convinced that the world around them was about to end and be replaced by a new kingdom; this was the message which it was their special duty to proclaim to Israel.

In 1947 and in the years following, a large collection of Hebrew and Aramaic documents was discovered in caves around the Dead Sea community of Qumran; popularly known as the Dead Sea Scrolls, these works have provided a flood of new information on Jewish life in the very period when the Christians were emerging as a sect within Judaism. They are likely to have been produced by a community of Essenes, and at first they seemed to suggest that Christianity had close links with such communities. After all, the Dead Sea Scrolls made it clear that those who read them had shared property, led lives of austerity and had a great interest in Old Testament prophecy, with a particular tradition that they had once had a Teacher of Righteousness who had suffered at the hands of the Jewish establishment; the Qumran community also believed in an imminent divine intervention in the world.

However, the differences in the attitudes of the Qumran community and of the first Christians are equally striking. There is certainly no hint of any continuity between the two organizations, and not much trace of borrowings in their literature. The Essene communities seem to have been preoccupied by the need for ritual purity in their lives, which meant a constant round of ceremonial washings, and Greek writers tell us also that they much concerned themselves with a scheme of naming objects and powers in this world and the next, distinguishing them from the outside world. Christian literature shows little trace of such interests; and above all, Christianity developed a very different attitude to the outside world, both Jewish and non-Jewish. Within Judaism, even when their founder Jesus had been executed at the instigation of the Jerusalem Temple authorities, the first Christians went on taking part in the worship of the Temple; we can see this from references in the Acts of the Apostles. Above all, they turned their face not eastward towards the great deserts on the edge of Palestine, but westward, into the teeming life of the Roman Empire and the Mediterranean basin. They sought to convert the mainstream of Judaism, the congregations gathered around the synagogues of Palestine and the whole network of Mediterranean ports.

In this aim they were largely unsuccessful. Different groups within Judaism would respond unfavourably to different parts of the Christian message. For the Sadducees it was too disruptive; after all, it had been the Sadducees who had instigated the arrest and victimization of Jesus. For the Pharisees, the Christians sat too lightly to the obligations of Jewish law: for the Essenes, they were too keen to embrace the everyday world and to spread their message through it. For the Zealots, they were deplorably hostile to violence. However, this failure in Judaism was the basis of the massive Christian success elsewhere. If Christianity had succeeded in capturing the heart of the Jewish people, it is likely that it would have remained a fairly selective body; Judaism has rarely shown the appetite for converts which has been a feature of Christianity for most of its history. In the decades after the death of Jesus, Christianity began turning its attention to the world beyond Judaism, particularly through the work and writings of a brilliant convert from the Jewish establishment, Paul of Tarsus.

This change of direction was not an easy one; it engendered debates which seem very decorous as they are presented to us in the Acts of the Apostles, but which are more immediately reflected in the occasional fiery phrase of Paul at his most aggressive: look for instance at his description of his clash with Peter and Judaizing Christians in Gal.2.11f. At stake was an issue which would trouble Christianity for one hundred and fifty years: how far should it move from its Jewish roots, if it started preaching the good news of Christ's kingdom to non-Jews? Straight away symbolic questions posed themselves: should converts to Christianity accept such features of Jewish life as circumcision, strict adherence to the Law of Moses and abstention from food defiled by association with pagan worship (virtually all meat sold in the non-Jewish world would fall into this category)? The long-term victory in this contest would go to those Christian communities which followed Paul: he would only allow that Christians should not eat idolatrous food, and he could be quite offensive about the Jewish Law.

In this Paul was opposed by the oldest and at first the most important Christian community, the church in Jerusalem, presided over by James the brother of the Lord. When he was executed by the Jewish authorities in AD 62, his place at the head of the Jerusalem congregation was taken by another kinsman of the Lord, Simeon; so there was a great deal of prestige attached to this community in the shadow of the Jewish Temple. What might well have happened would have been the development of two branches of Christianity in fundamental disagreement with each other about their relationship with Judaism: a Jewish church looking to the tradition represented by James and a Gentile church treasuring the writings of Paul. In fact this is not so; all Christians alive today are the heirs of Paul's church, and the other type of Christianity has disappeared. How did this happen? A great political crisis intervened to transform the situation.

The fall of Jerusalem and after

In 66 the nationalist revolt which had been threatening for decades in Palestine broke out. The rebels eventually took control in Jerusalem and massacred the Sadducee élite, whom they regarded as collaborators with the Romans. The Jewish Christian church, interestingly, fled from the city; it was sufficiently distant from the world of Jewish nationalism to wish to keep out of this struggle. The result of the revolt was in the long term probably inevitable: the Romans could not afford to lose their grip on this corner of the Mediterranean, and they put a huge effort into crushing the rebels. Jerusalem lay in ruins, and no substantial Christian community was to return to it until the fourth century. The Jerusalem

Christians regrouped in the town of Pella in the upper Jordan valley, and maintained contact with other Jewish-Christian communities in the Near East. Their refusal to become associated with the second great Jewish Revolt of 132-5 cost them dear, but even when the crushing of the rebellion brought them relief, their future was one of gradual decline. No longer did they have the prestige of a centre in the sacred city of Jerusalem. The fourth-century writer Jerome knew Jewish-Christian communities, and translated their 'Gospel according to the Hebrews' into Latin, but with that, they fade from history. The Gentile church, originally their daughter, rejected them as imperfect Christians, and soon took their ancient name of Ebionites ('the Poor') as the description of a heretical sect.

The catastrophe of Jerusalem's destruction had another important effect: it left the Jewish intelligentsia determined to make their peace with the Roman authorities, to preserve their religion and to give it a more coherent identity. Like the Jewish Christians, mainstream Judaism had to regroup away from the former capital, and it did so at the town of Jamnia near the coast – in the opposite direction from Pella! Here it established an assembly of religious leaders which was very influential in giving Judaism a unity of religious belief which it had not previously possessed. The Sadducee leadership had been destroyed, and so it was the Pharisee group which stamped its identity on surviving Judaism.

It is interesting to see this development reflected in the Gospels. although it had been the Sadducees who had been responsible for the train of events leading to the death of Jesus, it is the Pharisees who come in for most of the abuse recorded by the Gospel writers. When the Gospels were compiled, the Pharisees were the leaders of Judaism, a living force to which Christian communities were now strongly opposed. The growing coherence in Judaism, the narrowing in the variety of Jewish belief, meant that by the end of the first century AD a clear break had become inevitable between Christianity and Judaism. For most communities, the break probably occurred two or more decades earlier. The Roman authorities unwittingly encouraged the process by taking into their hands the receipt of the tax formerly paid by Jews to the Jerusalem Temple, now destroyed; for them it was important to know who was and who was not a Jew. A question from a civil servant demands a decision! Despite all the Jewish rebellions, tax-paying Jews continued to enjoy their status as an officially recognized religion (a *religio licita*); Christians who finally broke their links with the parent culture would find no such recognition from the Roman government.

Thanks to these developments, and thanks to the energy of Paul's work in reaching out to the Gentile world, the movement which had started as a Jewish sect had decisively shifted away from its Palestinian home. Its mission was now to conquer the whole world; and if it was to do so, it would have to conquer the capital of the known world, Rome. Even the great cities of the eastern Mediterranean, the old Seleucid capital of Antioch or the Ptolemies' former Egyptian capital of Alexandria would not do; while outside the Roman Empire, Babylon, home to a flourishing Jewish community, stoutly resisted Christian penetration. The church would have to encounter the city where the Roman Emperor himself presided over the power which held all the Mediterranean in its grasp. It was here that Peter and Paul met their deaths; the leadership of the Western Church would build on that memory over a thousand years to create one of Christianity's most noble and most dangerous visions, the Roman papacy. Without the tragedy of the destruction of Jerusalem, Rome might never have taken the unique place which it has held in the story of Western Christian faith.

Chronology for Chapters Four and Five

62	James the brother of the Lord put to death by Sanhedrin
66	Christians flee from Jerusalem in Jewish Revolt
c. 69	Ignatius succeeds Euodius as bishop in Antioch
c. 100	*I Clement* written to Corinthian church from Rome
c. 107	Ignatius writes seven epistles
c. 130	Justin Martyr becomes a Christian at Ephesus
c. 136	Valentinus the Gnostic arrives in Rome
c. 140	Marcion arrives in Rome
144	Marcion expelled from Christian community in Rome
172	Montanism comes to prominence in Phrygia
c. 172	Tatian leaves Rome for the East
177	Irenaeus becomes bishop in Lyon after persecution
c. 180	Montanists condemned by Bishop Eleutherius of Rome
c. 190	Theodotus arrives in Rome. Clement succeeds Pantaenus in Christian schools in Alexandria
c. 197	Tertullian becomes a Christian
202	Roman authorities persecute church, particularly in north Africa and Alexandria
c. 213	Tertullian writes abusive pamphlet against Praxeas
215	Origen preaches in Palestine: row with Demetrius
230	New Origen/Demetrius row: Origen leaves for Caesarea (Palestine)
250	Origen tortured by Emperor Decius
268	Paul deposed as Bishop of Samosata for monarchian views etc.

Chapter Four

Folly to the Greeks?
(AD 50 to 200)

Once it had broken with its Jewish parent body, Christianity started moving out into the Greek world, and by AD 200 it was a force which the Roman élite could no longer ignore. How did it achieve this success? Historians will not be faithful to their calling if they take refuge in statements like 'because it was true'; they can only gather the evidence which helps us to understand the very varied motives with which people embraced the Christian faith. To begin with, historians can point to the very favourable conditions which the church found for its mission. Augustus and his successors had torn down political frontiers throughout the Mediterranean, and by controlling piracy, they had made it comparatively safe and easy to travel from one end of the sea to the other.

Besides imperial security, the church could take advantage of the spiritual needs which it found in the Empire; I have already mentioned the pessimism of much Hellenistic philosophy and the blow which the establishment of the Empire dealt to the credibility of the official gods. Christianity offered more than most of its rivals; few even of the other eastern cults promised immortality, not even the minority which gained widespread popularity like Mithraism; they concentrated on the concerns of this life. Moreover, the church offered two things normally distinct in paganism: both cultic rituals and a philosophy of life which became increasingly intellectually satisfying as Christians reflected at length on their distinctive identity and the nature of their Saviour. A pagan might attend one or more cults to secure worldly ends, perhaps using the more sophisticated cults for more sophisticated requests, but it would be to the classical philosophers that he would turn if he was looking for guidance on how to conduct his life. The convert to Christianity got a package deal! Christianity's most dangerous rivals in the late Empire would be creeds like neo-Platonism which similarly combined cult and philosophy.

Such considerations might appeal to the well-educated and well-to-do; conversely, Christianity might win the very poor by its evident concern to look after its disadvantaged members; Christian charity came ruefully to be acknowledged, even admired, by pagans. The church would give its members a decent burial, and that was very important in the ancient world; probably the first grudging recognition which Christianity received in Roman official circles was as a series of burial clubs. Christian ideology would also be attractive to two great disadvantaged groups in classical society: women and slaves. Paul had proclaimed that in Christ there was neither Jew nor Greek, slave nor freeman, male or female (Gal.3.28); the Christian ethic of marriage insisted (with a novelty startling in Graeco-Roman circles) both that a woman had as much right to expect chastity from her husband as he from her, and that a slave had as much right to contract a full, indissoluble marriage as anyone else. There is evidence, for instance, to suggest that when the pagan Roman aristocracy finally and reluctantly succumbed to Christianity at the very end of the fourth century, one of the main impulses came from strong-minded female members of the great families who had converted first and who would not then take no for an answer.

On the other hand, the church was not revolutionary enough in its view of women or slaves fundamentally to challenge male superiority to both groups. It resolutely maintained a male clergy in the Jewish tradition. Although the New Testament has references to women playing quite significant roles in church affairs, they were still in a secondary place; although there were women deacons in some parts of the church, their main liturgical function seems to have been to look after female candidates in services of baptism, and their role seems to have lapsed after the first few centuries. Paul accepted the institution of slavery, which was after all the whole basis of ancient society; for his generation of Christians, who believed that the world was about to come to an end at any minute, there was no point in challenging any part of the existing social structure. By the fourth century, Christian writers like Bishop Ambrose of Milan were providing even more robust defences of the idea of slavery than pagan philosophers before them.

Christianity therefore appealed in all sorts of ways to all sorts of people. As it expanded into the Graeco-Roman society of the Mediterranean in the late first century, it was meeting a world very different from that of Judaism; at the same time, it was having to decide just how separate from Judaism it ought to be. As it claimed more and more converts, it was meeting people with a decent Greek education, with all the restless curiosity based on centuries of deep reflection on the meaning of life which Greek culture represented. It was therefore only natural for the church to try and explain its doctrines by reference to the thought and the categories of the Greek philosophers. Jews had found it difficult enough to understand how the man Jesus could also be God; for Greeks, with Plato as their guide to the nature of God, it was more difficult still. A supreme God was without change or passions, and his perfection demanded no division of his substance; how then could a Jewish carpenter's son, who had cried out in agony on a gallows and then died, really be God? The answers which modern Christians have inherited from the second-century church were only one set of answers to this embarrassing problem. There were many other answers among people who called themselves Christians or who were at least fascinated by the personality and the power of Christ; collectively these alternative answers have found a common label as Gnosticism.

The Gnostics

Who were the Gnostics? Their name simply comes from the ordinary Greek word for knowledge (*gnosis*), for they claimed to have special knowledge about the ultimate secrets of the world, of the Saviour, and of salvation, but that hardly helps us define them closely. There was never such a thing as the Gnostic church, with a set of rule-books and membership lists; Gnosticism ranged through a whole variety of sects and sets of belief, many of which are quite definitely not related to Christianity. It is this variety which has made it difficult to say how Gnosticism arose: scholars still argue. Some point to the affinities with Greek thought, others to the way in which Gnostic dualism (the idea of a struggle between good and evil, darkness and light) reflects the beliefs of

Near-Eastern religions like the Zoroastrianism of Iran. Some have pointed to far-off Hinduism, and admittedly such distant links are perfectly possible; the Greeks had reached India, and Roman traders carried on a flourishing trade with the sub-continent. Several influences probably made up the Gnostic family; rather than go into the details of the various belief-systems which these influences produced (in the followers of Saturninus, Basilides, Valentinus or Carpocrates, for instance), I shall draw out some of the common strands within Christian Gnosticism. The task has become easier over the last few decades; whereas previously we had to rely mainly on the hostile descriptions penned by main-stream Christian writers, in 1945-46 a large collection of Gnostic writings was discovered in Upper Egypt at Nag Hammadi, and we can hear them speak for themselves.

Basic to most Gnostic systems of beliefs was a distruct of the Jewish account of creation, as we will see. This is a clear sign that Gnosticism emerged in environments which were familiar with Judaism, and that Gnostics were people who found the Jewish message hard to take or had revolted from its content. Gnosticism was a creed for cultural frontiers, places where Judaism interacted with Greek culture, for example, and produced a hybrid of beliefs. So we find that Alexandria, with its great Greek university and influential Jewish community, was a home of Gnosticism, and we find that the early Christian fathers identified Samaria as one of Gnosticism's early centres. Samaria was the country of a people related to the mainstream Jews, but with a long tradition of hostil-ity to them. Thus like the Christians of the first century, Gnostics were on the edge of Judaism looking in, and objecting to what they saw; but their objections were more fundamental.

Perhaps one of the first things which makes people turn to consider religion is a consciousness of suffering and misery, and these themes were very much at the forefront of the Gnostics' thoughts. They asked why we are stuck in such an imperfect and contemptible world; they felt embarrassed by the human body, with all its diseases and petty lusts. The answer to these problems and embarrassments was one which would have been congenial either to Greeks, with their background in Plato's thought, or to many of the dualist cults of the East: what we see and experience with our senses is a mere illusion, a pale picture of a spiritual reality. It follows that this world as a whole is an inferior state of being, and that such a world could not possibly have been created by a supreme God. Yet the Hebrew Scriptures say that it was; in Genesis is the bold claim that God looked on this earthly creation and that it was good. What would the Gnostics do with this statement?

A whole series of conclusions followed from the Gnostics' firm rejection of the created world and of the Jewish affirmation that it was a good creation of God:

1. If the God of the Old Testament who created the material world said that he was the true and only God, then he was either a fool or a liar. At best he could be described, using Plato's term, as a *demiurge*, a craftsman. Beyond him there must be a Supreme Being, a first cause of all things which are real.

2. The Hebrew Scriptures make it clear that the God of the Jews either knew nothing of this supreme God or concealed his knowledge; the world of humankind was ignorant of the true God until the coming of Jesus Christ, who therefore had nothing to do with the God of the Jews.

3. Separating our created world from the Supreme Being was a complicated hierarchy of beings (described differently in different gnostic systems); the creation described in Genesis was a disaster, an interruption in the perfection and harmony of this original scheme.

4. Some elements in humanity were capable of avoiding the consequences of disaster and reaching their way back to the original perfection through *gnosis*; why this should be so was accounted for differently in various Gnostic systems, but was usually seen as the result of external fate: a sort of predestination. It was these people – the Gnostics themselves – whom Jesus Christ had come to save.

5. There could be no true union between the world of spirit and the world of matter, so Jesus Christ could never truly have taken on flesh, and he could never have felt any of the things which fleshly people feel – particularly the suffering of humanity. The passion and resurrection of Christ were therefore not real; they were just play-acting (the doctrine known as *docetism*).

6. If this was true of Christ, it is also true of the spark of true knowledge within the Gnostic believer. There is no solidarity between the divine element in the body and the matter which

clothes it like a prison. The mortal flesh must be mortified by asceticism because it is despicable, or contrariwise, the soul can be regarded as so independent of the body that anything goes; the most wild earthly excesses will not affect the soul's chances of salvation, and may even express the Gnostic's confidence in his redemption.

Such doctrines ran against the whole tendency of Jewish theology, with its earthy affirmation of created things and its constant theme of God's personal relationship with his chosen people. For the church it was particularly tempting to go down the Gnostic road. After all, in the last chapter we have seen the church moving steadily away from its Jewish roots and entering a Hellenized world; now, by the end of the first century AD, the Gnostics were saying to the newly independent Christian body that it should go the whole hog and cut the links with the Jewish past altogether. What could be more logical? It must have been particularly tempting in view of the way in which Gnostic beliefs were so congenial to people with a Greek background; it would give the church's message a relevance to those who might otherwise dismiss Christianity as a crude Jewish superstition. The Gnostics included people of sophistication and learning, probably more than the main Christian body in its first decades, and arguably they had a better solution to the problem of evil in the world than the Christian church has ever been able to provide. Christianity has always found it hard to reconcile its idea of a universe in which everything has been created by a good God with the existence of evil: why should a good God allow such a thing to happen? Such a question was easy for Gnostics to answer. Evil simply existed; it had not been created by God. Life was a battle between good and evil, in a material world which was wholly outside God's control, and beyond his interests. It all made good sense.

Marcion

Particularly tempting for the church was the approach adopted by a Christian thinker of the early second century named Marcion. The son of the bishop of the town of Sinope on the Black Sea coast, he made a tidy fortune out of shipping, and used this wealth to finance a career as a religious leader. He came to Rome about

140, but was eventually expelled by the Christian church there when the full radicalism of his approach to the faith became apparent. Opinions differ as to whether Marcion can be numbered among the Gnostics, but like them, he was determined to pull Christianity away from its Jewish roots. In characteristically Greek fashion, he found the Hebrew Scripture crude and offensive; he saw the God of the Jews as a God of law, rather than the God of love whom he saw perfectly revealed in Jesus Christ. So the books of the Septuagint he dismissed as 'Jewish fables', and in his condemnation of Jewish law, felt that he had found the perfect ally in the writings of Paul. Taking Paul's conflict with Judaism to its extreme, he came to the same conclusion as the Gnostics in saying that the created world so lovingly described in Genesis must be a worthless sham, and that therefore Jesus's human flesh can have been nothing but an illusion; his passion and death should be blamed on the Creator Demiurge.

Marcion was a literalist: he took the first apparent sense of scripture. If he found something in the Christian sacred writings which he found inexplicable or an embarrassment, he did not follow the Alexandrian line of finding an allegorical hidden truth inside it, but simply cut it out. The result was that all of what we call the Old Testament had to go, and all that remained of the New Testament were doctored versions of Paul's letters and a slightly edited Luke's Gospel – chosen perhaps because Luke was the Gospel with which Marcion had grown up, or because of the way in which Luke presents the picture of a spiritual Christ. To hammer home his anti-Jewish message, he added a Book of Antitheses pointing out the difference in approach between his selection of scripture and the Hebrew sacred books.

References to Christians opposing Marcion come from places as far apart as France and Syria, so it is clear that his teachings had an alarmingly widespread effect on the church, and needed to be met with a vigorous response. The Gnostics and the Marcionites presented the church with a crisis of identity. It must draw boundaries around itself, and make clear what its doctrines were. There were three main ways of achieving this: developing a canon of scripture, forming creeds and formulating a ministry. A canon (that is, a rule, from the Greek for 'straight rod') defined exactly which writings about the faith should be regarded as divinely inspired and therefore authoritative. Creeds formed simple statements of what Christianity meant. A single system of ministry developed authority so that certain people within the church could be regarded as guardians and teachers of true doctrine.

The Canon

In the first century, the Christian Bible had simply been the Hebrew Scriptures in the Septuagint version; this would come to be accepted by the church as its Old Testament. Alongside this were a great mass of different traditions about the sayings and doings of Jesus, passed on by word of mouth. The process of sorting out these sayings to give them an ordered place in the life of the church produced various collections, of which four became accepted during the second century as Gospels with a special authority. The surviving letters of Paul gained a central place already in the first century, for we find them quoted in Christian writings in the decades before AD 100; other works which are now in our New Testament, such as the Pastoral Epistles and St John, were gradually accepted into the canon. It was a slow and untidy process, given an urgency by Marcion's construction of his own canon, but even with that spur in the mid second century, the earliest complete list of our accepted New Testament books which we can find is as late as AD 367, laid down in a pastoral letter written by Athanasius the Bishop of Alexandria.

Even then, parts of the church continued to argue whether it was really necessary to have four Gospels which did not always agree with each other, and some churches went on into the fifth century using a harmony (the Greek word for this is *Diatessaron*) combining all four, produced by a Syrian writer named Tatian at the end of the second century. Besides this, some books drifted in and out of the canon: the church of Corinth long treasured and read as scripture the first of the two epistles written to them by Clement of Rome; the strongly anti-Jewish Epistle of Barnabas enjoyed great popularity and lasting influence. On the other side, some Christians regarded the Gospel of St John with suspicion, and the other New Testament writings attributed to St John were among the last to be universally accepted as scripture: Revelation as late as the fifth century in parts of the Greek East.

Creeds

The advantage of credal statements defining the faith was that they could be learnt quickly by virtually every believer as a way of excluding unorthodoxy. Probably credal formulae had been taught to new believers from the earliest days of the Christian sect; several can be traced embedded in the text of both Pauline and non-Pauline epistles. However, with the coming of the Gnostics, these creeds took on a new aggressive tone. Take for instance the credal statement set down by Bishop Irenaeus of Lyon in his influential book *Against Heresies* in the late second century: he says that the church has received the faith

> in one God, the Father Almighty, who made the heaven and the earth and the seas and all things that are in them; and in one Christ Jesus, the Son of God, who became incarnate for our salvation; and in the Holy Spirit, who proclaimed through the prophets the dispensations and the advents, and the birth from a virgin, and the passion, and the resurrection from the dead, and the incarnate ascension into heaven of the beloved Christ Jesus, our Lord, and his future manifestations from heaven in the glory of the Father to sum up all things and to raise up anew all flesh of the whole human race . . .

This Creed contains much less matter than later creeds, which were concerned to exclude other challenges to the church's identity; practically every clause in it hits at the Gnostics. No Gnostic could have asserted, for instance, that God made the earth or that all flesh could be raised anew; few would have wanted to say that the Hebrew prophets foretold the coming of Jesus.

The Ministry

The most effective answer to the Gnostics was to confront them in their bewildering variety with a single church which could not be diverted by their beliefs; the writers against the Gnostics all take as one of their main themes the unity of the Christian church. The way to emphasize this unity was to increase the authority and coherence of the ministry, a process which was very marked during the second century. By AD 200, virtually all the church took for granted the existence of a threefold ministry of bishop, priest and deacon, and there would be few challenges to this pattern for the next thirteen hundred years. When the pattern was challenged in the sixteenth-century Reformation, the opposing viewpoints all looked for proof of their own patterns of ministry in the early church, and it must be said that in the end no party could find complete satisfaction in the evidence. Let us briefly review what can be said.

The most important church of the first generation was Jerusalem, and it is clear that from the beginning this had a single head, first St Peter (cf. I Cor. 15.5), who presided over the remaining Apostles and a group of elders (the Greek is *presbyteroi*). In Chapter Three we saw how James the brother of the Lord came to share the authority of the Apostles, and how his successors also claimed kinship with the Lord. In addition to these there was a group of seven deacons (the word comes from the Greek *diakonos*, a servant): an equivalent in embryo, it might seem, to the later grades of bishop, priest and deacon. A similar picture emerges from one of the earliest Christian centres, Antioch in Syria, where the Christians were first nicknamed Christians. At first there seems to have been a group of 'apostolic' or inspired men at the head, but when the church at Antioch becomes visible to us once more at the end of the first century, we find a single bishop as at Jerusalem, Ignatius by name, sometimes calling himself Bishop of Syria, sometimes Bishop of Antioch; Ignatius was also assisted by presbyters and deacons. It might seem from this that the Catholic case for ministry is clinched, but we need to look elsewhere to find the full story.

Antioch and Jerusalem seem to have been finding their models for ministry in the organization of the Jewish Temple and its hierarchy, as one might expect from Christian centres so much resonating with the Palestinian past. The church elsewhere had spread mainly through the work of Paul and like-minded people, and was very quickly becoming more Hellenistic in its thinking. All sorts of patterns of ministry emerge from casual references in Acts and in various Epistles: talk of *charismata*, gifts of the Spirit, is frequent, and these gifts were not confined to the Apostles. Various churches seem to have prized different manifestations of the Spirit: Paul, for instance, had trouble tackling the emphasis on ecstatic utterance in the church at Corinth. Paul lists gifts of the Spirit more than once, and if you look at such lists, for instance, comparing the lists in I Cor. 12 and Eph. 4, you will see that these are not the same. They should not be considered as rigid technical terms, merely as ways of organizing a mission which constantly called for improvisation, just as John Wesley had to improvise an organization for mission in the conditions of eighteenth-century England

Gradually, however, the similar situations which the work of mission produced tended towards a standardization of language. The words *presbyteros* (elder) and *episkopos* (overseer) are found scattered through Acts and the Epistles, but it is quite clear that at this early stage they often described the same people interchangeably; so for instance in Acts 20, Paul is said to have addressed himself to the *presbyteroi* of Ephesus, but to have told them that the Holy Spirit had made them pastors or bishops (*episkopoi*) over their church. Again a comparison with the early development of Methodism may be helpful: here in the late eighteenth and early nineteenth century a mobile 'itinerant' ministry grew up alongside a locally-based one, that of the local preachers. A similar stage can be detected in the late first-century church: the mobile ministry included those known as apostles and prophets, the local ministry in particular communities consisted of bishops or presbyters and a separate function of deacon. The deacon was regarded as serving the other grade, particularly in the performance of the eucharist, the central Christian act, and also in the day-to-day running of church affairs.

It was perhaps not surprising that a mobile and a local ministry should sometimes come into conflict; they represented two different ways of presenting authority handed down from the Apostles. The tension is reflected in a curious but probably very early book about church life and organization called the *Didache* (that is, 'teaching'). For instance, the *Didache* lays down instructions for detecting false prophets, and specifies how prophets should be entertained; it also reminds its readers that the local ministry should be given just as much honour as the mobile ministry. It does not take much imagination to see why a community should have felt it necessary to commit such thoughts to writing.

How would this tension be resolved? Ultimately it would be the mobile ministry which would disappear from the mainstream church, leaving the local ministry as the only accepted form. Perhaps this was inevitable as the church began to settle down round local centres which had their own traditions and their own way of life, but the need to show a settled continuity of Christian doctrine against the alternatives offered by the Gnostics was a powerful incentive to shift the balance of authority in favour of the local ministry. This theme of continuity was especially prominent in an influential document of about AD 100, the epistle sent by Clement of Rome to the church at Corinth. There had been trouble at Corinth, which had resulted in the congregation dismissing their leadership and appointing others. Clement wrote from Rome in the most solemn terms to protest, not because the congregation was deviating in any way in doctrine, but simply because it was endangering the succession of authority from the Apostles. Break this, said Clement, and you endanger the succession of doctrine, which is the only way of making sure that doctrine remains the same in Corinth as in Rome and throughout the whole church. So here we see the characteristic Christian theme of unity in defence against doctrinal deviation, and for the first time we hear of apostolic succession. The Corinthians took the point; their old leaders were restored, and the prestige of the Roman church among its fellows had begun on its long march towards the medieval papacy.

Clement, it must be noted, assumed the twofold order of bishop/ presbyter and deacon which can also be seen in the *Didache*, even though most sources are agreed in regarding him as the Bishop of Rome. Another curious little work from Rome not much later than the time of Clement, the book by Hermas known as the *Shepherd*, also talks of a collegiate ministry of presbyter/bishops, even though the final version of the *Shepherd* was said in the late second century to have been written when Hermas's brother Pius was Bishop of Rome. So the two-fold and the three-fold view of the ministry could coexist happily side by side; yet the separation of one leading bishop-figure from the other presbyters would be virtually complete by the end of the second century. One powerful force in this development was the prestige enjoyed in all parts of the church by the seven letters written to various churches and to Bishop Polycarp of Smyrna by Ignatius, Bishop of Antioch. All of them relate to his journey from Antioch to Rome under arrest just after AD 100, and were written in the certain expectation, not to say joyful hope, of martyrdom for the sake of his faith.

In these letters, Ignatius spoke much of his concern at what are recognizable as early forms of Gnostic belief, including docetic views of Christ's passion. To combat this he emphasized the reality both of Christ's divinity and his humanity, which he saw best expressed in the church's continuing celebration of the eucharist, where spirit and flesh meet in a wonderful mystery. How should this doctrine be guaranteed, however? Ignatius pointed to the standard of doctrine set by the church of Rome, which he knew would be the city of his martyrdom; it is worth noting that there was no mention of the bishop of Rome, simply of the church. He linked with this the role of the bishop of each community, who should be the one person in every place responsible for handing on the faith and guarding against deviation. He was the obvious person, since he presided at the eucharist, and he should be the automatic source of authority: 'Follow, all of you, the bishop, as Jesus Christ followed the Father; and follow the presbytery as the Apostles ... Let no man do aught pertaining to the Church apart from the bishop.'

The cynical might say that it was easy for Ignatius to take this line, since there was already one bishop in Antioch and his name was Ignatius, but the passion of his arguments and the respect which his courage and death won for his memory made sure that this appeal would be heard. The advantages were obvious; it was much more straightforward for one person to act as a focus for the church in this way to resist new departures in doctrine, just as it made more sense for one man to preside over a community's eucharist than it did for a committee to do so. If churches started taking this line on the nature of ecclesiastical authority, it is easy to see that the alternative authority represented by the mobile ministry should come to seem unnecessary and even a threat to the good order of the church.

It is of real significance that there is no surviving debate about the gradual domination of church affairs in each community by one man in apostolic succession (monarchical episcopacy); the early Christians were not afraid to commit their disagreements with each other to writing, but in this case, they do not seem to have done so. The prestige and example of Jerusalem and Antioch must have helped; and by the end of the second century the pattern set by the discussion of apostolic succession in Clement and of monarchical episcopacy in Ignatius had taken over the whole Christian world. Big churches soon had many presbyters under the bishop's authority; deacons were the bishop's assistants, occasionally rising to be bishops, but never being made presbyters. Much later, the distinctive role of the deacon diminished, and already in the late Roman Empire there were examples of the diaconate being used as the first step in a successful clerical career through the presbyterate up to the rank of bishop, just like the various career grades in the Roman civil service.

Montanism

The disappearance of the mobile clergy was probably sealed by the defeat of the movement known as Montanism at the end of the second century. Montanus was a native of Phrygia in the mountains of Asia Minor, already a strong Christian centre in the second century. He was a convert, and like so many converts, a passionate enthusiast for his new found faith; some time between 150 and 180 he began proclaiming that he had new revelations to make from the Holy Spirit to add to the gospel story. At first what he said was fairly orthodox, and it was the medium rather than the message which worried the church authorities. By what right did this man with no commission, in no apostolic succession, speak new truths of the faith, and sweep crowds along with him in his excitement? What made it worse was that Montanus was accompanied by female prophetesses, who spoke in states of ecstasy. The church had set its face against women exercising authority in the community; it was too reminiscent of so many pagan cults in the world around. So the church in Asia became split down the middle about whether Montanus was a blessing or a danger. Both sides appealed to other churches round the Mediterranean, and to the great distress of the Montanists, they were condemned by Eleutherius the Bishop of Rome. As is so often the case, opposition and hostility drove them into ever wilder statements about their own mission; their total and final exclusion from the church by a Council of bishops was sadly inevitable after this. Only in north Africa, where high temperature religion would always be valued by Christians, would their passionate commitment to the Holy Spirit find a lasting sympathy within the mainstream church.

The Montanists' firm conviction that they were about to see the new Jerusalem descend on earth, and in particular near their main

Phrygian centre at Pepuza, contrasts with the church's gradual abandonment of its original keen expectation of an imminent return of the Lord Christ during the second century. Henceforward, such beliefs would be the property of groups marginal to the mainstream, and among the Montanists' contemporaries among the orthodox leadership, only Bishop Irenaeus of Lyon stands out as still enthusiastic for a vision of the world's last days coming in his own lifetime. One might regard the Montanist emphasis on new revelations of the Spirit as a natural reaction to the gradual closing of the New Testament canon: as was remarked by the north African theologian Tertullian, the most distinguished known convert to Montanism, 'Shall the devil daily devise new contrivances for evil, and can it be believed that the work of God shall stand still and make no countervailing advance?' However, equally natural was the church leadership's strong reaction against Montanus. The church was settling on one model of authority through the threefold order of ministry: the Montanists presented the model of authority conferred through the random gift of prophecy. The question of how authority is presented and derived in the church recurs again and again in its history; perhaps no completely satisfying solution can ever be found.

Gnosticism and Montanism thus had a marked effect on the church, shutting doors on all sorts of possibilities for new Christian identities and setting the direction in which Christianity would now go. The most dramatic effect of the fight against the Gnostics was to halt the church's march away from its Jewish roots, the process which had dominated its life during the first century; now it vigorously affirmed the worth of what it called the Old Testament. The defensive development of the local ministry into the exclusive structure of authority in the church was so marked as to make it reject the Montanist enthusiasm, and to put an end to any chance of the revival of a mobile ministry, where prophecy would have a leading part.

The outlines of a mainstream Christian faith had been set, a faith which we call 'catholic' ('universal') without any of the restricting overtones which that word has taken on in the last four and a half centuries. Nevertheless, the episcopal guardians of doctrine were still faced with the problem of presenting their faith to the world of the Greek and Roman cities where their congregations lived and worshipped. They had rejected some of the more extreme ways in which the Gnostics had adapted the Christian message to a classical system of thought, but large questions still remained about the relationship of the church to society around it.

Chapter Five

Talking about God (second and third centuries AD)

As the extent of the Christian sacred writings and the general shape of the doctrines which they contained became defined during the second century, Christian intellectuals were forced to begin thinking systematically how the Christian faith should be discussed both with non-Christians and with those who had accepted the faith. A great issue for these thinkers would be whether the legacy of Plato and Aristotle could be any help to them in organizing their thoughts: in other words, whether the revelation of God in Christ in the first century said everything, and the achievements of pre-Christian reason could be disregarded. Could wise and venerable men like Plato really be damned because they had not heard the Word of God? So right from the very early days of the church, Christians have needed to assess what place they give in their faith to human reason, alongside revelation. It is another of those debates, like the nature of the church's authority already mentioned, which remains as fresh now as it ever did.

Chief among the people engaged in this discussion were two groups, one working mainly in Rome and the churches of the western Mediterranean, the other based in the exciting intellectual world of Alexandria. From the first group we must briefly consider the leading figures, Justin Martyr, Irenaeus and Tertullian; from the second, the successive careers of Clement of Alexandria and Origen.

Justin, Irenaeus and Tertullian

To call our first group Westerners is misleading, because both Justin and Irenaeus were born and grew up in the eastern

Mediterranean; the fact that the main part of their work lay in the west is another instance of the way in which widely-separated parts of the church managed to keep a sense of unity and regular contact. Justin was born in Samaria; he tells us how he came to the faith in a little piece of autobiography which is also a parable of his view of the reason/revelation debate. In his search for truth in the university world of Ephesus, he started with a tutor in the Stoic tradition, who could tell him nothing about God; Stoicism was a philosophy whose chief concern was the self and self-regulation. He had no more luck with a follower of Aristotle, who was mainly concerned with fixing a fee for his services – perhaps a dig at the practical and systematizing concerns of Aristotelianism. A Pythagorean was no help to him, because he demanded that Justin should first become an expert in music, astronomy and geometry before contemplating the mysteries which these skills illustrated; finally he went to a Platonist, and found satisfaction in what he learnt here. He then happened to meet an old man on a beach near the city; the old man told him of the Hebrew prophets who had foretold Christ. Justin was converted, but in thus arriving at the end of his spiritual quest, he did not feel that he was rejecting the Platonic outlook. In particular, he was happy to explain the mysterious relationship of Jesus Christ to God the Father in terms which Plato would have understood, and which would therefore make sense to intelligent Greeks who were puzzled by Christian claims; he used Plato's concept of *Logos* (meaning 'Word'), to describe the work of our Lord.

For Justin, God the Father corresponded to Plato's discussion of a Supreme Being. Justin wanted to say with the mainstream church against the Gnostics that this supreme God had created the material world, and he tried to get over the problem of relating the two by seeing the Logos as a mediator between them. This Logos had been glimpsed in the insights of both the Hebrew prophets and great philosophers like Plato, who was thus happily enrolled among Christian witnesses as a Christian before Christ. The Logos was seen completely and finally in Jesus Christ, a person other than the Father, but derived from him with the fullness and intimacy of a flame which lights one torch from another: torchlight from torchlight, in the phrase which has become embedded in the creed we call the Nicene.

We may think that this 'Logos' solution to the Platonic difficulty of linking God with his creation solves very little, but it was a popular one in the second century, and is reflected in Justin's younger contemporary, Irenaeus. Probably from Smyrna on the west coast of Asia Minor, Irenaeus went westward (like so many Christians of his day) to Rome, where after some study he moved into southern France and the city of Lyon. When in 177 persecution devastated the Lyon Christian community and resulted in the death of Bishop Pothinus, Irenaeus succeeded as Bishop; all his career as a writer was determined by the practical concerns of a father in God for a flock troubled by official harassment and by the alternatives offered by Gnostic belief.

Irenaeus was not an innovative thinker like Justin, but as might be expected from one in his position, he defended Christianity against Gnosticism by emphasizing the tradition which the bishop embodied, just as Ignatius of Antioch had done; we have already met the credal summary of this tradition which he set down (above, Chapter Four). So the eucharist, and the symbolism which it gave to the bishop's role, were vital to him, and he was determined to stress the importance of flesh and matter which he saw proclaimed in the eucharist, against their rejection by the Gnostics. Like Justin, therefore, he talked of the gradual unfolding of God's purpose which was visible in world history. To emphasize the church's vital need of the Old Testament, he was fond of stressing the symmetries which its history revealed: thus the fall of the first man Adam was remedied by the rising of the second Adam, Christ, from the dead; the disobedience of the woman Eve remedied by the obedience of the woman Mary; the fateful role of the Tree of Life in the Garden of Eden remedied by the Tree of Life which was Christ's cross. Such symmetries, particularly delightful to a culture which was fascinated by the poetry of numbers and geometry, form the doctrine of recapitulation. It is all of a piece with Justin's and Irenaeus's lively interest in a coming earthly thousand-year rule of the saints (a *millennium*, hence the belief in such an event being known as millenarianism); we would expect God's purpose thus to be expressed on this earth, since this is where his plans have been demonstrated before.

Justin and Irenaeus were thinking and writing in Greek and ministering to Greek Christian communities in the Latin-speaking West, and the majority of Western churches must have remained Greek into the third century; a tiny fossil of this has been faithfully preserved in Roman Catholic and some Anglican liturgies through all the ages of services in Latin and other Western languages in the simple little threefold Greek prayer for mercy to Father, Son and Holy Spirit: '*Kyrie eleison, Christe eleison, Kyrie eleison*'. However, with Tertullian, we meet the first great thinker in the church's history who thought and wrote in Latin. Tertullian came from the important north African city of Carthage, which back in the third and second centuries BC had nearly succeeded in defeating the Roman Republic in a life or death struggle for control of the Mediterranean. Its conquest, destruction and refoundation as a Roman colony had been so thoroughgoing that it was now a centre of Latin culture, with its own flourishing university; it may be that it was here rather than in Rome that a Latin-speaking Christian church first emerged. The city's links with Rome were close, for it was the centre of the north African grain export trade which was a vital support for the Roman emperors in their constant task of keeping their huge capital city properly fed; the Christian churches of Carthage and Rome followed this pattern of trade in maintaining close if not always friendly links. Tertullian would have much to do with controversies which had Rome as their main stage.

Tertullian's pagan family background in the officer corps of one of the crack regiments of the imperial troops in north Africa shows us how the church was beginning to make an impact in influential circles. Converted to Christianity after a first class classical university education in Carthage, he continued to show his debt to the classical tradition in the brilliance of his Latin literary style; he writes in his numerous theological and controversial works with all the verve and energy of a very talented and very bad-tempered high-class journalist. He affected, unlike Justin, to despise the classical tradition – 'What has Athens to do with Jerusalem?' he once asked – but he could never escape it. He was a maverick Roman intellectual who spent his life in rebellion, even against the church itself, for he ended his days as a Montanist schismatic. Montanist enthusiasm appealed to him, and its restless energy and chafing against settled episcopal authority would remain a hallmark of the north African church, which treasured Tertullian's memory for centuries despite his schism.

This paradoxical rebel could in one work bitterly abuse the Bishop of Rome for his laxity in enforcing what Tertullian saw as proper Christian rigour in moral standards, and elsewhere could write movingly of the honour which attached to the role of the bishops in apostolic succession, including Rome itself. Supporters of Marcion, advocates of infant baptism, collaborators with the Empire, opponents of Montanism, all came under the lash of his pen; his advocacy of the view that the human soul is transmitted by parents to their children and is therefore inescapably associated with continuing human sin (the doctrine of 'traducianism') lay at the base of the pessimistic view of the human condition and its imprisonment in original sin which would be presented in its most extreme form by that later north African theological giant, Augustine of Hippo (below, Chapter Eight).

The Monarchian debate

Tertullian's particular value to later Christian discourse lies in the fact that he was the first writer known to us to develop a Latin vocabulary in which to discuss the nature of the Trinity. This discussion comes mainly from a typically abusive tract written against a Christian from Asia Minor called Praxeas. Praxeas represents an important school of thought within second-century Christianity called monarchianism; this was a reaction against the 'Logos' language used by theologians like Justin. Justin had been so concerned to stress the difference in the role of Father and Son in the Godhead that he had gone so far as to talk of the Logos as 'another God', although he had been quick to try and cover himself by adding 'other, I mean, in number and not in Will'. This did not satisfy some, who in a manner not unknown in the church today, thought that the Logos theologians were being too clever by half, and were endangering the basic Christian idea of the unity of God. In their anxiety to safeguard this unity ('monarchy'), they themselves were in turn in danger of losing any distinctiveness in the three persons of the Trinity – and the Trinity was the doctrine of the nature of God which the church had found best expressed its experience of his power as creator, redeemer and strengthener. So the 'monarchians' caused a reaction of extreme hostility, not simply in Tertullian, who was the first to use the term as an insult, but throughout the Christian world.

There were two main varieties of the monarchian models of God. The first, known as *adoptionist monarchianism*, explained the nature of Christ by saying that he had been adopted by God as Son, although he was a man; he was only God in the sense that the Father's power rested on his human form. Some early writers, such as Hermas in his book the *Shepherd*, had taken this view without being called heretical, but late second-century monarchians like Theodotus, an eastern visitor in Rome, took the idea much further: Theodotus could say that Jesus was a man like other men apart from his miraculous birth; at his baptism in the Jordan, the Holy Spirit had descended on him and given him the power to work miracles, but that did not mean that he became God. Because of this emphasis on the power of the Holy Spirit in Jesus's 'promotion', this theory is sometimes called *dynamic* (from the Greek *dynamis*, 'power').

The other monarchian idea was *modalism*, so called because the modalists held that the names of Father, Son and Holy Spirit corresponded merely to different aspects or modes of the same divine person, playing transitory parts in succession; there was no independent reality to each person. They also came to be known as Patripassians, since their beliefs seemed to make the Father suffer on the cross (Latin *pater*, 'father', and *passus est*, 'he has suffered', are the roots of this word). From Sabellius, a rather shadowy late second-century exponent of the idea, modalism has often been known as Sabellianism, a word which has been flung about as a term of abuse at various periods in the history of the church with about as much discrimination as the late Senator Joe McCarthy's use of the word 'Communist'. Both forms of monarchianism were separately condemned by the Roman authorities at the turn of the second and third centuries, but monarchian ideas continued to trouble the church, as is only natural in a faith which wants to talk of a God who is both one and three. In particular, many Christians associated one Greek word with monarchian thinkers: *homoousios*, meaning 'of one substance' and intended to emphasize the intimate and direct relationship of Father and Son. For many of the faithful, especially in the east, the use of this word would endanger the separate identities of the three persons of the Trinity, since it had been used by monarchians like Paul the Bishop of Samosata in third-century rows about the monarchian issue. We will meet it again, together with the fears which it aroused, in due course (see Chapter Seven).

Alexandrian theologians: Clement and Origen

In the Alexandrian school of theology we see the closest relationship which early Christian thought achieved with Greek thought without entirely losing contact with the mainstream Christian church. This was hardly surprising, since the Christian schools which Clement of Alexandria and Origen represented were sited in one of the greatest Greek university cities of the ancient world, where Jews and Greeks had lived side by side for centuries, and where many varieties of Gnosticism flourished. Indeed early Christian literature found in the sands of Egypt shows that for a long time there was no easily recognizable border between mainstream Christianity and Gnosticism. Clement in particular was fond of calling his Christian teaching 'the true *Gnosis*' in contrast with the Gnostics, but in the eyes of many later unsympathetic writers, both he and Origen had stepped over the borders which could be considered orthodox. It is no coincidence that much of Clement's and Origen's writing is lost to us; in a society where one manuscript might be the only source of a particular work and might easily crumble to dust in obscurity if someone did not think it worthwhile copying, it is clear that quiet ecclesiastical censorship made sure that many works of these dangerous and audacious masters remained uncopied, and disappeared from sight.

Clement succeeded his master Pantaenus (of whom we know little) as the leading figure in the Christian schools of Alexandria about 190. His career shows that he was no mere ivory-tower scholar spinning far-fetched theories in isolation from reality, for when he was caught up in a crisis of persecution for the church in 202, he distinguished himself far away from Alexandria in the Cappadocian city of Caesarea in Asia Minor, looking after the Christian community and bringing new people to the faith. For all this pastoral concern in response to a desperate situation, his writings show that he regarded knowledge not merely as a useful tool of analysis for a Christian, but as the door to a higher form of Christian life; like Plato, whom he much admired, he believed that knowledge increases one's moral worth. There is an intellectual élitism both in his writings and those of Origen which repelled many Christians – the very form of his writings encourages this élitism, for he was determined not to produce anything too straightforward to understand, a sort of idiot's guide to

theology, and he made his theological writings deliberately form-
less and difficult to follow: one of his major works is even entitled
Stromateis, which might be translated as 'miscellanies', but which
literally means 'laundry-bags'!

There were clear distinctions between Clement's élitism and the
élitist *gnosis* of the Gnostic sects. Although he does speak of
a special tradition handed down from the apostles to his own
teachers, this tradition is firmly that of all scripture, both Old and
New Testament: he emphasizes the Christian doctrine of creation
and the positive value of our life on earth. Indeed he does so by
presenting our life as a journey towards knowledge of God and
holiness, a progress which is the result of hard work and moral
progress, not through the sort of random external gift of a divine
spark of knowledge which was a favourite theme of gnostic sects.
This knowledge of God is seen both in scripture and in such
worldly achievements of the human intellect as the writings of
Aristotle and Plato. Clement was so concerned to emphasize the
Christian need to travel on a road of holiness as he moves to meet
God, that he saw the Christian's journey as continuing after
physical death, which was not a stage of ultimate importance:
'after he has reached the final ascent in the flesh, he still continues
to advance', he said. Clement would see this continuing stage of
development as like a purging with fire, not the fires of Hell,
but the fires of knowledge. It was a comforting doctrine for
those who feared a sudden death which might leave them helpless
before God without adequate preparation; it was therefore a
notion which took root in Christian thought, and in the course
of centuries it would flower into the complex family of ideas
about the afterlife which the medieval church collectively called
purgatory.

Because Clement so emphasized the idea of moral progress, he
wrote much about the way in which the Christian life should be
lived; he is of great value to us as one of the earliest Christian
writers on what would now be called moral theology. For instance,
he was concerned to affirm the value of sex, which many mainstream Christian writers as well as many Gnostics regarded as too
contemptible and dangerous to be worth their consideration;
admittedly, in discussing sex, he led the church towards an affirmation of it as justified only if it led to procreation, an attitude which
is much nearer the assumptions of the non-Christian Aristotle than

it is to the Old Testament or Paul. He could discuss worldly wealth, a very necessary concern in a church where there were more and more wealthy people, and in defending a Christian's responsible stewardship of riches, he would provide an extended framework for Christian views of money and possessions for centuries to come.

Origen

Origen was Clement's successor in the Christian schools of Alexandria, a boy from a devout Christian household thrust into a leading role while still in his late teens because of the disruption of the persecution of 202 and the absence of Clement. From then on his life was occupied in constant, restless intellectual exercise: research, presentation of the faith to inquisitive and intellectually-lively non-Christians, and missions as a one-man academic task-force in various theological rows throughout the eastern Mediterranean. His fiery nature had led him into near-destruction in the 202 persecution, for he was then only preserved for his later work in the church by his mother's hardheaded decision to hide his clothes when he wished to run out into the street and proclaim himself a Christian; embarrassment won out over heroism.

Later this combativeness would make Origen many enemies, not least his bishop Demetrius, who was doing his best to pull together the church in Egypt, laying the foundations of the formidable ecclesiastical machine which would later make the Bishopric of Alexandria one of the major powers in the church; it was not surprising that Demetrius should feel himself sorely tried by the independent-minded thinkers who followed Clement's line that what really mattered in the Christian life was the pursuit of knowledge. Demetrius and Origen clashed over what the Bishop saw as successive acts of insubordination while Origen was making visits to his friends in the Palestinian church; first they asked him to preach while he was only a layman, and in a ham-fisted attempt to get round the problem on a later occasion, they secured his ordination as presbyter without any reference to the authorities back in Alexandria. This second incident led to a complete breach between Origen and Demetrius, and the scholar retired permanently among his supporters, to continue his academic work at Caesarea in Palestine. His thirst for martyrdom, eloquently expressed in one of the writings of his middle age, was eventually fulfilled when he died as a result of the brutal maltreatment which he received in one of the mid-third-century persecutions.

Origen's importance was both as biblical scholar and speculative theologian, two halves of a career which seem to have puzzlingly little direct effect on each other. In his biblical work, Origen's concern was for exactness and faithfulness to the received text, something very necessary in an age when the text was still uncertain in many details for many Christian communities; in his theological work, he was prepared to make statements of extraordinary boldness, sometimes putting them forward simply as theoretical suggestions for solving a particular problem; so radical were some of these that a whole group of his ideas were labelled 'Origenism' and condemned at a council at Alexandria a century and a half after his death, in 400. Both halves of his work produced books in such quantity that they excited the awe of generations of theologians, but much remains now only in fragments.

This fragmentary survival is true of the crown of Origen's biblical labours, the *Hexapla*, so called from the Greek word for 'sixfold' because of its arrangement of the Old Testament in six different versions side by side. This arrangement was designed with the still continuing theological debates against Judaism particularly in mind. The Jews had ceased to trust their Septuagint Greek version of scripture precisely because the Christians used it; they found it too free a translation of the Hebrew originals, and consequently had turned to more literal versions. If Christians were to use their scripture effectively, they would have to meet Jewish criticisms of the Septuagint text with as full a knowledge of all acceptable versions as possible. The Hexapla marshalled the Hebrew text next to a transliteration of it into Greek characters, followed by the Septuagint and three other Greek versions. It is a mark of how far Christianity and Judaism had now drifted apart that, according to his great admirer the historian Eusebius, even this greatest of third-century Christian biblical scholars had an imperfect grasp of Hebrew.

If Origen had succeeded in establishing the text of Old and New Testament as accurately as was possible, how should this text be used? Even though Origen affected to despise the world of Greek thought (in sharp contrast to his master Clement), he shared all the Greek suspicions about the literal meaning of some parts of the

Bible. For instance, he said that it was absurd to believe that God had made a garden of Eden which had contained a real Tree of Life, or that he had walked in this garden and talked with Adam. Such things were true, because all parts of the scriptures were divinely-inspired truth, but they should not be read as if they were historical events, like the rise and fall of Persian dynasties were historical events. They contained a different sort of truth; this was even so in relation to some of the Gospel stories. Like the Jewish scholar Philo, he saw scripture as having several layers of meaning, and the innermost meanings, hidden behind the literal meanings, were not only the most profound, but were also only available to those with eyes to see; here once more we note the intellectual élitism which was such a feature of the Alexandrian theological outlook.

This method of analysing scripture, the allegorical method, would be very influential in the church, particularly in the Greek East; the Latin West tended to have more reservations about it, although the great Augustine of Hippo was among those who found it useful. In the East, thinkers who looked to the Syrian city of Antioch were not so influenced by the mystical Platonic ideas which so entranced Clement and which despite himself saturated Origen's thinking; perhaps because of their background in the Semitic cultures of the Near East, the practical analytical thought of Aristotle appealed to them more, and they were inclined to read the Bible as a literal historical record. The contrast in approach between Alexandria and Antioch, not merely to the Bible but to a whole range of theological issues, would in the long term result in some ugly power struggles for the Eastern church, as we shall see (below, Chapter Seven).

Origen's debt to Plato was as apparent in his work on systematic theology as in his biblical commentaries. Particularly in his book entitled *On First Principles*, one of the first attempts at a universal summary of orthodox or non-heretical Christian thought, we see him grappling with the old Platonic problem of how a passionless, indivisible, changeless, Supreme God communicates with this transitory world. For Origen, as for Justin, the bridge was the Logos; and like Justin, Origen could be quite bold in terming the Logos a second God, even tending towards making this Logos-figure subordinate to or on a lower level than the Supreme God, whose creature he is (the doctrine known as subordinationism). In his concentration on explaining this relationship of Father and Son, Origen has little to say about the Holy Spirit, whom he could quite boldly say was inferior to the Son, and whom he saw as concerned only with strengthening the faithful within the church. Few early Christian writers had much to say about the Spirit in the unhappy aftermath of the church's expulsion of the Montanists, with their particular devotion to the Spirit; Origen frankly admits that there are questions about the person and work of the Spirit which puzzle him and which still need clarification by the church.

One of the boldest parts of Origen's theological scheme is his suggestion as to how to relate the Fall and the Incarnation; he says that God created inferior spirits with free will, and that all abused this gift, following the example of a ringleader who was Satan; the degree of their fall then determined which part of the cosmic order, from angels through humankind to demons, they were to occupy. It is thus our duty to use our free will to remedy the mistake which we had made in this first fall (a fall of which Adam's fall was merely an allegory); once more as in Clement's scheme, humankind will be saved through its own efforts with the help of Christ, through purging which goes on after human death. Since the first fall was universal, so all, including Satan himself, have the chance to work back towards God's original purpose. All will be saved, since all come from God.

Most audacious of all was Origen's suggestion that one soul alone had not fallen in the original fall, and that it was this soul which the Logos entered when finally he decided that he must come himself to save humankind. The point of this idea was to safeguard Christ's free will in his earthly life; he enjoyed the free will granted to that soul, so he was making real choices, not playing a docetic charade as the Gnostics said. Thus our free will also has value, because it is seen most perfectly in Christ, and it is a gift for us to use properly. The whole scheme was intended to affirm the majesty of God, as did both Plato and Paul, but also to affirm the dignity of humankind; divine majesty and human dignity have never been easy concepts for the church to keep in balance.

The church turned its back on Origen's vision of a universal salvation; Augustine of Hippo was to call it a 'compassionate' belief, but went on to affirm the church's total rejection of it. By rejecting such notions, Christianity was committing itself to the idea of eternal choices made by God, a separation of all people into the saved and the damned, although the debate continued as to when and through whom (God or humankind?) this separation comes about. Perhaps if Christianity was to maintain its character as a religion hungry for souls, this drawing-back from universal salvation was inevitable: could there be an urgency in a mission to win converts, if the end of time and the cosmos would inevitably see the return of all things to their creator? Origen might say that the purpose of proclaiming Christianity was to proclaim truth and wisdom, regardless of any incentive like an escape from damnation. However, for the church as a whole, this delight in wisdom and its proclamation was not enough. Now Christianity was ceasing to be a rather inward-looking community, and its mission became more and more a mission of conquest of the entire known world and its peoples. Conquest there was, but who conquered whom? The next two chapters may provide some answers for this question.

Chronology for Chapter Six

c. 50	Claudius expels Jews from Rome after (?)Christian riots
c. 62–4	Paul and Peter martyred in Rome
64	Persecution by Emperor Nero
95	Persecution by Emperor Domitian
c. 107	Ignatius martyred in Rome
112–13	Correspondence about Bithynia between Pliny and Trajan
117	Trajan's conquests take Roman Empire's boundaries to maximum extent
c. 155	Polycarp martyred in Smyrna
167	Barbarians cross Danube and devastate Roman provinces
c. 170	Dionysius, Bishop of Corinth writing letters
177	Persecution in Lyon
178	Celsus writes attack on Christianity
192	Septimius Severus becomes Emperor after a year of civil war
c. 200	Christianity established in Osrhoene
211	Septimius Severus dies; political trouble resumes
226	Ardashir becomes first Sasanid King of Persians
244	Plotinus establishes school in Rome
247	Thousandth anniversary of founding of Rome
250	Emperor Decius orders universal sacrifice to Roman gods
251	Cyprian writes *On the Unity of the Church*
256–7	Row between Bishop Cyprian and Pope Stephen
260	Emperor Gallienus abandons persecution of Christians
262	Porphyry meets Plotinus in Rome
271	Emperor Aurelian begins walls for Rome
c. 280	Christianity becomes official religion in Armenia
284	Diocletian becomes sole emperor
303	Full persecution of church begins
312	Constantine defeats rival Maxentius in the West (at the Milvian Bridge)
324	Constantine defeats Licinius in the East

Chapter Six

Prisoner of the Roman World (first to third centuries)

What was the official reaction to the new religion as it grew in the two centuries after Christ's execution? It took the Romans some time to distinguish between the Christians and the other quarrelling segments of Judaism, but once the break was made, Christianity could not hope for any sort of official recognition. Normally the Roman authorities were tolerant of the religions which they found in their conquered territories; as long as a religion had a tradition behind it, it could be accepted in a vague and easy-going manner as having some relationship to the official gods of Rome. 'Anything for a quiet life' was the hallmark of most Roman colonial policy. All that was demanded was that subjects of the Empire accept in their turn some sort of allegiance to the official cult of the Emperors, alive and dead. Even a cult like Judaism, which refused to make this concession and which maintained an awkward insistence on regarding every other religion as untrue, could be accepted because it had a long pedigree; and one might say that the Romans usually regarded Judaism with remarkable good nature considering how troublesome it proved to them in successive revolts.

Christianity had no such tradition to excuse it; it made exclusive claims for its God which cut across the normal courtesies of observing the imperial cult, and which therefore made Christians a force for disruption in Roman life. No Christian of the first three centuries AD would fit easily into the army, since army life automatically demanded as frequent attendance at official sacrifices as today it does salutes to the flag and parades. What was worse, Christians caused trouble, and the Romans hated trouble. The first

Christian missionaries usually began their work of proclaiming the good news within the Jewish communities of the Mediterranean cities, and when they did so, they often provoked a riot from angry Jews. One of the first mentions of a Christian presence in Rome, for instance, is a remark by the second-century historian Suetonius that the Emperor Claudius (AD 41–54) expelled the Roman Jews for rioting 'at the instigation of Chrestus' — probably a garbled reference to Christian preaching.

Later, as Christian communities established themselves in cities, they did not endear themselves to people. This was not because they lived austere lifestyles which made a painful contrast with a world of debauchery and luxury round them; this is a later Christian caricature which ignores the austere and world-denying character of much pagan thought in the early Empire. What really offended was their secretiveness and obstinate separation. For Christians such separation was inevitable, given their sense of the falseness of all other religions; ancient life was saturated with the observances of traditional religion, and to play any part in ordinary life was to risk pollution, particularly in public office. Christians did not go to the public baths; and the full enormity of this refusal can only be appreciated if one visits the surviving public baths of Eastern Europe or the Near East and sees the way in which they serve as centres of social life, politics and gossip.

The Christians lived in their own world, a fact symbolized in a puzzling peculiarity of their literature; with remarkable consistency, from the first century they recorded their sacred writings not in the conventional form of the scroll, like their Jewish predecessors and like everyone else in the ancient world, but in gatherings of sheets of parchment or paper in the form of our modern book (the technical Latin name is *codex*). They also jealously guarded their ceremonies of baptism and eucharist from the uninitiated, and it is a proof both of their success and of their secretive intentions that these ceremonies were so thoroughly misunderstood by intelligent and sensitive Roman observers. Reports of incest arose from their talk of love-feasts, of cannibalism from the language of drinking body and blood, and it was a small step from there for suspicion and righteous indignation among their non-Christian neighbours to spill over into violence and riots. It was equally understandable for the Roman authorities, jittery about any secret organizations, to wish to suppress these troublemakers who wasted the taxpayers' money by provoking disturbances of the peace.

The Romans therefore came to look on Christianity with irritation, and sometimes this irritation spilled over into persecution. This could be cruel and intense, involving the deaths of such early Christian leaders as Peter, Paul, Ignatius of Antioch or Polycarp of Smyrna. More often, probably, it petered out rather inconclusively, as the Romans felt that they had better things to do than to try and wipe out a group of troublesome fanatics; one little instance of this is preserved by chance among the papers of a highly cultivated and conscientious Roman provincial administrator, the younger Pliny. Pliny, newly appointed about AD 112 to sort out the chaotic affairs of the Asia Minor province of Bithynia, found among a host of other problems a strong and aggressive Christian community, which was emptying the pagan temples and ruining local trade by boycotting meat previously offered in pagan sacrifice. He rounded up Christians who had been anonymously denounced to him and interrogated under torture some who appeared important, but he was puzzled as to what to do next with people who seemed to him crackpots but comparatively harmless. He consulted the Emperor Trajan, whose reply was soothing but hardly much help, since his most definite advice was to ignore anonymous denunciations about anyone.

There must have been many inconclusive encounters like this in the first and second centuries, and what persecution there was, was clearly not centrally directed; it came about as the result of some personal initiative, like the megalomaniac pogroms unleashed in Rome by the unbalanced Emperors Nero and Domitian, or the angry response of some local provincial governor to a particular outbreak of trouble, like the persecution which devastated the Christian community of Lyon in 177. However, this random response would change by the end of the second century. By then, Christianity had established itself throughout the Mediterranean world. It is impossible to estimate what numbers were involved; Pliny's experience in Bithynia would suggest that in Asia Minor at least, Christians could be very numerous right at the beginning of the second century. This is confirmed by the prominent part which Asia Minor played in the theological ferments which we have already discussed (above, Chapters Four and Five), and by archaeological finds which show that Christians in Asia Minor were putting up blatantly Christian tombstones, presumably in public places, during the third century; this was generations before the appearance of similar openly Christian material elsewhere. In Rome, too, Christians were numerous and the church wealthy, although in size it was dwarfed by the vast community of the capital as a whole.

Elsewhere, however, Christian communities were probably quite small, particularly in the west. What was impressive, and what was increasingly noticed by non-Christians, was not so much the numbers of any one community but the geographical spread of the church throughout the Empire. We have no definite evidence of Christianity in Britain before the early fourth century, and not much from the far end of the Mediterranean in Spain, but through other centres of the Empire it is in the late second and early third century that we find evidence of well-established communities, invariably with an episcopal organization, that had obviously existed for some time. This is true for instance in north Africa around Carthage, in Alexandria and in the south of France at Lyon; letters of the late-second-century Bishop Dionysius of Corinth shed similarly sudden shafts of light on the Christian communities of Athens and Crete. Most churches like this fabricated direct lines of succession back to the apostolic period — Athens, for instance, could point to Paul's convert Dionysius the Areopagite, while Alexandria claimed foundation by the evangelist Mark himself. The genuineness of such claims is less significant than the witness which they give to the way in which apostolic succession had established itself as a vital idea in the thinking of the church, and to the self-confidence which these communities could feel as the result of generations of tradition.

By the late second century, intelligent pagans were beginning to realize the significance of this self-confidence. Christianity offered a complete alternative to the culture and assumptions of the Roman establishment, an establishment which felt in no way threatened by the teeming ancient cults of the provinces, or even by the ancient and rather exclusive traditions of the Jews. Christianity had no national base; it was as open to those who wished to work hard to enter it as was Roman citizenship itself. Was it really trying to create a new citizenship for its own purposes, to create an Empire within an Empire? This was certainly the opinion of one late-second-century traditionalist Roman aristocrat called Celsus, who wrote a bitter attack on Christianity, paradoxically preserved for us in the text of a Christian answer by Origen decades later. Celsus loved the old gods of Rome because they were the pillars of the society which he loved, though he felt that certainty was unattainable in religious matters. He deplored the superstition of eastern mystery cults as much as he deplored Christian stupidity in paying divine honours to a recently executed Palestinian carpenter, yet what he saw as particularly dangerous about Christianity was its worldwide coherence; it was a conspiracy, and one which he saw as especially aimed at impressionable young people. The result of Christian propaganda would be to leave even the Emperor defenceless, 'while earthly things would come into the power of the most lawless and savage barbarians'.

Crisis in the Empire (166–285)

When Celsus wrote these words, about AD 180, they would have a new and terrible significance for his Roman readers. During the second century, the Empire ceased to expand; it reached its maximum extent under the Emperor Trajan (98–117), who annexed new territories in what are now Rumania and Iraq; after that, it was the people on the frontiers who began pushing back. On the northern frontier, a new phase in the long majestic process which pushed people after people westwards from the interior of Asia was causing disruption among the tribes on the Roman frontier, and was forcing them in their turn to look westwards for a refuge, inside Rome's territories. On the eastern frontier, matters were made worse from the early third century by a new dynasty in Persia, the Sasanids or Sassanians, who had regained Persian independence from their hated neighbours the Parthians and who were now determined to take their revenge on the world of Greece and Rome for the humiliations inflicted centuries before by Athens and by the Hellenistic monarchs. The dynasty's founder, Ardashir, made his intention plain by taking the name of the ancient Persian king and conqueror Darius. Decades before this, however, from the disaster of the winter 166–7, when on the northern border thousands from the tribes of the Langobardi crossed the frozen river Danube and devastated the Empire's central European provinces, Roman Emperors would face a constant battle to preserve their frontier secure.

This might not have been so bad if the Empire had contrived to remain united under capable rulers. Although several first-century Emperors had found the psychological strain of ruling the greatest Empire in Western history too much for them and had gone insane, the Empire had later enjoyed an exceptionally able and wise succession of rulers in the successive dynasties of the Flavians and the Antonines (69–192). However, the last of the Antonines, Commodus, had reverted to the pattern of madness, and had eventually been murdered by his mistress Marcia to stop him murdering her (she was a Christian, incidentally). From chaos and civil war during 192 there emerged an army officer of north African origins, Septimius Severus, who put his own family on the imperial throne. His sons displayed his ruthless brutality without his political good sense, and from Septimius's death at York in 211 to Diocletian's achievement of supreme power in 285, hardly any Roman emperors died a natural death. It was a terrible time for the Empire: a mute tribute to that is the fact that we know so little about it.

Political trouble was not confined to the Empire's leadership. The short-lived dynasty founded by Severus had been based on a military *coup-d'état*, and so were the regimes of most of his successors well into the fourth century; they could not appeal to any traditional legitimacy, and were therefore increasingly dependent on the goodwill of the army. 'Be united, enrich the soldiers and scorn the rest', Severus urged his sons on his deathbed; they listened to the second two clauses of his advice. The needs of the army, both in the constant frontier wars and in equally bitter civil wars, became all-important; to finance the soldiers, taxation soared, and many people fled their towns and villages rather than pay, turning to banditry. This in turn created a problem of internal policing which could only be met by increasing the power of the army; it was a vicious circle.

Not surprisingly in this situation, the imperial currency collapsed; even in the days of the 'good' Antonine emperors, there had been constant problems in financing the vast imperial machine, and from the late second century, the government resorted to the fatal expedient of debasing the silver coinage with copper. Increasingly large areas of Roman life reverted to an economy of barter, a process hastened by the demands of the all-powerful soldiery under Severus to be given a hedge against inflation by receiving their pay in kind.

All these pressures combined to ruin the delicate balance of city life which had been the basis of classical civilization since the great days of the Greek *poleis*; previously the round of civic office, the construction of beautiful city buildings and of roads, water supplies and bridges had been accepted voluntarily by wealthy citizens as necessary demonstrations of their public spirit. Now few were willing to undertake such things, and the government had either to force people to take on public office, or to send in its own bureaucrats to do the work with the backing of the troops. A melancholy symptom of the new situation was the fact that when third-century Roman cities showed any energy in building, it was only to put up city walls partly constructed out of civic buildings torn down for the purpose. Archaeologists have noted a particularly sinister feature of many of these new schemes of fortification; they enclosed only part of the old cities, the official headquarters and the wealthy parts: rather like building nuclear shelters today reserved for the élite. The old spirit of civic solidarity was dead.

It is a tribute to the strength of the Empire that it survived the third-century crisis at all. Survive it did, in its eastern part for more than a thousand years, but the price of this survival was that it became a police state. This was intensified rather than remedied when Diocletian restored long-term stability to the economy and in part to politics after 284. If the autonomous world of the *polis* was gone, this would have profound consequences for ancient religion; at every level, traditional cults were linked with local identities, and in the towns, with the self-government which had helped to sustain them. Even without the coming of Christianity, paganism would have changed. To bolster up their dubious regimes, usurper dynasties like the Severans encouraged the identification of different territorial gods as facets of one supreme God, and then identified themselves with this single figure: in the case of Septimius Severus, the Egyptian God Serapis. The worship of the sun became steadily more dominant, a natural universal symbol to choose in the brilliant sunshine of the Mediterranean; but this new religiosity was not just an official cult.

The third century has been seen as an 'age of anxiety' which drove people back to find comfort in religion; and although this idea has been challenged, the surviving writings of the upper classes show a new interest in personal religion, remote from the traditionalist respect for the old gods and the cultured cynicism which had been the received wisdom for second-century Golden Age aristocrats like Celsus. Intelligent people took a new interest in magic; they were also increasingly drawn to forms of philosophy which wore a religious and even magical aspect. Gone was the sceptical philosophy of Stoicism, which in the second century had boasted one of the greatest Roman emperors, Marcus Aurelius, as an exponent; now the intellectual fashion which captured the élite was neo-Platonism, a development of Plato's philosophy which empasized its religious side. Its greatest teacher was Plotinus, a contemporary of Origen's in the pagan schools of Alexandria; not surprisingly, his picture of the supreme God bore some similarities to that of Origen. He spoke in a trinitarian fashion of a divine nature consisting of an ultimate One, of Intelligence and of the Soul; the first represented absolute perfection, the second was an image of the first but was capable of being known by our inferior senses, and the third was a spirit which infused the world and was therefore capable of being diverse, in contrast to the Platonic perfection of the One and of Intelligence. There was no Christ-figure in this picture to be incarnate; it was the job of the individual soul by ecstatic contemplation of the divine to restore the harmony lost in the world, an ecstasy so rare that Plotinus himself had only achieved it four times in his life. Neo-Platonism was largely independent of the old religious forms, though it would coexist perfectly happily with traditional gods by enrolling them as manifestations of Intelligence. The writings of Plotinus's successors, particularly his somewhat self-important biographer Porphyry, encouraged this tendency, which was yet another force uniting paganism. Now the pagan élite would begin reacting to the Christian threat.

Crisis for the church

For the first time persecution of Christians came on an Empire-wide scale. The new earnestness and personal commitment in pagan religion in any case spelled trouble for the Christians, but the situation was made worse by the celebrations surrounding the thousandth anniversary of the foundation of the city of Rome in 247. It was a time for Romans to take a long cool look at the history of their beloved Empire, and in the atmosphere of crisis which we have described, the picture was not a pretty one. This was especially apparent to the energetic senator and provincial governor who seized imperial power in 249: Trajan Decius. Decius was a conservative who blamed the Empire's troubles on the morrow of its thousandth decade squarely on the Christians; the old gods were angry because Christians were causing their sacrifices to be neglected, and so they had afflicted the Empire as a sign. For Decius the solution was simple: enforce traditional sacrifices on everyone. This he proceeded to do with bureaucratic efficiency in 250; those who sacrificed were issued with certificates of proof, some of which have been preserved for us in the rubbish pits and desert sands of Egypt. The order was coupled with severe repression, usually imprisonment, for those Christians who refused; two subsequent Emperors, Trebonianus Gallus and Valcrian, revived the policy in 252 and 257 in the intervals of their many other responsibilities, and it was only abandoned by Gallienus in 260 because there were so many other pressing dangers for the Empire.

In the meantime the church had suffered a terrible blow, not so much in terms of death and suffering, for few died outside a small group of the leadership, but in terms of morale. The overwhelming majority of Christians gave way; this might have been predicted, because the same thing had happened when Pliny had arrested those Bithynian Christians back in 112. It was only natural to wish to obey the Emperor: most Christians felt a deep reverence for the Empire which is obvious from their leading writers' rather confused and contradictory statements about the limits of the obedience due to it. Moreover, the church as a whole was not used to persecution, certainly not a systematic campaign directed from the centre. The real damage to the church began when persecution ceased and the leadership began picking up the pieces. The bishops' authority was at stake; after all, some bishops had followed the command recorded by the Evangelist John to suffer martyrdom bravely and had been killed (including the Bishops of Antioch, Jerusalem and Rome); others had followed the precisely opposite advice to be found in Matthew's Gospel to flee from city to city, including such important figures as the Bishops of Carthage and Alexandria. The latter group were likely to come in for criticism from those who had stayed and suffered ('confessed') for their faith; these 'confessors' provided the troubled church with an alternative sort of authority, particularly when it started deciding how and how much to forgive those Christians who had lapsed. Many of the lapsed flocked to the confessors to gain pardon and re-entry to the church, and the bishops did not like this at all.

Especially important rows broke out over the issue of forgiveness in Rome and Carthage. Faced both with defiance from some of the confessors and with the election of a rival bishop by those opposing him, Bishop Cyprian of Carthage engaged in a warfare of pamphlets, producing statements about the role of the bishop in the church which were long to outlive this particular dispute: he came to see authority for forgiveness of sins as vested in the bishop, and he emphasized the bishop as the focus for unity in the whole church, a successor of the Apostles in every diocese. It was yet another stage in the discussion which we have seen begun by Ignatius and Irenaeus. In Rome, the row was mainly over whether there could be any forgiveness at all for those who had lapsed. Novatian, a hardliner on this issue, opposed the election as bishop of Cornelius, who held that forgiveness was possible through the bishop, and the church was bitterly divided as to who to support. Cyprian and Cornelius, who had arrived at similar views about the bishop's powers, allied with each other, and the supporters of Novatian found themselves an isolated minority.

Subsequent developments made matters worse, for in their initial enthusiasm, the Novatianists started holding missions and baptizing converts in north Africa as well as in Rome. When many of them decided that the division had gone too far, and the newly baptized applied to rejoin the mainstream church, Rome and Carthage were faced with the problem of deciding the terms: was Novatianist baptism valid? Cyprian thought not; a new Bishop of Rome, Stephen, wishing to be conciliatory to those who were coming in, disagreed with him. A furious row broke out between them, partly an expression of Rome's growing feeling that the north African bishops were inclined to think too well of their own position in the Western church: Stephen not only called Cyprian Antichrist, but in attempting to clinch the rightness of his own opinion, he appealed to the Matthean text 'Thou art Peter, and on this Rock will I build my church'. It is the first time known to us that the text had been thus used by a Roman bishop: another significant step in the gradual rise to prominence of Rome. In the end, north Africa and Rome agreed to differ on this issue, the north Africans saying that valid baptism could only take place within the Christian community which is the church, the Romans saying that the sacrament belonged to Christ, not to the church, and that therefore it was valid whoever performed it if done in the right form and with the right intentions.

Although comparative peace then descended on the church for several decades, exactly the same pattern of unhappy internal disputes would break out in the wake of the last and most serious bout of persecution designed to wipe out Christianity in the Empire: that of Diocletian. Diocletian made it his life's work to restore the glory of the old Rome, and although the oppressive bureaucracy which emerged from his efforts was very different from the early Empire, he was determined to honour the old gods: he distrusted all religious novelty, not just Christianity. Only gradually did his undemonstrative religious conservatism turn into active persecution of the Christians, when in the last decade of the third century he came increasingly to be influenced by a clique of army officers from what is now Yugoslavia, headed by Galerius, one of the colleagues whom Diocletian had chosen to help him govern the Empire. Gradually these rabid anti-Christians, some of them neo-Platonists, persuaded Diocletian to follow his inclinations, and from 303 a full-scale attack was launched on the Christians, beginning with the clergy. Churches were torn down, pagan sacrifices ordered and sacred books confiscated. Things were not so bad in the west, where Diocletian's colleague Constantius had some sympathy with Christianity, but elsewhere things particularly intensified after Diocletian retired from public life in 305. It would take a series of military victories by Constantius's son Constantine I (the Great), not ending until 324 in the east, before the Christian church was safe from the effort to destroy it.

In the meantime Christians quarrelled about how to heal the wounds caused by persecution. In Egypt, hardliners were so shocked at the Bishop of Alexandria's willingness to forgive the repentant lapsed that one of them, Bishop Meletius of Lycopolis, founded his own rival clerical hierarchy; while an even more serious split occurred in the north African church. Here complicated rows about who had done what in the crisis combined with personality clashes to produce a disputed episcopal election for Carthage. Bishop Caecilian was recognized by Rome and other churches, one of the prices of this recognition being his abandonment of Cyprian's views of baptism; while the opposition, furious at what they saw as this final proof of his unworthiness, rallied behind the rival Bishop Donatus. The Donatist schism in the north African church had begun, and would never be completely healed before the Islamic Arabs swept all Christianity from north Africa in their seventh- and eighth-century conquests.

Who conquered whom?

The pagan Empire's third-century struggle to the death with the church contained the irony that in some ways the Empire had already conquered Christianity. The patterns of expansion in the easy, settled conditions of the second-century Empire had decided this; the church had travelled a long way from its rural Palestinian roots, and had become based in an urban Mediterranean setting. Christians of the first three centuries were mainly city folk, and that was emphasized by the triumph of the organization by bishops, who were almost invariably leaders within a city community. This became so much a habit both in the Roman and the Eastern churches that when Rome started sending missionaries into northern Europe during the sixth and later centuries, it still sent bishops to find cities as their bases, although there were no cities to speak of.

What is striking about the expansion of the church in the second century is that despite its wide geographical scale, hardly any of it was outside the Roman Empire. The one important foothold which it gained was in the Roman client state of Osrhoene, on the eastern border near where modern Syria, Iraq and Turkey join; Osrhoene was incorporated within the Empire after Christianity arrived, but it remained substantially outside the dominant Greek tradition of the Eastern Church, to become the home of Syrian-speaking Christian tradition. Beyond this, the independent Armenian kingdom to the north of Osrhoene was brought to Christianity by the conversion of its king Tiridates III in about 280, making it the first country in the world to make Christianity an official religion. However, in these crucial first three centuries, Christianity had no other successes outside a Roman context. For all the church's problematic relations with the imperial authorities, the barbarians on the frontiers would have had great difficulty in seeing the missionaries of the church as anything else but part of the imperial culture.

We have already seen the way in which Christian thinkers of the second century could not escape the influence of classical thought in their theology, and that was true in a whole host of other ways. Eventually the church would be so identified with the Graeco-Roman world that in the Christian West, almost fifteen hundred years after the disappearance of the last Western Roman Emperor, schoolboys and schoolgirls would still be learning Latin as a necessary qualification for entry in any subject to two of Britain's leading universities. Has that world now gone? Is the Western church now emerging from a Roman prison? If it is, the imprisonment began very early, long before Constantine I revolutionized the position of Christianity within the Empire in 312.

Chronology for Chapter Seven

c. 285	Anthony retreats to the Egyptian desert
306	Constantius I dies at York
312	Constantine I defeats rival Maxentius at the Milvian Bridge
313	Edict of toleration at Milan
314	Council of Arles fails to end Donatist schism
c. 318	Arian controversy breaks out
c. 320	Pachomius founds first monastic community
324	Constantine defeats Licinius at battle of Chrysopolis
325	Council of Nicaea
330	Dedication of Constantinople
337	Constantine I dies: Empire divided once more
351	Constantius II defeats usurper Magnentius: master of whole Empire
359	Homoean formula of Creed accepted by two Councils (Ariminum and Seleucia)
360	Gaulish troops mutiny to back Julian as Emperor
363	Julian killed in battle against Persians
366	Damasus elected Bishop of Rome
c. 372	Martin, a monk, elected Bishop of Tours
374	Ambrose unexpectedly elected Bishop of Milan
378	Emperor Valens defeated and killed by barbarians
379	Theodosius I becomes Eastern Emperor
381	First Council of Constantinople. Council of Aquileia
386	Priscillian of Avila executed by usurping Emperor Magnus Maximus
392	Pagan-backed *coup d'état* defeated by Theodosius I's intervention
c. 415	John Cassian founds two monasteries near Marseilles
428	Nestorius made Bishop of Constantinople
431	First Council of Ephesus: Nestorius condemned
449	Second Council of Ephesus: a Monophysite triumph
450	Pulcheria seizes power in Constantinople on her brother's death
451	Council of Chalcedon
459	Simeon Stylites dies

Chapter Seven

The Christian State (306 to 451)

In 306, as persecution of Christians gathered momentum, the last thing which anyone would have expected would have been for the church to enter an alliance with the Roman state. Yet by the end of the century, that alliance was so complete that it would govern the way the church thought of itself down to the present day; Europe would become a self-proclaimed Christian society, although the forms which that society have taken have often seemed remote from the teachings of the Sermon on the Mount. Only now are the long centuries of 'Christendom' apparently coming to an end, and all the consequences of this new stage in Christian life have yet to be assessed.

306 was a crucial year in this transformation because in that year Diocletian's Western colleague Constantius I died at the British military headquarters at York (the second Roman Emperor to do so), and the British army proclaimed his son Constantine as Emperor. Diocletian had instituted a team of four emperors under his own leadership (the 'Tetrarchy') in the hope that it would make the Empire more manageable and stable; now that he had retired, the Tetrarchy in fact led to further civil war. In the complex series of manoeuvres which followed, by 312 Constantine was leading his army to face the army of his rival Maxentius at the Milvian Bridge which barred his passage into Rome; in this battle he was completely victorious. Constantine's troops won this victory with their shields bearing a symbol which would come to be seen as a hallmark of the Christian faith: the Chi Rho (✗), the first two letters of Christ's name in Greek. In the following year Constantine and his ally for the time being, Licinius, proclaimed an equal toleration

for Christians and pagans by an edict at Milan; and as Constantine won further victories against the pagan clique who were still persecuting the church in the Eastern Empire, it was again after his troops had been ordered to say a prayer to the God of the Christians. When in turn Constantine's alliance with Licinius cooled and they eventually clashed in open war, Constantine once more waged his campaign as a Christian crusade, while Licinius threw his weight on the side of the pagans; Licinius's defeat and murder in 324 was the final defeat of the pagan assault on the church begun by Diocletian in 303.

What lay behind this remarkable reversal of fortune for the church? Many people have seen Constantine as undergoing a 'conversion' to Christianity; this is an unfortunate word, because it has all sorts of modern overtones which conceal the fact that Constantine's religious experience was like nothing which would today be recognized as a conversion. Most obviously, the Emperor associated the Christian God with the military successes which had made him able to destroy all his rivals from Maxentius to Licinius; the Christian God was the God of Battles. Constantine himself later told his friend the Christian historian Eusebius that one of the crucial experiences in his Milvian Bridge victory had been a vision of 'a cross of light in the heavens, above the sun, and an inscription, CONQUER BY THIS'; the association of the cross and the sun was no accident. A military leader and a ruthless politician rather than an abstract thinker, Constantine was probably not very clear about the difference between the pagan development of a universal sun-cult and the Christian God, at least to start with, and as he began showering privileges on the Christian clergy, it is unlikely that many of them considered whether the Emperor should be given a theological cross-examination before they accepted their unexpected gifts.

What interested Constantine was the Christian God rather than the Christians. It would hardly have been worth his while from a political point of view to court the Christians' favour, for they were still a decided minority in the Empire (perhaps forming as little as a tenth of its population) and they were noticeably weak in these crucial power blocs, the army and the western aristocracy; in any case, a simple grant of toleration would have been enough to delight the battered church. Constantine went much further than that. As his reign went on, he gave the church an equal place alongside the old pagan religious structure, and lavished wealth on it; he favoured Christians in senior positions and went as far as being baptized just before his death. He founded a new Eastern capital, Constantinople, on the superb strategic site of the old city of Byzantium at the entrance to the Black Sea; Constantinople could be seen as a new Rome without the pagan tradition, although it centred on a statue of Constantine shown with attributes which called to mind both Christ and Helios the Sun God. Despite all such ambiguities, Constantine's frequent and important interventions in Christian affairs show a particular concern for the church's unity, for unity was an obsession of his. If he knew nothing else about the Christian God, it was that he was One; oneness was in any case a handy emphasis for the Emperor who had destroyed Diocletian's Tetrarchy to replace it with his own single supreme power. Anything which challenged unity was likely to offend the supreme God, and that might end Constantine's run of favour.

Very quickly the Emperor was to learn to his cost that Christians were often inclined to imperil the unity which their religion proclaimed. The first instance of this came with the Donatist row in north Africa; desperately concerned to end this split in the church, Constantine adapted the favourite north African device of holding a council of bishops to decide the issue, with the great difference that now it was the Emperor who summoned the bishops. This Council, which met at Arles in 314 (incidentally including three British bishops among its number) did not succeed in appeasing the Donatists, and in the course of much muddled negotiation with Donatist leaders, Constantine was provoked into ordering in troops to enforce their return to the mainstream church: the first official persecution of Christians by Christians thus came within a year or two of the church's first official recognition. Most Donatists stayed out, nursing new grudges against the Catholics.

Arianism

Constantine's next intervention in a Council was even less successful in bringing peace to the church, though it would leave lasting fame in the church's memory. The occasion of this was a dispute in the church of Alexandria. An austere and very able priest of the church there called Arius was concerned to make his presentation of the Christian faith intellectually respectable to his contemporaries. To achieve this, he would have to wrestle with the old Platonic problem of the nature of God. If God is eternal and unknowable, Jesus Christ cannot be in the same sense God, since we know of him and of his deeds through the Gospels. This means, since the Supreme God is one, that Christ must in some sense come after the Father, even if we argue that he was created or begotten before all worlds. 'There was when he was not' became Arius's slogan. Moreover, since the Father is indivisible, he cannot have created the Son out of himself; if the Son was created before all things, it would therefore logically follow that he was created out of nothing.

Here, then, was Arius's Christ: inferior to the Father (as indeed Origen and other earlier writers had been inclined to say), and created by the Father out of nothing. It has recently been argued that Arius was not merely preoccupied by logic, but had a warm concern to present Christians with a picture of a Saviour who was really like them, to the extent that Christ too was part of the created order, not simply an image of God. Arius certainly found an affectionate following among ordinary Alexandrians, teaching them simple songs about his ideas. Whatever his motives, he quickly provoked an infuriated opposition in Alexandria, including his bishop. Finding himself condemned by a synod of Egyptian bishops, Arius appealed to his many friends further afield, not least the wily and politically-minded Bishop of Nicomedia, the former eastern Imperial capital: this was Eusebius, not to be confused with the historian Eusebius who was Bishop of Caesarea in Palestine – Eusebius was a common name. Eusebius was in a powerful position to rally support for Arius, so the dispute was overtaking the entire Eastern church. Constantine was now consolidating his power in the east after Licinius's destruction, and he was determined to reunite these warring churchmen. His instinct was to try the tactics of Arles a decade earlier and settle the dispute with a council, but his first plans in 324 to summon a council to the city of Ancyra were pre-empted by Arius's enemies, who seized the chance of the death of the Bishop of Antioch to gather at Antioch both to choose one of their supporters as the new bishop for this key diocese and to condemn Arius's views once more.

Furious, the Emperor now summoned a Council at which nothing could go wrong, since for the first time in Christian history, he himself would be presiding over the debates. He chose the city of Nicaea, conveniently near his headquarters at Nicomedia, and it was he (probably on the recommendation of his ecclesiastical advisor, the Spanish Bishop Hosius of Cordova) who proposed a most significant clause in the creed which emerged as the Council's agreed pronouncement: the statement that the Son was 'of one substance' (*homoousios*) with the Father. Faced with the awe-inspiring presence of the Emperor of the known world, there could be little opposition to this: only two bishops are recorded as standing out against it. With the passage of much important legislation on other matters, the first Council of the church reckoned in later ages as oecumenical (world-wide) came to an end.

However, this was not the end of Arianism, although Arius himself faded from public life and died obscurely. The problem with the word *homoousios* (the '*Homoousion*') was that it had a history, which we have already touched on when discussing the Monarchian heresies (above, Chapter Five). For many Eastern bishops, not least Eusebius of Nicomedia, it was a word tainted with monarchianism, and the effort to get rid of it from the Christian credal statements was to give the Arian cause another half-century and more of life within the Empire. The Arian party around Eusebius of Nicomedia was successful in winning influence around Constantine in his last years, and gained support from several of his successors in the east when the imperial power was divided once more. Their opponents in the church leadership, often harried out of their dioceses and forced to flee, were led by Athanasius the Bishop of Alexandria, who allied ruthlessness to an acute theological mind and a fixed determination to defend to the last the idea of one substance in the Father and the Son.

In the course of the struggle, many Arians became ever more extreme, some saying that the Son was actually *unlike* the Father (hence their Greek name 'Anomoeans' and their Latin name 'Dissimilarians'). A middle party was concerned to unite as much of the church as it could, and backed the formulation of creeds which blandly said merely that the Son is 'like' the Father (from which comes the party's name 'Homoean', from the Greek word for 'same'). Its greatest triumph was to win the backing of the Emperor Constantius II, who through his military victories reconquered the whole Empire in both East and West and was therefore able in 359 to dictate a Homoean formula to two Church Councils representing East and West, in an effort to settle the dispute once and for all. This statement, named the Creed of Ariminum after the Western Council which had been steamrollered into accepting it, remained the central statement of Arianism.

However, the radicalism of some of the victorious Arians had alienated many Eastern church leaders from their cause; this group, the 'semi-Arians', was concerned to hold on to the view that the Son and the Father are *similar* in essence (*homoiousios*), and this concern drew the Semi-Arians nearer to Athanasius and the remaining champions of the *homoousios* view. The problem for many of these easterners had been their uncertainty about the philosophical implications of the word *ousia* (essence); the eventual solution to their worries was to take the word *hypostasis*, which had previously been used with little distinction in meaning from *ousia*, and assign to the two different words two different technical meanings: the Trinity consists of three *hypostaseis* in one *ousia* — three Persons in one Essence. The disintegration of the Arian party in the East was completed by a political revolution in 378: the Eastern Emperor Valens, an Arian sympathizer, was defeated in a disastrous frontier battle and killed, and the Western Emperor Gratian sent his Spanish general to sort out the resulting chaos as the Emperor Theodosius I. Theodosius had scant sympathy for the Arians, reflecting the general Latin and Western impatience with Greek scruples about language; he convened a Council at Constantinople in 381 at which Arian defeat was inevitable.

Not only Arianism was outlawed at the Council of Constantinople, but also two other tempting new directions in which the doctrine of the Trinity might have been led. The first came to be known (for reasons which are still obscure) after an Eastern church leader called Macedonius, but its supporters are more accurately described by their nickname of *Pneumatomachi* ('fighters against the Spirit'), because their development of the subordinationist idea took them in a different direction from Arius; they denied the equal status of the Holy Spirit in the Godhead, seeing him merely as the pinnacle of the created order. The second heresy, ironically, was an effort to combat Arianism by a distinguished Lebanese theologian who became Bishop of Laodicea, Apollinaris: he wanted to emphasize Christ's divinity and hence his consubstantiality with the Father by saying that in

Jesus Christ there had been a human body and soul, but that his human mind or spirit had been replaced entirely by the divine Logos. The danger of this anti-Arian enthusiasm was to lose any real idea of Christ's humanity. Both the Pneumatomachi and the Apollinarians were condemned; at the same time, a Western Council of Aquileia (also 381) dealt with the remaining Western Arians.

This first Council of Constantinople saw the formulation of the fully-developed creed which we call the Nicene, and at much the same time the rather shorter creed which came quickly to be known as the Apostles' Creed was evolved in the West. After this Arianism was dead in the Empire, yet paradoxically it survived across the northern frontier among barbarian tribes, who had been evangelized through an uncharacteristically visionary initiative of Eusebius of Nicomedia. The barbarians came to see their theological difference from the Empire as an expression of their racial and cultural difference.

It will be quickly apparent even from this brief summary of the Arian entanglement how much imperial politics now affected church affairs: theology, always hotly debated in church circles, was now often decided in circumstances which remind one more of Al Capone's Chicago than the shores of the Sea of Galilee. This is even more painfully apparent if we consider the collection of disputes which go under the name of the Monophysite controversy. In these, the focus of theological debate shifted from the relationship of Son to Father, as in Arianism, or of Spirit to the Trinity as a whole, as in the views of the Pneumatomachi, to the way in which Christ combined both human and divine elements: but behind this lay several hidden agendas which were as much to do with power politics as with theology.

In the church of the eastern Mediterranean there had previously been two great centres, Antioch and Alexandria, which as we have noted (above, Chapter Five), took very different approaches to theological questions. Now added to this was the new power of the Bishop of Constantinople, which the older sees (that is, dioceses) resented, particularly as Constantinople preened itself on the title 'the New Rome'. Additionally, the Emperor Constantine I and his mother Helena had both invested a great deal of emotional energy in promoting the glory of Jerusalem, previously a fairly obscure see since the destruction of the Jewish capital. They encouraged

Christians in a passionate interest in pilgrimage to the Holy Land which gave successive Bishops in Jerusalem ambitions to revive the prestige which they had known in the very earliest days of Christianity. All these four dioceses would therefore be jostling for power at the same time as they fought to establish what the most adequate view of Christ's humanity and divinity might be.

The basic difference lay between an Alexandrian and an Antiochene viewpoint. Alexandria, following Origen's line, tended to stress the distinctness of the three persons of the Trinity, so Alexandrians were reluctant to stress a further distinctness within the person of Christ. Antiochenes, taking their cue as Syrians from the Near East's ancient concern with monotheism, tended to stress the oneness of the whole Godhead, so they were much more prepared to talk of two natures in Christ, human and divine, language which patriotic Alexandrians found blasphemous. The real flashpoint came when in 428 an Antiochene called Nestorius was chosen Bishop of Constantinople. This was bad enough for Cyril of Alexandria, one of a line of wily and power-conscious politician-bishops in Alexandria, but Cyril was particularly outraged when Nestorius aggressively promoted his Antiochene views by attacking a widely-popular title of honour for the Virgin Mary: *Theotokos*, or Bearer of God. This was the age in which devotion to Mary was becoming prominent in the church; Nicene churchmen encouraged it, as a way of safeguarding Christ's divinity against the Arians through emphasizing the unique favour granted his earthly mother. Nestorius, however, said that talk of *Theotokos* was a nonsense: a woman could not be bearer of God.

The ensuing row once more plunged the entire Eastern church into a bewildering welter of intrigue and complication, which once more drew in the Eastern Emperor, in sheer self-defence, to stop his Empire being ripped apart. After a Council at Ephesus in 431 and negotiations over the next two years, he forced a compromise on the opposing sides which vindicated the title *Theotokos*, ruined Nestorius's career for good and left Nestorian theology permanently condemned, but also left many Alexandrians outraged that their own theology had not been fully vindicated; these were the Monophysites (*monos* and *physis* = single nature). Their grumbling discontent took the form of further political manoeuvres which culminated in a second Council of Ephesus (449), humiliating all opponents of Alexandrian claims and outlawing all talk of two natures. So extreme had the Alexandrians by now become that they ignored a moderate statement of the Western view of the nature of Christ produced by delegates of Leo the Bishop of Rome, infuriating and alienating a see which had been their traditional ally. However, it was once more a political revolution which proved their downfall. A palace coup on the Emperor's death brought to power his formidable sister Pulcheria, a bitter enemy of the Monophysites' political backers in Constantinople; she selected a tame husband for herself, and in 451 the new regime called a Council to a city where the imperial troops could keep an eye on what was going on: Chalcedon, near Constantinople.

The main concern at Chalcedon was to persuade as many people as possible to accept a middle-of-the-road settlement. The statement presented by Leo's envoys at Ephesus two years before (his 'Tome'), was accepted as orthodoxy, and a carefully balanced definition of the faith was constructed which still remains the standard by which the mainstream Christian church measures discussion of the person of Christ. In the manner of middle-of-the-road settlements, the Chalcedonian Definition left bitter discontents on either side. On the one hand there were Nestorius's followers (Nestorius himself continued to suffer a humiliating Egyptian imprisonment with great dignity), holding to a view of Christ's natures which has been likened to a vessel which contains a mixture of oil and water, mingling but not mixing. On the other hand, there were Monophysites who treasured the memory of Cyril and his campaign against Nestorius: their view of Christ's humanity and divinity has been likened to a vessel which contains wine and water, perfectly and inextricably mixed.

Both sides nursed their grievances and sought to recapture their power in the Empire; the Monophysites in particular often seemed to be on the point of destroying the Chalcedonian settlement in the East over the following century. However, their eventual failure meant that both defeated sides saw the Empire as an oppressor and a source of heresy, and both increasingly withdrew from the world of Greek Christianity which had dominated the Eastern church for so long, taking refuge in Persian, Syriac and Egyptian Coptic-speaking areas. Therefore neither Monophysites nor Nestorians were especially anxious to defend the Empire when the Islamic Arabs began attacking the imperial frontiers in the seventh century; the rapid caving-in of the Empire's Egyptian and Syrian provinces to Arab attack has much to do with these festering Christian discontents, and the isolation of large sections of Christian opinion from their former Mediterranean roots.

The Nestorians showed what this severing of links with the Graeco-Roman world might mean for Christian mission when they established their main centre in Persia. They engaged in vigorous missionary work in Arabia, India and even in China; in fact they were more successful in these areas than any subsequent mission from Western churches, the heirs of the Roman Empire, has been since. It was only the ferocity of the Mongol invaders, converted to Islam in the thirteenth century, which shattered their work. Like the Nestorians, the Monophysite churches in Egypt, Syria and Armenia have had to fight for an existence down the centuries against Islam; in the rest of the world, Christianity is the property of the heirs of Chalcedon.

Politics and the church: Damasus and Ambrose

If the bishops involved in these fourth- and fifth-century Eastern disputes were now frequently politicians playing a power-game, the same was true also in the Latin West; it would have to be, because the Emperors had forced the church into a political position. It was all the more so because in the police state which the Empire had now become, the church was about the only place where people might still make decisions for themselves or have any control over their own lives. Bishops were not mere tools of the government; very frequently now they behaved like and often emerged from the upper aristocracy, and it would take more than an emperor to overawe them. The Bishops of Rome, for instance, began developing a spiritual role for themselves which very quickly gave them a leading place in their city; Rome had become nothing more than a ceremonial capital for the Empire, occasionally visited by Emperors whose main concern was to face the constant demands of the frontiers, and the Emperor's secular representative in Rome was no match for the Bishop. Damasus (Bishop of Rome 366–84) is important in this process, for after a highly discreditable election in which his supporters massacred supporters of a rival candidate, he sought to highlight the traditions and the glory of his see.

Damasus encouraged the new Christian enthusiasm for pilgrimage to the graves of the martyrs, placing a new emphasis on the role of Peter rather than Paul in the Roman past. This would have an obvious usefulness for the successor of Peter, and it is in Damasus's time that the Bishop started using the distant language favoured by the imperial bureaucracy in his correspondence; increasingly the old affectionate nickname of 'papa' (father), the Pope, previously used in the West for any bishop, became a title of honour confined to the Pope of Rome. All this was not merely for the Pope's greater glory, however; it was a conscious effort to show that Christianity had a past as glorious as anything that the old paganism could offer. It was no longer an upstart, but could be a religion fit for gentlemen.

Bishop Ambrose of Milan also illustrates this tendency. Brought up a Christian but very much the gentleman, he was the son of the Praetorian Prefect (Governor-General) of the vast imperial province which included the modern France, England and Spain. This great aristocrat predictably went in for a military career, equally predictably ending up as governor of the province whose capital Milan was the chief imperial headquarters in the West. Here in 374 things took an unexpected turn. The Christian population had gathered to choose a new bishop (incidentally showing that the church still had genuine choices to make even in a key strategic city); however, since they were bitterly divided, there was no agreement on who should be bishop, and in desperation the crowd turned to Ambrose, who had come along at the head of his troops to keep order. Consecrated Bishop after a rather indecently hasty progress through baptism and ordination, Ambrose proved a remarkable success, but it was not surprising that this nobleman who in other circumstances might have bid for the imperial throne was quite capable of bullying pious Christian emperors into doing what he thought was right for the church. To our eyes, the results seem ambiguous; in two famously contrasting instances, Ambrose both forced the Emperor Theodosius to cancel an order for compensation to a Jewish community whose synagogue had been burnt down by militant Christians, and on the other hand, successfully ordered Theodosius to do penance for his vindictiveness in massacring the rebellious inhabitants of Thessalonica. The church had come a long way from the days when the Roman authorities had seen it as a minor nuisance.

Pagans fight back

Was there any chance that paganism could reverse this steady Christian takeover? The one substantial attempt at halting the tide came when Julian came to power as Emperor. Julian is a fascinating character, one of the great might-have-beens of history: an intellectual, a pagan theologian, a soldier. All he lacked was time. One of the few members of Constantine's family to escape being murdered on the old man's death, he spent his childhood resisting either secretly or openly all attempts to impose Christianity on him; what came to fascinate him was the ancient culture of Greece and in particular, Christianity's great intellectual rival, neo-Platonism. In his efforts to conceal his true beliefs he even became a Reader in the Christian church. His chance to throw off deception came in 360, when the troops whom he was commanding in Gaul mutinied and proclaimed this popular young general their Emperor. The death of Constantius II the following year left him supreme, and he hastened to weight the balance against Christianity.

There was little violent persecution in the Diocletianic manner; with wry humour, the Emperor let the Christians alone to fight amongst themselves, for this was the height of the Arian dispute. He also did nothing when pagan mobs took the law into their own hands to take revenge for decades of Christian aggression, and meanwhile he launched his own positive campaign to produce a coherent paganism. Partly this was through the organization of an alternative pagan church; Diocletian's assistants Galerius and Maximin Daia had started on this idea fifty years before, but now Julian tried to improve on what they had done by searching out priests distinguished by virtue rather than by aristocratic birth, and making his paganism as full of good works as Christianity at its best. Imitation is the sincerest form of flattery; paganism was at its most organized in this last throw against the Christians. At the same time, the Emperor himself mounted a one-man literary campaign against the Christians. For many pagan noblemen it was all rather embarrassing, particularly when they saw their Emperor going on preaching tours proclaiming the virtues of the old gods and of the Unconquered Sun, or indulging in a pamphlet war with one of his own cities, the Christian centre of Antioch. Perhaps he would have won over aristocratic paganism in time, but within three years he was dead, struck down by a Persian arrow in a battle on the eastern frontier. The Christians did not hide their glee at his passing.

Despite this setback, the aristocracy in the West remained determinedly pagan through the later fourth century, and their last attempt at regaining power came with a *coup d'état* in 392 backed by a barbarian general of the Roman army named Arbogastes. He murdered the legitimate Western emperor Valentinian II, and replaced him with a mild-mannered academic of pagan sympathies named Eugenius. Moves to restore honour and equal treatment to paganism had not got very far when Theodosius I intervened from the east and destroyed the new regime. His reaction, naturally enough, was to confirm and extend the commanding role of Christianity, so that it is in the 390s that one can talk without qualification of Christianity as the established religion of the Empire. Ambrose of Milan was now free to complete the campaign which he had long waged against pagan survival in the corridors of power; and now most of the pagan aristocracy accepted defeat and joined the church with suspicious rapidity. Temples were pulled down, allowed to fall down, or turned into Christian churches, the famous Parthenon in Athens for instance turning from a shrine of the virgin goddess Pallas Athene to a church dedicated to the Virgin Mary. Heresy laws were enacted outlawing both Christian sects and many other religions, including the latest form of Gnostic dualism, the influential belief system of eastern origins known as Manicheism after its Babylonian founder Mani. Already Diocletian had issued furious condemnations of the Manichees, and like him, the Christian regimes of Valentinian I and his successors laid down that those found guilty of professing Manicheism should be subject to the severest penalties, including being burnt alive.

Early Monasticism

Influential paganism was thus finally defeated by the end of the fourth century; henceforth pagan cults would be the religion of the humble, those outside the cities — literally the countryfolk (*pagani* in Latin). Now Christianity, far from putting down the mighty from their seats and sending the rich empty away, was the religion of the powerful. However, by this time, a reaction against this new-found power and status had set in within the church itself: monasticism, what the spiritual writer A.M.Allchin has called 'the silent rebellion'. What he means is that all monasticism is an implied criticism of the direction which the church has taken in becoming a large-scale and inclusive organization. In its early years, the church was a small community which found it easy to guard its character as an élite consisting of spiritual athletes proclaiming the Lord's coming; its links with Gnosticism encouraged this feeling, and also pushed Christians in the direction of austerity of life and self-denial, just like so much contemporary pagan philosophy. This stance became increasingly hard to maintain as Christian communities grew and all sorts of people started flocking in; even the long process of instruction and preparation for baptism and admission to communion which was then customary could not prevent this process. How much could the church retain its character as an élite?

There had been rows over this in Rome as early as the end of the second century, when the sternly austere priest Hippolytus had furiously attacked his bishop Callistus for what he regarded as laxity in imposing penances on church members who had fallen into serious sin. At the root of this quarrel, which resulted in Hippolytus severing his links with the mainstream church, was the issue of whether the church of Christ was an assembly of saints, handpicked by God for salvation, or whether it was a mixed assembly of saints and sinners. The same issue lay behind the rows which led to the Novatianist and Donatist schisms of the third century which we have already mentioned (above, Chapter Six). It was probably inevitable that the hardliners from Hippolytus to Donatus should lose the argument and leave the mainstream, for Christianity was already set on course to be a religion constantly in search of converts; if it applied the sort of rigorous moral standards which the purists wanted, there would hardly be anyone left in the church.

Nevertheless there would be some who without wishing to go to the extreme of cutting themselves off from the general fellowship, would wish to lead a separate Christian life to the highest standard they could; to do what the Essenes had done in relation to mainstream Judaism and withdraw. The situation for many reached crisis proportions when the Roman establishment jumped on the Christian bandwagon at the end of the fourth century, but the impulse is already perceptible in Egypt during the third century; again, it is worth remembering that it was in Egypt that the Gnostics and their denial of the material world had had the strongest influence on Catholic Christianity. In addition, the geography of Egypt, with its narrow fertile strip along the Nile backed by great stretches of desert, meant that it was easy literally to walk out of civilization and get away from it all. The first great names of Christian monasticism were both Egyptians, Anthony and Pachomius, pioneers respectively of two very different forms of the monastic life, that of the hermit and that of the community. Anthony might today have been under the care of a medical social worker from an early age, for contemporary stories about him make it clear that he was a compulsive loner who shunned human company. Eventually his desire to live a Christian life out of touch with anyone else led him into the desert, where after twenty years of solitude, he was faced with a new problem: hordes of people were coming out to join him. The persecution of Christians by Diocletian and the sheer burden of taxation in ordinary society were powerful incentives for many to flee into the wilderness.

The solution to Anthony's problem which Pachomius devised, way to the south of Anthony's homeland in the deserts beyond Upper Egypt, was to organize these crowds into communities of hermits living under a simple set of common rules: the first monasteries. His sister founded female communities along similar lines, with a programme of manual work and study of scripture. Egyptian hermits and monks became famous for their austerities during the fourth century, vying like athletes in outdoing each other for God's glory in such exercises as standing day and night, or eating no cooked food for years on end. This spirit fired imitations in the deserts of Palestine and Syria, where the most bizarre form of ascetic exercise, sitting for years on end on top of a specially-built stone column, was devised by Simeon the Stylite ('pillar-dweller'). In Asia Minor, the climate in winter was much harsher than further south, and community life was much more practicable than the life of a hermit. It was here that most of the monastic rules were devised from which form the basis of modern Eastern monastic rules, emphasizing the regular life pioneered by Pachomius rather than the individualism of Anthony or Simeon. The disruption caused by the controversies of the early fifth century forced one monk from Asia Minor, John Cassian, to flee to the West, and it was he who founded the first Western monastic community to follow Asian lines, in the south of France, about 415. The hermit's life also quickly attracted Westerners, and so by the fifth century the whole church had accepted the institution as part of its structure.

It is perhaps difficult for us, who accept monasticism as a traditional feature of Christianity, to see that this acceptance was not inevitable. A 'silent rebellion' might well have been seen by the church as a threat, particularly since a hermit's life denied the whole basis on which the church had come to be organized: the eucharistic community presided over by the bishop. How could Anthony receive the eucharist out in the desert, and how therefore did he relate to the authority of the bishop? As it happened, Anthony proved himself in the eyes of the church authorities by leaving his isolation during Diocletian's persecution to comfort the suffering faithful in Alexandria; he also became a great friend of Bishop Athanasius and was such a constant support to him in his long struggles against the Arians that the Bishop wrote an admiring biography of him; the desert monks were a constant, not to say a militant, source of support for the hierarchy during the fourth century. Nevertheless, there were conflicts, as is demonstrated by the sad case of Bishop Priscillian, a pioneer of the monastic life in Spain, whose (now somewhat obscure) theological ideas were so world-denying that he was widely accused of Manicheism; through the politicking of some of his fellow-bishops he was eventually executed for alleged sorcery by the then Western imperial authorities in 386.

The case of Priscillian was an embarrassment to the Western church authorities, and his enemies were roundly denounced by no less an establishment figure than Ambrose of Milan. Monasticism had come to stay, as was symbolized by the fact that more monks became bishops in the West. Martin, who became Bishop of the French city of Tours and a noted evangelist among the pagan Celtic peasantry, is an example of this process; the popularity of his absurdly sensationalized life-story by his friend Sulpicius Severus was a sign that the monks had achieved respectability. It was very fortunate for the Latin West that they had, for as they established themselves, the structure of the Western Roman Empire was giving way. It would be monks who carried what remained of its legacy into the future, as we shall see.

Chronology for Chapter Eight

382	Jerome begins work on Vulgate
384	Augustine arrives in Milan
386	Augustine converted to Catholic Christianity
391	Augustine becomes coadjutor Bishop in Hippo
410	Sack of Rome by Alaric the Goth
418	Final condemnation of Pelagius by Pope Zosimus
430	Augustine dies during Vandal siege of Hippo
c. 433	Controversy between Prosper of Aquitaine and Vincent of Lérins
451	Council of Chalcedon
c. 460	Possible date of death of Patrick in Ireland
476	Deposition of Romulus Augustulus, last Western Emperor
493	Theodoric the Ostrogoth becomes King in Italy
c. 530	Abbey at Monte Cassino founded (?)by Benedict
533	Emperor Justinian makes Byzantine counter-attack in Italy
c. 550	Marked decrease in copying manuscripts begins in West
590	Gregory becomes Pope
597	Gregory sends Augustine to Britain
622	Muhammed flees to Medina (Hijra): Islamic era dated from this event
680	Third Council of Constantinople
698	Carthage falls to Islamic forces
726	Byzantine Emperor Leo III orders the destruction of all icons
732	Charles Martel defeats Arabs at Battle of Poitiers
774	Charlemagne conquers Lombard kingdom in Italy
800	Charlemagne crowned Holy Roman Emperor
1000	World fails to come to an end, despite much excitement
1054	Pope Leo IX excommunicates Patriarch of Constantinople
1066	Battle of Hastings: William the Norman conquers England

Chapter Eight

The Parting of the Ways
(350 to 1000)

Diocletian's reforms in government in the late third century led to a division between East and West which became more or less permanent under the successors of Constantine I; only occasionally and for short periods would the Roman Empire again be united, and never after the end of the fourth century. From then on the histories of the surviving Eastern and Western Empires would be very different; in the Greek East there would be a Byzantine Empire based on Constantinople, with an Emperor in direct succession from the Roman imperial throne, for the next thousand years. In the Latin West, the state machine which had looked so stable in the 390s quite suddenly suffered terrible damage from successive barbarian invasions in the first decade of the fifth century. The barbarian pressure continued after the most humiliating blow of all, the capture and sack of the city of Rome itself in 410; gradually central government disintegrated. In 476 the last Western Emperor, a mere boy with the grand old names of the Roman founder Romulus and the first Emperor Augustus, was deposed by his barbarian mercenary troops, who came to a conveniently vague arrangement with the Eastern Emperor recognizing him as sole Emperor. In fact most of what had been the Western Empire was by then under the control of barbarian kings, and although the Byzantines would make several successful conquests in the West, they never regained these territories for long.

All this was the background to a long process of disengagement and separation of the Eastern and the Western Christian churches. We have already seen the beginnings of this by considering some of the great names of the Western church: Damasus, Ambrose and Martin of Tours. Previously the Latin Western church had seemed a poor relation of the Greek East, in terms of traditional prestige, numbers or theological sophistication, but Damasus had emphasized Western Christian tradition, Ambrose had masterminded the official establishment of the church, and Martin had been used by his biographer to show that the West could produce a holy man who was the equal of the holy men in the East. Additionally, the fourth century had given the Western church a Latin Bible which would have an unchallenged place at the centre of its culture for a thousand years. Much credit for this can go to Damasus, who in 382 persuaded his secretary, a brilliant but quarrelsome scholar called Jerome, to undertake this massive task of revision and editing, to replace several often conflicting Latin versions from earlier centuries. The result, the Vulgate version (from the Latin *vulgata*, meaning 'generally known' or 'common'), was as great an achievement as Origen's work in producing a single Greek text a century and a half before.

Augustine of Hippo

However, the most significant individual to symbolize the new self-confidence and separate identity of the Western church was Augustine, a Latin-speaking theologian from north Africa who had little interest in Greek literature, hardly spoke the language, read virtually nothing of Plato and Aristotle and had very little influence on the Greek church. By contrast, his impact on Western Christian thought can hardly be overstated; only his beloved example Paul of Tarsus has been more influential, and in any case Westerners have generally seen Paul through Augustine's eyes. One modern church historian, Jaroslav Pelikan, has gone so far as to say that the bitter disputes between Catholic and Protestant in the sixteenth-century Western Reformation were first and foremost a dialogue between different parts of the writings of Augustine. What is more, Augustine is one of the few early Church Fathers who wrote works of which some can still be read purely for pleasure.

Augustine's life was played out against the background of the rise, final splendour and terrifying fall of the Christian Western Empire, but apart from these great political traumas, his whole life's work can be seen as a series of responses to a series of conflicts both internal and external. The first conflict was with himself: what did he want to be, and how would he find a truth which would satisfy him? He had been brought up in small-town north Africa; his father Patricius was a pagan, his mother Monica (a tougher character) a deeply pious if not very intellectual Christian. Augustine reacted against her unsophisticated religion, and after his parents had scrimped and saved to send him to the University of Carthage, he was increasingly drawn by the excitements of university life to the philosophy and literature of pagan Rome. The world was at his feet; like many young intellectuals of his day, he settled down with a mistress who bore him a son. But even as he began an exceptionally promising career as a teacher of rhetoric (the language studies which lay at the heart of Latin culture), he was becoming tormented by anxieties which would lie at the heart of his theological preoccupations all his life. What was the source of evil in the world? It was the ancient religious question which the Gnostics had tried to solve, and it was the Gnostic religion of his day, the semi-secret sect known as the Manichees, which first won his allegiance; they held him for nine years.

Nevertheless Augustine became increasingly unsatisfied by Manichean belief, and as he pursued academic success in Rome and Milan, he was haunted by doubts and anxieties about the nature of truth, reality and wisdom. As he ceased to find Manicheism of use, he turned to neo-Platonist belief, but in Milan he also became fascinated by the personality of Bishop Ambrose. Here for the first time he met a Christian whose mind and thinking he could respect, whose sermons, sonorous and rich, made up for the crudity and vulgarity of the Bible which had long distressed the young Augustine. These contradictory influences came to tear him apart, especially as he became drawn back to Christianity and felt that his loyalty to his mistress was the only barrier keeping him from a full faith.

In a state bordering on nervous breakdown, he arrived in 386 at a crisis which was to bring him a new serenity and a new certainty: the crucial turning-point was the impulse which led him to read Paul's words of Romans 13, from verse 13: 'Let us behave with decency, as befits the day ... ' It was enough to bring him fully back to his mother's faith, and it meant that the mistress had to go.

She has seldom got the sympathy which she deserves, as she left behind her teenage son, and left the man who lived with her for fifteen years, swearing to remain faithful to him. In the autobiographical *Confessions* in which Augustine describes all this, she is never given her name. When in later years Augustine came to discuss original sin, he saw it as inseparable from the sexual act, which transmits sin from one generation to another: a view momentous in its consequences for the Western church's attitude to sexuality.

For Augustine, his conversion was a liberation from torment. He was determined now to abandon his teaching career and to express his new-found Christianity in a community life with cultivated friends back in his home town: a life which would bring the best of the intellectual world of old Rome into a Christian context. However, the turbulent church politics of north Africa soon ended this ambition: established Catholic Christianity was faced with a self-confident and aggressive Donatist church, cherishing grievances a century old, and enjoying increasing support from the semi-independent north African regime of Gildo from his takeover in 387. In 391 Augustine happened to visit the struggling Catholic congregation in the town of Hippo Regius, the second most important port on the north African coast; the Bishop, an eccentric but shrewd old Greek named Valerius, encouraged his flock to bully this brilliant stranger into being ordained priest, and soon Augustine was coadjutor (that is, assistant) Bishop in the town. From Valerius's death until his own in 430 he remained Bishop of Hippo, and all his theological work would be done against a background of busy pastoral work for a church in a world which was collapsing.

The next phase of his theological work would be dominated by the very practical problem of the Donatists, particularly the differences between their concept of the nature of the church as a gathered pure community and his own idea of what 'One, Holy and Catholic' might mean. In 401, the Donatists' run of luck under Gildo ended when his rebel regime was destroyed by imperial troops: now the Catholics found themselves in a position to dictate terms. Over the previous decade, Augustine had done much to prepare for this moment, in co-operation with the statesmanlike Bishop of Carthage, Aurelius; now he tried to bring the Donatists back into the Catholic fold by negotiation. A series of conferences failed; the old bitterness lay too deep for reconciliation to be easy. Faced with government repression, the Donatist leadership began relying on guerrilla warfare and terrorism, and the behaviour of both sides began deteriorating in the miserable cycle of violence familiar to us today in Ulster or the Lebanon. By 412 Augustine's patience with the Donatists was at an end, and he was backing new harsh government measures repressing them, even providing theological justification for the repression. He pointed out that our Lord had said 'Compel them to come in'; it was the duty of a Christian state to support the church by punishing heresy and schism, and after all, such unwilling adherence might be the start of a living faith. It would be a side of Augustine's teaching which would much appeal to Christian regimes for centuries to come.

The 'City of God'

At the same time, Augustine was faced with the problem of explaining how God's providence could allow the collapse of the manifestly Christian Roman Empire, and in particular, how God could have allowed the disaster which overtook Rome in 410. Quite naturally, pagans were inclined to say that it was Rome's flirtation with the Christian church which was at the root of the problem; but even Christians could not understand how a heretical Arian like the Goth Alaric had been allowed to plunder Catholic Rome. Part of the Christian response was to argue from history: a Spanish protegé of Augustine's called Orosius wrote a 'History against the Pagans' designed to show from a brief survey of all world history that there had been worse disasters in pagan times.

However, Orosius's work seems thin stuff indeed compared with the response which Augustine was making at the same time: *The City of God (De Civitate Dei)*. It was his most monumental work, and it took him thirteen years from 413 to write. Although it starts with a consideration of Roman history, and ridicules the old gods, its preoccupation quickly becomes wider than the single disaster of the sack of Rome, or even the whole canvas of Roman history. It turns to the problem which was at the centre of Augustine's thought: what is the nature and cause of evil, and how does it relate to God's majesty and all-powerful goodness? For Augustine, evil is simply non-existence, since God has given everything existence; all sin is a deliberate falling-away from God towards nothingness. Only half-way through the work, at the end of fourteen books, does Augustine begin explicitly to take up the theme of two cities: 'the earthly city glories in itself, the Heavenly City glories in the Lord'. All the institutions which we know form part of a struggle between these two cities, a struggle which runs through all world history. No institution, not even the church itself, can without qualification be identified as the City of God. In this Augustine is occasionally incautious, and the visible church is indeed identified with the Heavenly City; ironically, much of the influence of *The City of God* over the next thousand years would come from the eagerness of medieval churchmen to expand on this identification in their efforts to make the church supreme on earth, equating the earthly city with opponents of ecclesiastical power like some of the Holy Roman Emperors.

The Pelagian controversy

Yet another side of Augustine's energies were occupied in the same years with a fierce controversy over the teachings of a British monk called Pelagius. Pelagius was a favourite spiritual director in upper-class circles in the Rome of the last decades of the fourth century, and was naturally concerned with the implications of the new established status of Christianity: were the affluent people among whom he moved simply joining the church as an easy option, without any real sense that they must transform their lives in the process? Pelagius was particularly concerned at what he read of the earlier works of Augustine; Augustine's preoccupation with God's majesty seemed to leave humankind helpless puppets, who might easily abandon all responsibility for their conduct. Talk of original sin, as it is developed in the writings of Augustine and other like-minded contemporaries, equally seemed to Pelagius to create the same result. He was determined to say that our natures are not so completely corrupt that we can do nothing towards our own salvation. As the controversy developed, his followers pushed the implications of this further to insist that although Adam sinned, this sin did not transmit itself through every generation, but was merely a bad example, which we can ignore if we choose. We can choose to turn to God. We have free will.

Pelagius's views have often been presented as rather amiable, in contrast to a fierce pessimism in Augustine's view of our fallen state. This is not so; Pelagius was a stern Puritan, whose teaching placed a terrifying responsibility on the shoulders of every human being to act according to the highest standards demanded by God. The world which he would have constructed on these principles would have been one vast monastery; the mixed human society of vice and virtue which Augustine presents in the 'City of God', where no Christian has the right to avoid everyday civic responsibilities in this fallen world precisely because we are all caught up in the consequences of Adam's fall, would be impossible. Some Pelagians were indeed revolutionaries in their wholesale condemnation of the world. One British writer living amid the country estates of fabulously wealthy Romans in Sicily advocated the confiscation of rich people's property – more thoroughgoing social change than is to be found in any other early Christian writer. The row over Pelagianism represents part of the wider unrest which the growth of monasticism brought to the church, the destruction of Priscillian (above, Chapter Seven) being another example.

The fall of Rome in 410 produced a scatter of refugees throughout the Mediterranean, and it was this which began spreading the dispute from Pelagius's Roman circle. One extremist follower of Pelagius, a lawyer named Celestius, arrived in north Africa and began expounding Pelagius's views to the extreme point where he left no possibility of affirming original sin; hence he said that there was no sin to remit in baptism. There could not have been a more sensitive issue to choose in north Africa, where much of the argument between Catholics and Donatists had been around who was the true heir of Cyprian's third-century teaching on baptism as the only way to gain salvation. It was therefore these statements of Celestius which first provoked Augustine's fury. Over the next few years a complicated series of political moves and counter-moves by both sides raised the temperature to new heights of bitterness; Augustine's crusade against the Pelagians eventually resulted in their defeat and the dismissal from church office of all their highly-placed supporters. In the process, Augustine's thought about the nature of grace and salvation had been pushed into ever more extreme positions, which can be traced both through *The City of God* and the long series of tracts which he wrote attacking Pelagian thought. Eventually he could say not simply that all human impulses to do good are a result of God's grace, but that it is an entirely arbitrary decision on the part of God as to who receives this grace. God has made the decision before all time, so some are fore-ordained to be saved through grace – a predestined group of the elect. The arbitrariness is fully justified by the monstrousness of Adam's original fall, in which we all have a part.

There was much criticism of this view at the time, and it has alternately repelled and fascinated both Catholic and Protestant down to the present day. Contemporary opponents, in particular the clever and outspoken Pelagian Julian, Bishop of Eclanum, pointed to Augustine's personal history and his involvement with the Manichees, with their dualist belief in the eternal struggle between equally-balanced forces of good and evil; such critics said that this was the origin both of his pessimistic view of human nature and of his emphasis on the role of sexual reproduction in transmitting the Fall. After Augustine's death one of his followers in France, Prosper of Aquitaine, came under attack from Vincent, a monk of the monastery in the French islands of Lérins; Vincent felt that Augustine and Prosper had gone beyond the bounds of doctrine as understood in the universal church, and he gave a definition of how doctrine should be judged properly Catholic or universal: it should have been believed everywhere in the church, always and by everyone (*'quod ubique, quod semper, quod ab omnibus creditum est'*). On the criteria of this 'Vincentian Canon', Augustine's theology cannot stand unchallenged, yet its influence remained profound. Augustine's early grounding in neo-Platonism undoubtedly stayed with him; references to the heritage of Plato, and Platonic modes of thought, shape much of his writing; amid many approving references to Plato in the *City of God*, he can say that Platonists are near-Christians. This meant that Plato would remain at the heart of Christian thinking through the medieval period, even when Christian thinkers began to be excited by their rediscovery of many lost works of Aristotle during the twelfth and thirteenth centuries.

It is easy to find Augustine unsympathetic and harsh, particularly if one reads the later phases of his writings against the Pelagians, where the historian Gerald Bonner has spoken of his 'love grown cold'. What we always need to remember is that Augustine's bleak view of human nature and human capabilities was formed against the background of the destruction of the world he loved; in one of the greatest disappointments ever experienced by the church, the Western Empire under Theodosius and the other emperors of the 390s, which had promised to be an image of God's kingdom on earth, had disintegrated into chaos and futility. Augustine himself died in 430 during a siege of his beloved Hippo by the Arian people known as the Vandals, who would capture all north Africa and horribly persecute the Catholic church there for sixty years. It was as if the nuclear winter had descended on classical society. Augustine stands between the classical world and a very different medieval society, sensing acutely that the world was getting old and feeble: a sense which would hardly desert Western Europe down to the seventeenth century.

Aftermath of Empire (400 to 800)

The centuries after the fall of the Western Empire up to the eleventh century have often been called the Dark Ages: there can be few more misleading names in history, concealing a rich and creative period in the development of the West. 'Early medieval' might be a better, more neutral description of this age, but how do we date it? A pleasant game for historians is to argue about when the classical world ended and the medieval world began. The general consensus at the moment is that something recognizable as classical society survived in the western Mediterranean well after the collapse of the central administration, and that it is only in the second half of the sixth century that this society decisively changed. The Roman aristocracy was then shattered by repeated wars in Italy, ironically mostly resulting from attempts by the emperors in Constantinople to restore the old Italy under their own rule; a similar process happened in north Africa. Perhaps most significantly, in the decades after 550, Latin culture came within a hair's breadth of extinction; the laborious process of copying manuscripts, the only way in which the fragile products of centuries of accumulating knowledge could be preserved, virtually came to an end and would not be taken up again for two and a half centuries. This was the period in which much of classical literature was lost to us for ever.

Politically, the area of the former Western Empire was transformed into a series of barbarian kingdoms, mostly ruled by Arians, who preserved their Arian faith as a mark of their cultural distinction from the Catholic Christians of the old Latin world. The two worlds remained curiously separate side by side, with the

Latins excluded from military service and paying tribute to the barbarian leaders. Frequently bishops of the Catholic church were the only form of Latin authority left, since the imperial civil service had collapsed; often Roman aristocrats would become bishops because they saw the office as the only way to protect what survived of the world which they loved. How would the Catholic church as a whole react to this new situation? Would it look to the Greek East, and identify itself wholeheartedly with the efforts of the Byzantine emperors to reconquer the West? Would it disappear, like all the other institutions of the Western Imperial structure? Would it be replaced by a series of Arian churches, separated into the various ethnic groupings which now occupied the West?

In fact the church chose a middle path; it abandoned for the time being the vision of a Christian empire, but it stood aloof from the Arianism of the Gothic tribes. This cautious approach to the new world became apparent when a kingdom was set up in the old imperial capital at Ravenna by an Ostrogoth military leader named Theodoric, owing an extremely loose allegiance to the Byzantine emperors who had backed his enterprise against their own Western enemies. Theodoric's acceptance of a sophisticated culture can be seen from the superb religious buildings which survive from his rule in Ravenna; Roman aristocrats entered his service, and although he remained an Arian, he could be seen as the protector of the Western Catholic church because he remained distant from the Eastern Emperor, who was then scandalizing Western Catholic leaders by making concessions to the powerful Monophysite grouping in the East. After this beginning of co-operation, there was modified rapture among Catholic Christians when in 533 the Eastern Emperor Justinian I (527-53) began a programme of reconquest in Italy. For the first time since the days of Constantine, there was a division in the church leadership's attitude to the Emperor: some saw his arrival as a threat to the new order, and his conquest as an alien occupation. It was particularly difficult further west in Gaul and Spain to relish any contact with the Emperor. Increasingly the survivors of the classical Western World would feel that if anything was to remain from the old culture, it would be dependent on the barbarians.

As Justinian's conquests in Italy and north Africa melted away in the ruinous wars of the later sixth century, it was inevitable that

the Bishop of Rome should come to play an increasingly important role in the Western church. Unlike the competing claims of
great churches in the East, there was no rival to his position in the
West, particularly as the north African church disintegrated under
the impact of the seventh-century Arab invasions. The church's
constant search for a source of authority to solve its disputes
encouraged the process. For all the honoured achievements of
great oecumenical councils like Nicaea and Chalcedon, the age of
the Councils had revealed evident drawbacks in this method of
decision-making, as we have already seen when considering
the long-drawn-out struggles over Arianism and Monophysitism
(above, Chapter Seven). The growing prestige of the Bishop of
Rome was both symbolized and encouraged by the pontificate of
Gregory I (590-604). He was Pope when the Byzantine power in
Italy was shattered by the people known as the Lombards; although he had represented the church of Rome at the Byzantine
Court for six years, he had no great affection for or high opinion of
the Greek East, and he certainly did not see the Lombard victory
as a final catastrophe as many had seen Alaric's sack of Rome. In
592-3 he more or less made a separate peace with the Lombards,
ignoring the Byzantine imperial representative in Ravenna. Here
was a very different world even from that of Augustine of Hippo,
who had been fully trained in the classical tradition as a professional teacher of rhetoric.

It was also Gregory who launched the celebrated mission of
another Augustine to the former Roman province of Britain in
597. During the fifth and sixth centuries, most of the Western
church had been too preoccupied with survival to undertake much
missionary work to expand its frontiers or to recover lost ground,
but now that its position was becoming more secure and the Arian
tribes were increasingly becoming reconciled to Catholic Christianity, Roman Christendom started to seek converts once more.
For all his timidity and frequent dependence on detailed advice
from Gregory back in Rome, Augustine's mission was a remarkable success-story; he became the first archbishop at Canterbury,
headquarters of the Kentish kingdom. He and his successors won
over the pagan leadership of the Anglo-Saxon kingdoms which by
now dominated the main part of Britain, and with this aristocratic
backing, they were able to found a church which proved its
remarkable vigour by itself rapidly becoming a missionary church
in central Europe.

However, there was another parallel missionary impulse in Europe which owed nothing to Roman initiative; it came from Ireland. Ireland was the first non-Roman outpost of Christianity in the West, for it had never formed part of the Empire; how Christianity arrived there is not certain, nor are the exact dates of its most prominent early figure, a Cumbrian missionary named Patrick. What is clear is that during the sixth century, when everywhere else in Western Europe, Latin culture was fighting a struggle merely to survive, in Ireland there had developed a flourishing and original intellectual life centred on monasteries. Appropriately for a non-Roman church, in a land where there were no towns to speak of, this church did not organize itself round the person of a bishop taking his title from a city, though there were bishops in Ireland. Instead the leading figures were abbots and abbesses; the distribution of their monasteries reflected the tribal centres of power in the country, and they were the driving force behind new missions.

It was perhaps this characteristic which made the Irish such effective missionaries in the lands of northern Europe which also lay beyond the city-dominated world of the Roman Empire. Irish missionaries brought Christianity in turn to Scotland, northern England and then to central Europe. It is worth noticing that it is in the heartlands of this Celtic Christianity, Ireland, Scotland, Wales and Cornwall, that the episcopal system favoured by Anglicanism and borrowed from Roman Christianity has had least success! There were many tensions when the Celtic and Roman missions found their work overlapping both in the British Isles and on the Continent, and it would take centuries before steady pressure from Rome made Celtic Christianity conform to the standard episcopal mould.

While Christianity was thus beginning to regain ground that it had lost in the north and also to expand into new areas, in the south and east of the Christian world there was a new and wholly unexpected catastrophe in the shape of the coming of Islam. Politics in the Near East at the beginning of the seventh century were dominated as they had been for centuries by the struggle between the Byzantine and the Persian Empires, a struggle which seemed to be going in favour of the Byzantines; then, out of the network of towns in western Arabia came a new monotheistic religion proclaimed by the prophet Muhammed. There had long been contacts with and an Arab racial presence inside the Roman Empire; now the Arab world burst upon the Byzantine with a new militance and coherence, born of its new-found faith. Within a decade of the first proclamation of Islam, Alexandria had fallen to Muslim armies; soon Antioch and the Roman Empire's ancient enemy Persia would follow. The Arabs left the remainder of the Byzantine Empire fighting for its life, while they swept through north Africa, destroying the church which had nurtured Tertullian, Cyprian and Augustine of Hippo. During the eighth century they crossed the Straits of Gibraltar (itself an Arab name dating from their conquest) and dominated Spain; they were only stopped from spreading into central Europe by their defeat in central France by the Frankish ruler Charles Martel at the Battle of Poitiers in 732. The earliest Christian lands would remain under Islamic control into the twentieth century; soon this unlikely military and religious confederacy would form a culture which far outclassed the struggling Latin Christianity of Western Europe.

Islam struck a great blow against the power of the Byzantine Emperor, and the possibility of a Christianity of East and West united under Greek imperial leadership became still more remote. During the seventh century, the possibility was still there; after all, the West hardly seemed the equal of the ancient and wealthy state based on Constantinople. Seventh-century Popes still acknowledged the Byzantine emperor as overlord, and if anything, contacts seemed to be growing. Eleven out of seventeen Popes in the period 650–750 had a Greek or an Eastern background; the third Council of Constantinople in 680 was a united attempt by Eastern and Western leaders to solve the controversy over the view of Christ's nature and of his will known as Monothelitism, in which Roman representatives joined eastern bishops in condemning as heretical both four patriarchs of Constantinople and one Roman Pope.

Yet by the 720s, the Popes had decisively quarrelled with the authorities in Constantinople, the main issue being the great controversy in the Greek church about the use of images (icons) in worship. The Popes were both shocked by the ruthless action of successive Byzantine emperors in backing the image-breakers (Iconoclasts) and worried by the implications which the emperors' ordering of such changes in church practice had for their own spiritual authority. The Popes turned westwards from this distasteful situation, and began to play off one western barbarian kingdom, that of the Lombards of north Italy, against another, the Franks, who would guarantee them independence both against the Lombards and the Emperor; in 774 Pope Hadrian I saw the fruits of this policy when with his encouragement the Frankish king Charles (grandson of Charles Martel) conquered the Lombard Kingdom.

Charlemagne and the Holy Roman Empire (800 to 1000)

Hadrian's backing of Charles was to have fateful consequences for the future of the church. With Charles we have come a long way from those Arian chieftains who had burst in to smash the central structure of the Roman Empire, for Charles was obsessed with ancient Rome. Small wonder that generations to come nicknamed him Charlemagne – Charles the Great. As military triumph followed military triumph, he built up a state which stretched beyond the Pyrenees and into the heart of modern Germany; on Christmas Day 800, Hadrian's successor Pope Leo III crowned him as the first Holy Roman Emperor. The Empire would remain part of Western Europe's dream of recapturing the golden Roman past for centuries to come. It was a brutal break with the claims of the Eastern Empire, and much resented in Constantinople; it was equally a dramatic assertion of the papacy's new self-confidence, and the returning vitality of the Latin West.

Charlemagne was no mere military leader; his new title was a conscious manifesto of his aim to restore past glories. What followed has been described as almost like a miracle, and with reference to the later movement of rediscovering the classical past in the fourteenth century, it has been called the Carolingian Renaissance (Carolingian after Charles himself). Charlemagne's buildings proclaimed his intentions: his imperial private chapel at Aachen was a copy of a church which the Emperor Justinian had built in Ravenna three hundred years before, and throughout the lands where he had control, he and his associates built monumental churches which imitated the forms and the plans of churches from the early Christian past. Most importantly, the long haemorrhage of written information from the classical past was brought to an end; Charles encouraged a massive programme of copying manuscripts, his scribes devising a special script

('Carolingian miniscule') which was so influential that it is the direct ancestor of the typeface which you are looking at now. Virtually nothing more of classical literature or early Christian writing has been lost since that burst of copying energy in the ninth century. This 'information explosion' was the basis of an attempt to remodel and to instruct society on Christian lines; Charlemagne's favourite bedtime book was Augustine's *City of God*. The church's liturgy was reformed, and the Emperor's advisers drew up systems of law to regulate all life by what they saw as the commandments of God.

Charlemagne's chief agents for this heroic programme of social engineering were monks (and nuns) of the Benedictine rule. Benedict himself is a shadowy figure who may not even have been a single individual, but the bundle of ideas attributed to this 'blessed one' (*benedictus* in Latin) came during the sixth century to form the Rule of St Benedict to guide the monastic community on Monte Cassino in south Italy. The Rule was comparatively simple; a skin of parchment would suffice to copy it out, but because of this simplicity, it was very adaptable, and has proved the basis of much Western monastic life in societies very different from the decaying classical world of the sixth century. Its spread for the next few centuries was slow, but the vision of order and regularity which it represented was just what the rulers of the eighth and ninth centuries were looking for. Charlemagne was a great patron of the Benedictines, and encouraged them to reform older monastic communities which to his eyes were chaotic and decadent. The Christian aristocracies of Europe enthusiastically followed his lead in endowing Benedictine monasteries with vast estates which would free the monks from financial anxiety and allow them to get on with the vital business of regular prayer; they could also be centres of intellectual life and education.

Prayer mattered to the Carolingian upper classes; Hell was very near. They were very conscious of the powers of spiritual evil, who were as real enemies to them as an invading army on their territory. A Benedictine monastery was therefore a fortress with which they could attack the Devil, using the monks as their soldiers, armed with prayer. In addition, the church instilled in these fierce warlords a healthy sense of their own sinfulness and in particular a sense of the profound sinfulness of war. Noblemen were in a cleft stick; they constantly had to fight to survive and gain wealth, but if they did fight, the church imposed on them drastic penances, such as severe fasting for long periods of the year spread over several years. The historian Sir Richard Southern points out that if the Norman armies who won the battle of Hastings in 1066 had carried out the penances which contemporary manuals of penance (penitentials) laid down as a punishment for their fighting, they would have been too weak to go on to conquer England!

The great advantage of the monasteries was that they could use their round of prayer to carry out these penances on behalf of the noblemen who had earned them. This was a society with a weak conception of individual identity; in early medieval eyes, God would not mind who actually performed the penance demanded, as long as it was done. So the regular round of communal prayer demanded by St Benedict's Rule was an excellent investment for the upper classes; it saved them from the powers of Hell. The highest form of prayer was the mass (the eucharist had come to be called the mass in the Western church during the fourth century, from the form of dismissal, '*missio*' in late Latin, with which it ended). Demand for the mass therefore grew, and this changed its character. Monks had rarely been ordained priest in earlier centuries, but now they were ordained so that they could increase the throughput of masses in a monastic community. The mass began to change from being the weekly sung celebration of the eucharist which had been the centre of congregational life in the early church, and became a said service, the 'low mass', to be said as often as possible, with a server as token congregation. Side-altars began multiplying in Charlemagne's great abbey churches, so that alongside the sung High Mass for the whole of the community at the main altar, many low masses could be said. This never happened in the Eastern church, where the eucharistic service like all others is still always sung.

Another very useful function for monasteries was as a way of cutting down the numbers of claimants to a noble family's lands: send spare sons or daughters off to a convent, for what more honourable life could there be than that of a monk or nun? It is also clear that during the early medieval period, the monastic life offered a golden opportunity for talented upper class women to lead an emancipated, active life as abbesses, exercising power which might otherwise be closed to them: take for instance a formidable figure from a royal house of Anglo-Saxon England like the princess Etheldreda, who in the seventh century founded her own double monastery for monks and nuns at Ely on the frontiers of her family's East Anglian kingdom, and became its first abbess. Such ladies were not to be trifled with.

None of the functions of a Benedictine monastery just described had formed any part of or received any mention in the Rule of St Benedict. Nevertheless, because of them, the ninth to eleventh centuries were a golden age for monasteries of the Rule; the survival of European civilization would have been inconceivable without them, and contemporaries regarded them with reverence. If we look at a surviving plan of the ninth century which was drawn up as an ideal rebuilding of the Swiss monastery of St Gall, we see a layout which would remain standard to these houses for centuries: church, dining hall, dormitories and assembly hall (chapter house) grouped round a central cloister yard, with around them a host of lesser buildings and gardens to service the community. It is all very different from the haphazard collection of cells and buildings which formed the early Christian or Celtic monasteries; it speaks of order, just like the majestic cycle of the liturgy in the great monastery church, to a world which neurotically sought order and reassurance in the middle of disorder and fear, and which dreaded the approaching end of the world which many saw as coming when the Christian era would reach its thousandth year. Such communities seemed like the City of God itself; they were an image of Heaven. It is not surprising that people came to feel that regulars (clergy and people living under a monastic rule) were especially close to God, and that it was much more difficult for lay people in the ordinary world to gain salvation. During the High Middle Ages (1000–1300) this would produce a reaction both among the secular clergy (those clergy not living under monastic discipline) and among layfolk at large, as we shall see in Chapter Nine.

The Holy Roman Empire did not long survive Charlemagne's death as a single political unit, but the succession of Emperors went on down to 1806, by which time the title had become an empty dignity for the Habsburg family whose power had come to have other bases. The fact that it existed at all was a symbol that the Christian worlds of East and West, whose story we have so far followed as intertwined narratives, had begun to take decisively different directions. A bitter theological disagreement between

East and West was encouraged by Charlemagne's Court in the matter of the 'Double Procession' of the Holy Ghost, an addition to the text of the Nicene Creed. Where the original text agreed at the end of the fourth century had talked of the Holy Spirit proceeding from the Father, an influential work on the Trinity by Augustine of Hippo had encouraged the idea in the West that the Spirit proceeds from the Father *and the Son* (in Latin, *'filioque'*). The phrase seems first to have been added to the liturgical recitation of the Creed in the seventh-century Spanish church, but it was given universal respectability in the Western church because Charlemagne had it used in his private chapel. The Eastern churches were infuriated at what they saw as this unwarrantable addition to a statement of faith, and the disagreement has remained permanent. Rome was one of the last places to adopt the 'Filioque Clause', but when it did in the early eleventh century, it was a sign that papal relations with the East had reached a low ebb.

Further proof of this came in 1054, when prolonged negotiations to settle the differences between Rome and Constantinople disastrously broke down, and the Pope formally excommunicated the Patriarch of Constantinople. At the time the rift was not considered either particularly serious or permanent, but in fact it would not be healed until the twentieth century, and the work of repair is not complete yet. With this, we must leave the history of the churches of the Eastern Orthodox World. Complex and important though that story is, it had increasingly less effect on the development of the Western church from the eleventh century, and it is on the West that the remaining two parts of our survey will concentrate.

Part II

Through Two Western Reformations 1000–1700

Chronology for Chapter Nine

1002	Christian victory against Muslims in Spain at Calatañazor
1022	Cathar heresy first condemned by Council at Orleans
1054	Pope Leo IX excommunicates Patriarch of Constantinople
1059	Augustinian monastic rule approved at Lateran Synod
1073	Hildebrand becomes Pope Gregory VII
1076	Gregory VII's first excommunication of Emperor Henry IV
1084	Carthusian Order founded
1095	Pope Urban II proclaims First Crusade
1098	First Cistercian house at Citeaux
1099	Crusaders capture Jerusalem
1139	Second Lateran Council declares clerical marriage invalid
1204	Fourth Crusade sacks and conquers Constantinople
1208	Albigensian Crusade begins
1216	First formal papal sanction for Dominican Order
1223	First formal papal sanction for Franciscan Order
1231	Teutonic Knights begin 'Crusades' in northern Europe
1260	Nothing much happens, despite Joachim of Fiore's calculations
c. 1272	Thomas Aquinas begins *Summa Theologiae*
1274	Council of Lyon defines teaching on Purgatory. Reunion negotiations between Eastern and Western Churches fail
1291	Last Crusader outpost in the Holy Land, Acre, falls to Muslims
1318	Spiritual Franciscans condemned by Pope John XXII

Chapter Nine

The First Reformation
(1000 to 1300)

The idea of a Reformation in the sixteenth century is probably a familiar one, but it must be realized that an equally crucial Reformation took place in the Western church during the eleventh and twelfth centuries. It was not a rebellion in the ranks like the second Reformation; on the contrary, it was directed from the top of the church, and it resulted in the creation of the most magnificent single structure of government which Christianity has ever known. Whether we approve of this achievement or not, it deserves the title of Reformation just as much as the actions of Martin Luther and John Calvin.

Just as with the second Reformation, where individuals like Luther and Calvin symbolized a much wider process which had its own momentum apart from them, the first Reformation has one individual who was at the centre of its energy: Hildebrand. An Italian, he was in papal service from the 1040s, and his ideas were already influencing successive Popes before he in turn became Pope Gregory VII in 1073. He was then free to begin a programme of reform which had all Europe as its canvas, and which was centred on a vision of the Pope as a universal monarch in a world where the church would reign over all the rulers of the earth. This one man's vision can be compared in its influences over centuries with the vision of Karl Marx eight hundred years later.

What was so revolutionary about Hildebrand's ideas was that the Papacy had never before made such universal claims. We have seen the ways in which the position of the Bishop of Rome in the church had gradually changed so that in the centuries after the Western Empire's fall, no other churchman of the West could equal him; he was the guardian of the tomb of St Peter, in an age when the bones of saints had as much power over the minds and imaginations of people as an army of soldiers had over their bodies. He was indeed the Vicar of Peter (*vicarius* is Latin for 'substitute'). However, in the early medieval centuries, this had not implied much real power in the church for the Pope, just a position of great honour. He had not appointed bishops, for instance; that had normally been done by lay rulers like Charlemagne, who were also perfectly capable of calling together Councils of their bishops to decide on church law and policy, even contradicting papal opinions from time to time. Lay monarchs enjoying this sort of power had come to have a sacred position, just as sacred as that of the clergy. Against this trend the Pope had tried to assert his prestige; crowning Charlemagne as Holy Roman Emperor had been one way of doing this, though in fact Popes soon found to their annoyance that Holy Roman Emperors had minds of their own, and were really more trouble than they were worth.

Another assertion of papal power came in a forged document probably of much the same period as the Holy Roman Empire's creation, although it pretended to date from 313 and to represent a gift from the Emperor Constantine to the then Pope of pre-eminence in the church and actual imperial rule over all the Western Empire; hence it is known as the Donation of Constantine. Such forgeries were quite common in the church of the Middle Ages, though none other was as important in its consequences; we have to realize that their authors would not have seen what they were doing as in any way criminal. They were working for the greater glory of God as they understood it; they lived in an age when documents from the past were few, and what they were doing was providing a document to prove something which they felt in their bones was true. In this case the forger was passionately devoted to the Papacy, and was convinced that a holy man like Constantine would have wanted to do what the Donation said that he had done.

Gregory VII went much further. The trouble with the Donation was that it still represented a gift from a secular ruler to a Pope, and for him, that was the wrong way round. His predecessor in 1054 had had the courage to excommunicate the Patriarch of Constantinople; during his time as Pope, Gregory VII went so far as twice to excommunicate the Holy Roman Emperor, who was daring to invest senior bishops with their sacred symbols of office when they were appointed. Bishops should be appointed by the Pope, and directed by him too – gradually this must come to apply to all clergy. Gregory's successors took a new title: more comprehensive than 'Vicar of Peter', which would perfectly express Gregory's ideas: 'Vicar of Christ'. The Pope was not merely the successor of Peter, but Christ's ambassador and representative on earth. His duty was to lead the task of making the world holy, and that first meant making the church holy. The age when it had been dominated by emperors, kings and noblemen must end, and the clergy should justify their new position by keeping to the highest possible standard set by the most worthy monasteries.

Reforming clergy and laity

One thrust of the Gregorian reforms was therefore to centralize the church under papal control and to bring a new wave of rationalization and regulation to church life. The system of local organization by parishes was patiently extended, and a long battle began to forbid all the clergy, not just monks, to marry – making them celibate. There had been occasional efforts to achieve this before, and the Western church had from the fourth century generally prevented higher clergy from being married, but now in 1139 the second Lateran Council declared all clerical marriages not only unlawful but invalid. The aim was to further the separation of the clergy from the laity, and also to preserve the sanctity of church property. Married clergy might well found dynasties, and might therefore be inclined to make church lands into their hereditary property; secular families were, after all, doing this at the same time with the estates which their lords had given them. The struggle was a bitter one, but even in countries like England where the married clergy put up fierce resistance, celibacy had largely won by the thirteenth century.

However, it was not just the clergy who were thus regulated: holiness was the duty of the laity too. The church's concern shifted from the kings and noblemen who had won early medieval Europe to Christianity, to have a much more active preoccupation with the laity as a whole. In particular, during the eleventh and twelfth centuries it mounted a determined campaign to take over the most intimate part of human lives, sexual relationships and marriage. It was in this age that the church successfully fought to have marriage regarded as a sacrament (there is no trace of this idea before the ninth century), and hence to bring it under the church's control; the only failure was in not being able to impose the doctrine that the priest performed the marriage rather than witnessing a contract between two people.

At the same time, the church greatly extended the number of relationships which could be considered incestuous and therefore a bar to marriage, taking these well beyond what even contemporary theologians could claim were scriptural guidelines. Modern historians like Professor Jack Goody have made out a good case for saying that one of the chief motivations in this, as with much of the church's concern to regulate marriage, was a desire to see property left to the church rather than to a large range of possible heirs in the family: the more limits were placed on legal marriage, the more chance there was of there being no legal heir, and the more likelihood that land and wealth would be left to the church for the greater glory of God.

In this aim, the church's preoccupations at first clashed with the wishes of the European higher nobility, who were not always pleased to see their estates being swallowed up by priests, and who by the early eleventh century were faced with a further crisis as their lands were broken up by the old custom of letting every member of the family take a share. It was only when a new custom of 'eldest takes all' (primogeniture) was established that European aristocrats could breathe easily again and know that their estates could pass as a unit from generation to generation; in this more relaxed atmosphere, achieved by the end of the twelfth century, they could see the church's new attempts to regulate sexual life as a source of stability for their society, and they began to support the newly established rules. This eleventh- and twelfth-century revolution was one of the most important periods in the history of Western marriage.

All this new regulation had the effect of creating a great bureaucracy at the centre of the church. It was not just the new regulation of marriage which brought legal business to Rome; in all sorts of ways, Rome's new importance in the everyday life of the church all over Europe meant that it was worth taking the long journey into central Italy to get something done. A monastery might seek a privilege to stop a local bishop interfering with it; an illegitimate boy might need a dispensation to get round the church's rules excluding bastards from the priesthood. A nobleman, desperate for a legitimate heir, might need to have his childless marriage declared non-existent. A thousand and one reasons, both creditable and discreditable, drew business to Rome; it was no coincidence that all the Popes between 1159 and 1303 were first and foremost trained as experts in the law of the church (canon law). Naturally, the unified church of Gregory's reforms needed a single system of laws by which universal justice could be given; so the twelfth century is the first great age when such a body of law began to be put in systematic form, particularly in the work of the Italian monk Gratian.

This was equally true at a local level all over the Continent. The eleventh-century success of bishops in asserting their position in the church against the Benedictine monasteries meant that they too developed bureaucracies; not only that, but kings and noblemen in Europe saw the usefulness of these well-trained clerics to improve their administration, and drafted them in to build up their own civil service. Often this might take a bishop away from his duties in his diocese, so administration might have to carry on without him. Usually it did so quite successfully, but an efficient office system is hardly very spiritually inspiring. Even though they generally tried to be real fathers in God to their dioceses, bishops were increasingly trapped in a world of fixed routine – faced with demands from both Pope and lay rulers, and remote figures to their flocks. It was not a healthy development.

The church in a new world

The Western Europe which Hildebrand and his successors were bringing to heel was newly prosperous, expanding and restless. In the early medieval period, the chief way of gathering wealth was by warfare, which produced plunder and slaves; kings survived by giving handouts to their warlords. By the eleventh century this system was coming to an end, a change symbolized by the collapse of central authority in many European kingdoms at this time. Free to go their own way, and with their estates newly secured by the device of primogeniture, the nobility of Europe turned to exploiting their lands through farming; this produced new wealth and better food supplies. Trade benefited from this new atmosphere of stability, and Western Europe, on the defensive for so long against Islam, began showing more aggression to its neighbours. The nobility of Germany began casting covetous eyes on the Baltic pagan lands to the north-east; in Spain, the eleventh century was the decisive time when the balance between the Muslims and the Christians tipped back in favour of Christianity, and Western Christendom began a long task of rolling back the Islamic conquests.

How would the church react to this wealthy and aggressive society? We can trace several effects, first on the whole way in which the church was organized and financed, and in turn, on the way in which it used the laity. In Chapter Eight we saw that the backbone of the early medieval church was the select group of kings and noblemen who had financed the growth of Benedictine monasteries and had generally directed church affairs. Now the church was organizing its life round the parishes, and either as cause or effect of this new development, it found that there were new sources of wealth on a much wider scale. In the parishes it could tax the new farming resources of Europe by demanding a scriptural tenth of wealth – the tithe. Here was a huge new source of money for the church, and one which involved many more of the laity than the old aristocratic minority. This was one good reason for extending the church's pastoral concern to a much wider section of the laity than the founders of Benedictine monasteries. Sir Richard Southern argues that this led to a profound shift in the church's theology.

The essence of Southern's argument is that in the earlier Benedictine phase, few people expected to escape Hell: mainly the clergy and those wealthy enough to finance monks to pray for them and perform the very heavy penances which the church demanded of the sinful. When the church's pastoral care extended to those with much smaller resources than the nobility, as the parish and the tithe system developed, this old approach would not do. Some other way must be devised to cope with the hopes and fears of a sinful population about the next world. This was where the doctrine of purgatory was so useful and comforting. Few people ever feel that their trivial sins justify hell fire, but most would follow Clement of Alexandria in thinking that their life on earth could do with further improvement after death. To expect a set period of time in purgatory before entering God's bliss satisfied this very basic instinct, and so the long-established notion of purgatory which we have seen pioneered by Clement (above, Chapter Five) and which was encouraged by some of the writings of Augustine of Hippo, came in very useful for the worried laity and their anxious clergy in the eleventh-century church. Purgatory became firmly established in the popular imagination.

Another new element in the church's thinking which was encouraged by the new assertiveness in Western European society was a dramatic change in its attitude to war. From being deeply hostile to warfare during the constant fighting of the early medieval period, the church came to see warfare as something which it might use for its own purposes; the notion of holy war, crusade, was born. The first impulse in this was to recapture the Holy Land from the Muslims: part of the great counter-attack which the West was now beginning against Islam. In 1095 Pope Urban II proclaimed the first Crusade, and within four years, Western expeditions had captured Jerusalem itself, at the price of vicious and ruthless fighting. Western Europe established a Latin Kingdom of Jerusalem and a territorial presence in the eastern Mediterranean which would only be extinguished when the Turks captured the island of Cyprus from the Venetian government in 1571, although Islamic armies had pushed Westerners out of the mainland by 1291. In connection with the wars which raged through these years, the church turned the monastic ideal in a new direction by allowing the setting-up of monastic orders of knights dedicated to fighting on behalf of Christianity, principally the Orders of Knights Templar and Knights Hospitaller. Their very names reveal their fixation: the Templars took their name directly from the Temple of Jerusalem, and the Hospitallers theirs from their Hospital headquarters in Jerusalem.

Ironically, one of the most prominent achievements of the Crusaders was fatally to weaken the Christian Empire of the East. The Byzantine Empire flourished during the twelfth century under the Comnenian dynasty, but in 1204 a Western Crusade which had begun with the aim of attacking Muslim Egypt turned to Constantinople, had no hesitation in sacking it and set up a 'Latin' Empire there. The result was to divide the Byzantine state and to set it on a path of decline which only ended when the Muslim Turks captured the last remnant of territory and Constantinople itself in 1453. The attack also led to deep bitterness among the Greeks against Westerners which ruined the last negotiations for church reunion with any chance of success. With this failure, sealed by the Greeks' furious rejection of the terms of reunion agreed by their negotiators at the Council of Lyon in 1274, all hope of Greek East and Latin West combining against the Islamic threat was at an end.

However, the Crusader ideal was not confined to the East; in the thirteenth century the Order of Teutonic (that is, German) knights turned its main attention from the Near East to the frontiers of northern Germany and the conversion of the pagan cultures there. The effort was brutally successful, mainly thanks to the Order's great advantage in military technology over its enemies, and it created a series of colonies around the Baltic Sea which were as much German as they were Christian. A further crusading enterprise at much the same time was designed to wipe out the Cathar heretics of southern France, and although begun at the Pope's call, it eventually turned into a war of conquest on behalf of the king and the aristocracy of northern France. As a war of genocide and cruelty, this 'Albigensian Crusade' (the city of Albi was a Cathar centre) ranks as one of the most discreditable episodes in Christian history. During the thirteenth century the idea of crusade reached its most strained interpretation when successive Popes proclaimed Crusades against their political opponents in Italy. For the Papacy, this was just as much a logical defence of the church as crusades in the East, but the failure of these Italian Crusades to solve any of Italy's problems was probably a major factor in disillusioning Western Europe about the whole idea.

The Crusades must be seen as another aspect of the process of making salvation a recognized possibility for a much wider variety of people than in the earlier medieval period. Noblemen and humble folk alike flocked on crusade because they were excited by the Pope's promise that this was a sure road to salvation; right from the start, Urban II had made it clear that to die on Crusade in a state of repentance and confession would guarantee immediate entry to heaven, doing away with any necessity of penance. Parallel to this was eleventh-century Europe's obsession with pilgrimages; the impulse to travel to find salvation shaded into the crusading impulse, and reflected the new mobility and dynamism of society. Relics of the saints had played an important part in the church's life since the fourth century; to look on the bones of a saint was to look on someone who could be said with certainty to have won salvation and to have entered heaven.

Now as travel became easier, northern Europe wanted to have its share in the saints of the south, and also to create its own places where famous saints were buried; the reconquest of Jerusalem provided an incentive, and at much the same time the centre of Christian Spain, Compostela, began attracting people from all over Europe to the tomb said to be that of St James the Apostle. Many of the greatest surviving churches of the period were built as stages or goals on pilgrimage tracks, and they themselves reflect this urge to travel: go through the main entrance of Ely Cathedral, St Sernin in Toulouse, the abbey church at Vezelay or Compostela Cathedral, and you find yourself beginning a cavernous vaulted road which takes you on a journey to the high altar in the far distance, and which at the far end of the church provides you with a passageway drawing you round that high altar on a complete circuit of the church building. The entrances of such churches were topped by majestic sculptures of Christ in majesty or God the Father judging all creation, a powerful reminder to the awestruck pilgrim of the object of the pilgrimage: the distant goal of heaven.

Many Benedictine monasteries themselves sheltered the bones of saints which were part of this pilgrimage industry: in this country, St Cuthbert at Durham, for instance, St Thomas Becket at Canterbury or St Edmund at Bury St Edmunds. The greatest abbey of all, Cluny in Burgundy, much developed the Compostela pilgrimage, and from the tenth century Cluny was a major force in renewing the Benedictine observance: the magnificent liturgy of its church (the largest in Europe at the time) centred on an unbroken round of masses and inspired many imitators, while its austerity of life was a great influence on Hildebrand's reforms. Yet despite all these links between the Benedictines and the pilgrims, the pilgrimage crowds were part of the new spirituality which went beyond the aristocratic, Benedictine ideal and which said that ordinary lay people had their own spiritual life. For many, the Benedictine abbey with its sprawling estates and its hordes of servants no longer seemed the perfect mirror of God's purpose for the world, and fewer aristocrats were prepared to make the lavish gifts of land which would support new foundations like this.

New monastic orders (1100 to 1200)

Reaction against the Benedictine style came both in renewals of monastic life and in new initiatives among the ordinary laity. Benedictine houses did not disappear – they were too powerful and well-established for that – but alongside them came new religious orders, seeking to change the direction of the monastic ideal. An explicit return to the roots of the Benedictine rule came with the Cistercian Order, so called from its original house at Citeaux (*Cistercium* in Latin) in Burgundy. Cistercian houses generally required endowment with lands on the same heroic scale as older Benedictine foundations, but they felt that contact with the sinful world had been their predecessors' downfall, so they sought lands far away from the centres of population life, in wildernesses; indeed, they would go to the length of creating wildernesses for themselves by destroying existing villages within their estates, as did for instance the Cistercian abbey at Fountains in Yorkshire. This ruthlessness in the service of Christ is a mark of the militance which they brought to the religious life; in this, they reflected the new aggressiveness of Christian spirituality which can also be seen in the crusading movement and which was one of the main characteristics of their most formidable twelfth-century leader, Bernard of Clairvaux.

The Cistercians made enemies, but their spiritual severity won them much admiration, particularly because they appealed to the new, more broadly-based spiritual hunger of the time and made the spiritual benefits of the Benedictine Order available to all; by basing the everyday work of their houses on teams of lay-brothers sworn to a simpler version of the monastic rule than the fully-fledged monks, they opened the monastic life to illiterate ordinary people. By the end of the twelfth century a Cistercian had been elected Pope, and there were 530 Cistercian houses throughout Europe, tightly organized into a single structure centred on Citeaux which was the first operative international corporation in the Christian world – a practical reflection on a smaller scale of Hildebrand's dream of universal monarchy, and as single-minded in its aims as modern international campaigning organizations like Campus Crusade for Christ.

The downfall of the Cistercians would come by the end of the thirteenth century, when their decline in popular esteem was registered by the drastic fall in those willing to be their lay-brothers; the reasons can be found in the sad dilemma which their success brought them. They farmed their estates with such energy, pushing forward the commercial development of English sheep-farming, for instance, that they found themselves making huge profits. The world which they had rejected thus came back to take its revenge, and their houses became little different from the magnificent Benedictine institutions which they had begun by criticizing. It took another twelfth-century religious order to make a permanent success of a return to the original simplicity of Benedict's Rule: the Carthusians, who like the Cistercians took their name from their first house, the Grande Chartreuse (*Carthusium* in Latin). Their proud motto was 'never reformed because never in need of reform', and the secret of their success was that they avoided the temptations to slackness which in-evitably haunt every religious community by insisting that all their members remain hermits, living in individual cells within the monastery and only meeting on a day to day basis for worship. This deliberate return to the earliest forms of Christian monastic life meant that they would never be a numerous order, but they always remained widely respected; their continuing spiritual fervour was shown in England at the sixteenth-century Reform-ation, when they were among the few religious to put up any resistance to Henry VIII's dissolution of the monasteries.

Yet another product of the rich diversity of eleventh- and twelfth-century monasticism was the Augustinian movement, so called because its appeal to the past was not to Benedict but to a series of remarks supposedly made by Augustine of Hippo as the basis for religious communities under his control. This Augustinian Rule appealed to people because it was even more general and brief than the Rule of Benedict, and could thus be adapted as the basis of community life in a wide range of different circumstances. Augustinian communities were distinguished by the flexibility and variety of their organizations, and their attitude to the world was precisely opposite to that of the Cistercians. They sought out the newly-developing towns; they planted their houses beside the castles and houses of the wealthy, and were received with enthusiasm because they satisfied the universal hunger for the prayers of holy people. Their communities were very rarely as large or as wealthy as the houses of the Benedictines or the

Cistercians, and thus they could supply spiritual services at what seemed like cut-price rates: the gift of a field from a modestly-well-off knight here, or there a legacy of a town tenement from a merchant's widow: a few pence in a poor man's will.

Lay restlessness: heresy and the universities

We have now seen various expressions of the ways in which people searched for salvation in this anxious, busy age: crusades, pilgrimages, new monastic initiatives (including several lesser orders which I have not described). The trouble was that there was no tradition of using the participation of the laity in the life of the church, and Hildebrand's reforms worked against a full use of such energy by separating out the clergy and emphasizing the superiority of their position. It was not surprising that much lay enthusiasm for Christian faith and lay yearnings to win eternal life ran beyond the structures which the church was building, and turned against those structures into forms which the church labelled heresy. The new boom towns which were springing up throughout Europe, and the new industries which serviced Europe's growing population, particularly in clothing, were difficult for the church to cope with; its developing parish system operated best in the stable life of the countryside. Now many people found themselves faced with the excitement and terror of new situations, new structures of life; their uncertainties, hopes and fears could be exploited by maverick clerics who had themselves rebelled against the system. So religious fervour could just as readily turn against the church as be absorbed by its rich variety of religious life.

Mass movements of heresy developed throughout Europe, particularly its most prosperous and disturbed parts, from the early eleventh century. The Cathars were a sect reviving all the dualistic ideas and rejection of the flesh of the Gnostics, although it is not clear how they connect up with earlier groups; their particular strength in the twelfth century was in southern France, although they were to be found in Italy and Germany as well, and they constructed an entire alternative church whose hierarchy was a gesture of total rejection of established Christianity. The Bogomils of Eastern Europe troubled the Eastern churches in a similar fashion, and they formed links with the Western sects; through much of Europe, self-appointed leaders roamed preaching mystical beliefs of inner light which often seem to have been full-scale pantheism, seeing God's Spirit in all things. These very loosely organized and often totally independent 'Brethren of the Free Spirit' could whip up mass support in times of crisis, often announcing that such disruptions heralded the beginning of Christ's reign on earth; much of their excitement became mixed up with the Crusades and the struggle to defend Jerusalem.

All this was terrifying to the church authorities, particularly since this religious enthusiasm shaded off without an easily definable break into the new release of religious energy which had brought so much of the official structures into being. What was worse was that much of the intellectual ferment of the age seemed in danger of slipping from the church's control. No longer were the Benedictine monasteries at the heart of Europe's cultural activity. They had first been displaced by the rapid development during the eleventh century of schools attached to the cathedrals; this was a natural reflection of the shift of power within the church from Benedictines to the structure of Pope and bishop which Hildebrand did so much to encourage. At least these were contained within the institutions of the church; in Italy, however, there were cities which were greater in size and wealth than anything in northern Europe, and during the eleventh century these developed their own schools. The first universities were coming into existence. Some cathedral schools developed into universities as well, as in Paris; the university there became the leading centre of theological exploration in twelfth-century Europe, much used by Popes when they needed specialist theological expertise. However, in contrast to this great French university, when England developed two permanent universities during the twelfth and thirteenth centuries, it was in provincial towns which had no strong ecclesiastical corporation to interfere with them: Oxford and Cambridge.

It was not simply that there were new institutions of learning, but these institutions represented a new intellectual life. Central to this was a new stage in the ancient dialogue between Plato and Aristotle; now Aristotle came to excite and inform those whose business was ideas. Previously Plato had dominated Christian thinking, particularly thanks to Augustine of Hippo; only one major Christian writer, the sixth-century Boethius, had dealt much with Aristotle's intellectual systems. Otherwise the West knew little of Aristotle's work; he was therefore mainly seen through Boethius's eyes, particularly when Boethius's writings were energetically promoted by scholars of the Order of Cluny in the tenth century. However, in the Islamic world and also among many scholars of the Jewish communities, there was direct knowledge of and keen interest in works of Aristotle which remained unknown in the early medieval West. Gradually these works reached the West, partly through contacts established in the Crusades (one of their less bloody results) and they were translated into Latin, the language which all educated Westerners could understand.

The effect was profound; once more, the West was stimulated to look for manuscripts containing classical learning, to produce another movement of renewal which has been called the twelfth-century Renaissance. Despite much official hostility, now Aristotle and his analytical approach to the world, his mastery of the possibilities of logical thought, would be an influence to match the Platonism of Christian theologians. The debate which based itself on Plato, Aristotle and Boethius, and which increasingly found itself discussing the work of Arab and Jewish commentators on classical thought, was centred on the old problem of how to relate the work of reason to the revealed truths of Christian faith; although the participants in this debate often bitterly disagreed with each other to the extent that on occasion they would secure their opponents' condemnation as heretics, the whole intellectual movement can be summed up in the term 'Scholasticism': that is, the thought and educational method of the new university schools.

The coming of the friars (1200 to 1300)

How could the church cope both with the challenges of widespread heresy and with the potentially uncontrollable life of scholastic thought in the universities? None of its existing institutions seemed very well adapted to the purpose, and its first reaction to the growth of heresy was to indulge in repression, seen at its worst in the Albigensian Crusade. However, at the end of the twelfth century two great religious leaders emerged who would give the church a more worthy response: Dominic and Francis. Though startlingly different personalities, they founded in parallel the first two orders of friars (an English version of the word *fratres*, the Latin for 'brothers'). Dominic was a Spaniard who became a priest in a community living under the Rule of St Augustine; he was drawn into the campaigns to win back the south of France from the Cathar heresy. The work was having little success, and Dominic realized why: it was being led by churchmen who conducted their work like the great prelates they were, surrounded by attendants and all the magnificence of their rank. Nothing was less calculated to win the affections of the resentful and terrorized people of southern France, familiar with the Cathar expressions of contempt for the corruption of the Catholic church.

To this situation Dominic brought the practicality and closeness to ordinary life which characterized his Augustinian background. He got official permission to start a new effort: a campaign of preaching in which he and his helpers would live a life so simple and apostolic as to outdo the Cathars. Not only that, but his preachers would have the best education that he could devise. Although his efforts in southern France were undermined by the selfish ferocity of official repression there, his idea blossomed into a new Order of Preachers (quickly nicknamed Dominicans) who had an impact all over Europe; they soon took the universities as one of their chief targets, and gained a brilliant reputation both as intellectual defenders of orthodoxy and often also as restlessly original thinkers.

It could not have been predicted that the fascinating, maddening and lovable eccentric Francis would end up creating a very similar organization to that of Dominic. He was brought up in a town of central Italy which typified the new wealth and success of Europe in the High Middle Ages: Assisi, where his father was a well-to-do cloth merchant. When Francis reached an emotional and spiritual crisis in his twenties, he took it as his divine mission to turn upside down the central obsession of his father's world, the creation of wealth: he would gather together people who would strip themselves of all possessions and become those who had nothing.

It is dangerously easy to sentimentalize Francis. The famous story of his preaching to the birds, for instance, is perhaps better understood if we see that he had turned in disgust from preaching to townsfolk who were complacent and well-fed, and instead brought God's good news to the graveyards, to birds of prey who tore at the decaying flesh of corpses, or perhaps to men who were so destitute that they too gnawed at dead human flesh like birds of prey. Against the Cathars who said that the world was evil, Francis passionately affirmed that all created things – Brother Sun, Sister Moon – were good. He was then horrified to find that the followers who had flocked to his message were beginning to organize themselves into another religious order, demanding a structure and everyday leadership; he handed over that leadership to someone else. Within little more than a decade of his death in 1226 a great church had been built over his tomb, its foundation stone laid by a Pope, its magnificence a strange comment on his life and work. He had created the Franciscan Order.

It was probably inevitable that the Franciscans should become a formal religious order if they were to survive, because the joyous anarchy of Francis's early supporters might have seemed more of a threat than a help to the official church. For all his personal friendship with Cardinals and even with one Pope, Francis's followers included crowds who were more part of the wild underworld of thirteenth-century religion than part of the establishment. His movement split between those who wished to remodel the order to make it much more like the Dominicans, and those 'Spirituals' who wished to reject all property, and by implication, all ordered society.

The Spirituals took up the teachings of a mystical Cistercian abbot of south Italy, Joachim of Fiore, whose broodings on the course of human history had convinced him that it was divided into three ages, dominated in turn by Father, Son and Holy Spirit; he thought that the third Age of the Spirit would begin in 1260 and would be an age when the world would be given over to the monastic life. Joachim's prophecies caused great excitement, particularly among disturbed and poverty-stricken groups, and his work would influence a great variety of movements well into the sixteenth-century Reformation. The wilder sections of the Spirituals became increasingly mixed up in the battles between successive thirteenth- to early-fourteenth-century Popes and Holy Roman Emperors; eventually Pope John XXII, a strong-minded and not always admirable cleric, was driven in 1318 to condemn the Spirituals as heretical, and four of them were burnt for proclaiming the doctrine that Christ had lived in absolute poverty. The most extreme Spirituals came to lead savagely violent mass movements dedicated to the destruction of all authority, which produced equally savage repression.

For all these tragic divisions, the surviving Franciscan Order performed a great service to the church in harnessing much of the religious energy of thirteenth-century Europe. Like the Dominicans, the Franciscans became deeply involved in the university world; both orders made an especial point of siting their houses wherever there were people, so that one can tell whether or not a settlement was important and wealthy in the High Middle Ages by seeing if any friaries were founded there. Unlike most religious orders, the friars welcomed people into their communities for spiritual counsel and discussion, and they usually deliberately built their dining halls where people could walk in off the street to see them, while their churches were built as spacious halls so that crowds could hear their sermons: the ancestors of the nonconformist or Methodist preaching-house! Franciscans and Dominicans were often bitter rivals, and it is a symbol of that rivalry that the two great opposing figures of thirteenth- and fourteenth-century thought should be respectively a Dominican and a Franciscan: Thomas Aquinas and William of Ockham. Ockham belongs to the next phase of our story, but we must consider the work of Aquinas; it is the culminating achievement of the first Western Reformation.

Aquinas was the son of a nobleman from Aquino in south Italy. His career illustrates the international flavour of Western Europe in the High Middle Ages, when a knowledge of Latin would be enough to make one understood by everyone who mattered in society from Stockholm to Seville; having joined the Dominicans, he went on to study and work not just in Italy but also in the universities of Paris and Cologne. His output of writings, which was very extensive, marks the height of Western Europe's enthusiasm for the rediscovery of Aristotle, and it was he who encouraged the translation into Latin of all Aristotle's works then known. The result of his efforts, after much opposition, was in the long run to end the official church's fears about the challenge which Aristotle's thought appeared to present to faith; Aquinas took as the ground of his work that the systems of thought and reasonable analysis presented by Aristotle did not deny the central place of faith, but illustrated, perhaps even proved, its truths. In the end faith was always the key: so in his great hymn about Holy Communion 'Pange lingua' (Hymns and Psalms 624; English Hymnal 326) he can sing that faith alone is adequate to understand this great mystery. Nevertheless, nothing should be argued which is contrary to our reason, and it is through reason that we approach the truths of faith: for Aquinas, this is the path which God has given us.

It was in the process of approaching faith through reason that Aquinas found Aristotle so useful, particularly in Aristotle's newly translated works on logic and metaphysics (that is, the science of being and knowing). Building on Aristotle's idea that everything which is created must have a cause from which it receives its existence, he could construct a system in which everything that is and which can be described is linked back in a chain of causation to God, the first cause of all things. This system is seen at its fullest in his great work the *Summa Theologiae* ('The Sum Total of Theology'), which was still not quite finished at his death. The *Summa* deals with the most abstract questions of being and the nature of God, yet it also extends to very practical discussions of the way everyday life should be viewed and how we should live as part of God's purpose. In its three-part structure, the harmony of God's earthly and heavenly creation mirrors the universe in which the successors of Gregory VII saw themselves as the earthly peak of God's system; the *Summa* is still officially at the centre of Roman Catholic doctrinal study. Yet Thomas's thought ('Thomism') never went unchallenged, and it would be opposed by new answers to the problem of the relationship between faith and reason even in his lifetime. Similarly, by the end of the thirteenth century, the immense and complicated ecclesiastical machine which was the fruit of the first Western Reformation would find itself subject to strains which in the end were to burst it apart.

Chronology for Chapter Ten

1274	Death of Thomas Aquinas
1309	Pope Clement V moves to Avignon
c. 1310	Dante writing the Divine Comedy
1318	Pope John XXII condemns the Spiritual Franciscans
1319	Petrarch begins studies at Montpellier University
1328	John XXII excommunicates William of Ockham
1337	War breaks out between England and France ('Hundred Years War')
1348	Black Death reaches West
1377	Pope Gregory XI moves from Avignon back to Rome
1378	Two rival Popes elected
1384	John Wyclif dies, unmolested by the church
1387	Augustinian house at Windesheim founded
1401	First vigorous persecution of Lollards in England
1406	Thomas à Kempis takes full monastic vows at Zwolle
1407	Bibles in English banned by Council of Oxford
1409	Council of Pisa fails to solve competing claims of rival Popes
1412	Anti-Pope John XXIII excommunicates Jan Hus
1415	Council of Constance resolves rival papal claims: Hus burnt. Wyclif declared a heretic
1431	Lollard-supported uprising in England fails: movement goes underground
1440	Lorenzo Valla exposes Donation of Constantine as a fraud
1452	Most of Hussite settlements in Bohemia wiped out
1453	Turks capture Constantinople
1457	Bishop Pecock of Chichester accused of heresy. First surviving dated printed book (the Mainz Psalter)
1460	Pope Pius II condemns Conciliarism with the Bull *Execrabilis*.
1486	Erasmus becomes Augustinian Canon at Steyn
1501	Martin Luther begins studies at Erfurt University
c. 1510	Thomas Cranmer begins studies at Cambridge University
1516	Erasmus's New Testament published
1529	Erasmus flees Basel for Freiburg im Breisgau
1549	Publication of first English Book of Common Prayer (work of Thomas Cranmer)

Chapter Ten

The Failure of Centralization (1300 to 1500)

By the end of the thirteenth century, nearly all the structures had been created which would shape the Western church down to the sixteenth century. However, these products of the energy of the first Reformation became as much of a hindrance as a help during the fourteenth and fifteenth centuries. The vision of a universal papal monarchy depended on a stable, unchanging society, but Europe continued to change rapidly, and the church's institutions did not change with it to keep pace.

Part of the change was beyond anyone's control. From the mid-thirteenth century Europe's climate generally got worse. This was bad for great monasteries which depended on the agricultural produce of their estates for their prosperity and which had little other means of improving their fortunes; it contributed to their loss of vitality. It was bad for ordinary people; population growth had been pressing on the land resources available for two centuries, and a food crisis would probably have been inevitable without the problems which climatic change brought. Population growth was therefore already levelling out, and the population's resistance to disease probably already weakened by bad diet, when a massive disaster hit Western Europe from the East in 1348: a wave of disease, generally thought to be Bubonic Plague, which quickly came to be known as the Black Death. Its effect in Europe was more thoroughgoing than any other recorded disaster; proportionally it was far more destructive than the First World War would be, with perhaps as many as one in three of the population dying.

In terms of morale the blow was terrible. In Asia the sickness had been equally devastating, yet it generally seems to have been accepted fairly calmly as a judgment from God; by contrast, Europe's reaction was one of hysteria. Here too, people looked to God's wrath, but they also noted that the official church seemed as helpless as anyone else in dealing with it. Desperate crowds looked instead to a series of unofficial groups calling the world to penance, and in particular, seeking to turn away God's wrath by ritual public scourgings; these were the groups known as the Flagellants, whose members travelled through much of Europe, probably un- wittingly doing much more to spread the plague than to prevent it. Their activities were linked with attempts to find some culprit to blame for the disease; frightened people will often turn to theories of conspiracy, and try to find some identifiable minority to attack. In this case Jews (and to a lesser extent, lepers) were a favourite scapegoat. Antisemitism (hatred of Jews) had become an ugly feature of European life during the twelfth century, and had undoubtedly been much encouraged by the preaching of the friars; now the Flagellant movement was frequently involved in vicious attacks on the Jewish community, linking their destruction with prophecies of the imminent end of the world. Adolf Hitler's campaign against the Jews could draw on at least eight centuries of folk-memory in Western Europe.

The Black Death therefore left the population exhausted and frightened, disrupted long-established social relationships and made people feel that accepted institutions had been of little use. The sufferings of those terrible years were long reflected in Western European piety and in the religious art which it produced; devotion and art both emphasized the sufferings of Christ for all people, and the sufferings of Mary his mother when he died. This emphasis on Christ's death and on his atoning work continued beyond the Reformation into the writings and preaching of the Protestant Reformers; it can be found, for instance, in the liturgy produced for the reformed English church by Thomas Cranmer in the sixteenth century, which in this respect reveals its continuity with the late medieval world.

The power of the church thus shaken by the Black Death also met new challenges from Europe's lay rulers. The Popes had seen most of the kingdoms of early medieval Europe fall into decay in the tenth and eleventh centuries; when the kings lost their power, they had lost much of their sacred quality, and had ceased to rival the Papacy's growing influence in the church. From the eleventh to the thirteenth century successive Popes had frequently engaged in vicious conflicts with the Holy Roman Empire originally created by the Pope himself; the struggle was enough to break the supreme power of the Holy Roman Emperor within his Empire by the end of the thirteenth century. From then on, the Emperor would constantly be jockeying for position with his leading subjects, and he would never again be the effective ruler of all central Europe. Yet in the fourteenth century other kings began to build up power once more, and this time the church would not succeed in imposing Gregory VII's dream of papal monarchy.

The change was much encouraged by major developments in military technology brought about by the introduction of gunpowder in the West during the fourteenth century. Artillery was complex to produce and expensive; only the most wealthy could command it. With it, a king could much more easily destroy the fortifications of an over-mighty subject, and it also made the old aristocratic skills of hand-to-hand combat increasingly irrelevant in warfare. Moreover, kings had an incentive to build up their power to tax their subjects because they needed to find the money for the new technology of the gun and the cannon, or for the hire of professional soldiers skilled in the new patterns of warfare. All this meant that strong centralized states began developing throughout Europe, and they would take a fairly cool view of the papacy's universal claims. In the end, the crisis of the sixteenth-century Reformation would lead many of them to break with the Pope altogether, and even those monarchs who remained supporters of the Pope after the Reformation would offer him no backing in his eleventh- and twelfth-century vision of ruling the world. The Papacy would quietly drop such claims during the seventeenth century.

Papal troubles and the Conciliar Movement

Already in the fourteenth century, Gregory VII's dream had been made to look absurd by first the Papacy's move from Rome to Avignon in southern France and then the emergence of more than one Pope. There were many good reasons why the Pope should make the move to Avignon in 1309; it got him out of the constant infighting of politics in Rome, and since the papal court was now the centre of a complex bureaucracy which affected all Europe, it made sense to find a more accessible centre from which the Pope's officials could operate. However, the move caused great indignation in Italy, where the great patriotic poet Petrarch called it 'the Babylonian captivity', and it showed how far the Pope had moved from the intimate association with the body of St Peter which had given him his power in the church to begin with. Although Gregory XI tried to cure the wars in his Italian possessions by moving back to Rome in 1377, the situation which emerged from the political wrangles of the late fourteenth century was still worse; from 1378 there were two rival Popes, both lawfully elected by the College of Cardinals. An attempt to solve the situation at the Council of Pisa in 1409 only resulted in a third candidate emerging, and although this double schism was resolved in 1415, the damage to the Papacy's reputation remained; all reality had gone out of the universal monarchy. Even when the Popes were firmly re-established in Rome during the fifteenth century, changes in contemporary politics made their position newly difficult: through most of the fourteenth and fifteenth centuries most of the turbulence of European politics had been concentrated around the North Sea, for instance in the so-called 'Hundred Years War' between the kingdoms of England and France. In the late fifteenth century, the rivalry between the King of France and the Holy Roman Emperor for control of Italy became more important than conflicts in the north, and this concentration on Italy naturally affected the Pope. The Pope's answer was to involve himself in the revolution in military technology and to take an active role in the wars which disrupted Italian life; in particular, the military exploits of Pope Julius II (1503–13) made the Popes seem just one Italian power politician among many. The scandalous personal life of some late fifteenth-century Popes and senior clerics in Rome did not ease the situation.

All this shows how the Papacy was now becoming the victim of changes outside its control, rather than playing a leading role in change as it had done in the twelfth century. Equally, rather than leading and encouraging changes in Western thought, it opposed them or condemned them. In Chapter Nine we have seen how John XXII condemned the Spiritual Franciscan movement, and he also condemned their supporter the great Franciscan theologian and philosopher William of Ockham. Later in the century the Papacy would find itself opposing major movements of rebellion inspired by the Englishman John Wyclif and the Bohemian Jan Hus, while in the fifteenth century it rejected the movement called Conciliarism which might have proved a way of altering the structure of the church without the destruction and violence of the Reformation.

Conciliarists were those who wished to modify the theories of authority pioneered by Gregory VII and to say that ultimate authority in the church should rest not with the Pope but with a General Council. Some thirteenth-century theologians had been speculating about this as an answer to the theoretical problem of how the church would deal with a heretical Pope, but the scandal of the Great Schism from 1378 persuaded many devout churchmen that this was the only way forward. It was indeed a General Council of the church at Constance in 1415 which brought the Schism to an end, but this very success meant that successive Popes were in a better position to stop the theory having further influence. In 1460 Pius II, himself a Conciliarist theologian before his election as Pope, published a Bull *Execrabilis* formally forbidding appeals to a General Council (a Bull is the most solemn form of papal pronouncement; it is generally known by its opening Latin word or phrase). From then on, all appeals to a General Council were by definition a crime against Canon Law.

The Papacy had thus rejected one of the most promising ways in which the church could have gone on reforming itself from above in the twelfth-century tradition. It was far more inclined to meet opposition with force, in the manner of the twelfth-century defeat of the Cathars, when it had pioneered the system of investigation and punishment of heresy later formalized as ecclesiastical and royal Inquisitions. Nevertheless, the Papacy could not stop people thinking new thoughts. One of these schools of thought, nominalism, survived John XXII's condemnation of William of Ockham to become one of the most influential intellectual forces in late medieval Europe; two others, the Lollardy of Wyclif's supporters and the Hussite movement, were crushed by authority but not forgotten.

New thoughts: the nominalists, Wyclif and Hus

Let us first consider nominalism. The word is based on the Latin word for 'name' (*nomen*), which in the thought of the time stood for the universal concept of a particular phenomenon: the word 'tree', for instance, is the *nomen* which unites our perception of every individual tree and points to the universal concept of a tree. Fourteenth-century nominalists, however, denied that there was any universal reality behind such a *nomen*; for them it was simply a word which organizes our thinking about similar phenomena – in the example we have already used, about individual examples of trees. The effect of this was to make it impossible to construct overall systems of thought or explanation by the use of reason. In particular, God was so beyond the thought processes of human beings that it was out of the question to apply reason to understand him; all we know of God must come from faith. This denied the value of Aquinas's work, with its majestic system of relationships throughout the cosmos; it implied that the line of analytical thought derived from Aristotle was pointless.

The leading figure in this development of thought was William of Ockham; although modern philosophers have pointed out that strictly speaking he and his followers did not hold views which would now be termed nominalist, the old label of nominalist is best retained for them. Ockham spent much of his career supporting the Spiritual Franciscans and the Holy Roman Empire against papal claims, and he died still condemned by the Papacy for his attacks on the idea that it could exercise any power in the world. Many of those attracted by the Conciliar Movement used his arguments, but the effect of his thought was wider than the Conciliar debate. The radical scepticism of his denial that universals had any real existence would mean that none of the church's doctrines could be approached through the methods of reason championed by Aquinas. A frequently-quoted example is the discussion of one of the central questions of the Christian faith: what happens when bread and wine are consecrated in the eucharist? If they become the body and blood of Christ, as virtually all medieval theologians agreed, how can this be explained? Aquinas could talk about this problem in language which he inherited from Aristotle: a particular phenomenon like bread has both 'substance' (its fundamental nature or universal quality as bread) and 'accidents' (the qualities of that individual piece of bread, such as its appearance or its weight). Using this distinction, Aquinas could say that when bread was consecrated in the Mass, its accidents remained unchanged, but its substance had become the body of Christ and was no longer bread. Ockham denied the usefulness of the language of substance and accidents, so he had no way of constructing such an explanation. This doctrine could only be taken on faith, relying on the authority of the church: and what would happen if one felt that the authority of the church was at fault?

Consequently nominalism was a corrosive doctrine for the certainties of medieval Christianity; it split apart the concerns of philosophy and theology. Nominalists denied that human reason could solve theological problems, so being unable to solve these problems, they turned to matters which were remote from them: logic and the study of meaning. Hard facts were the only things which could be analysed; abstractions could not. Yet this hard-headed philosophy was in effect anti-rational, since it denied the power of reason to know anything of God, and so nominalism found links with the mystical, non-rational piety which became so prominent in the fifteenth century: the *Devotio Moderna* (see below in this chapter). What is more, despite Ockham's condemnation by the Papacy, his followers came to dominate the universities of northern Europe during the fifteenth century, wherever the Dominicans could not defend the standing of their hero Aquinas. Nominalist scepticism would influence Reformers like Martin Luther or Thomas Cranmer, who were students in universities where nominalism was strong.

For all its disruptive effects, nominalism survived and prospered. John Wyclif's Lollardy and the Hussite movement started in the same academic world, but by contrast, official opposition and repression forced them far from it. Wyclif, an Oxford man, was one of the most distinguished academic philosophers of the late fourteenth century, although this side of his work has been overshadowed by the later stage of his career, when he began turning his attention to the shortcomings of the institutions of the church. His opposition was based on his philosophy: he condemned not merely the church's everyday faults, but its whole foundation. Philosophically he championed the idea that there were indeed universal, indestructible realities (in this he was far from the nominalists). These realities were greater than concrete individual objects. Similarly he contrasted the invisible true church with the false church of the ordinary world. He maintained that the true church consisted only of those who were saved, not just in the next world but here and now; there were some people, probably most, who were eternally damned and therefore never formed part of the church. No one could know who was damned and who was saved, and therefore the visible church, the institution presided over by Popes and bishops, could not possibly be the same as the true church, because it claimed its rule over the whole world.

Like the Spiritual Franciscans, Wyclif said that Christ had lived a life of absolute poverty, and the church which he had left us had been a purely spiritual body, without any worldly possessions. The church of the present age used force and elaborate codes of law to support its doctrines; these were anti-Christian. In place of this false authority, people should turn to the Bible, reading it and understanding it, for this was the only true standard of divine truth. If they did so, they would see that the Mass, on which so much of the church's power was based, was a distortion of the eucharist which Christ had instituted, making it into a miraculous transformation of substance rather than a moral and spiritual gift. Wyclif deeply loathed the eucharistic doctrine of transubstantiation.

Wyclif's doctrines would have surrendered all power to lay rulers, and this attack on the church's position made his teaching very attractive to noblemen and princes; he was given patronage by the sons of the King of England, and their support against his outraged opponents in the church hierarchy saved him from any serious trouble in his lifetime. However, his increasingly extreme attacks on the church, especially on the monastic life, were bound to lead to the condemnation of his ideas, and it is surprising that he was not finally declared a heretic until thirty years after his death. His followers, who were given the contemptuous nickname of 'Lollards', became mixed up with the losing side in early fifteenth-century English politics, and their victorious enemies co-operated with the church in purging the universities and the upper classes of any Lollard influence.

The reaction of the church in England was so extreme that it was not content with destroying the Lollards' political power. Wyclif's admirers had followed his teaching on the unique authority of the Bible by producing the first translations into English so that all might have a chance to read it and understand it for themselves; now, in 1407, all versions of the Bible in English were officially banned, and remained so until Henry VIII's Reformation. No other country in Europe went to such lengths, but the English church was so scared of what Wyclif had said that it ruthlessly suppressed any sort of criticism over the next century. Even a pious and conscientious Bishop of Chichester, Reginald Pecock, was accused of heresy in 1457 and forced to withdraw his views when in an attempt to defend the church against the Lollards, he made some mild criticisms of ecclesiastical faults. As a result, Lollardy only survived among secretive groups of ordinary people, who were less easy to supervise than the top ranks of society; they kept in touch over wide areas, and they cherished their English Bibles and increasingly tattered copies of Wyclifite tracts right down to the coming of a new Reformation in the sixteenth century. However, the remarkable lack of any new writings from these groups is some indication that they were more inclined obstinately to cling to the glorious past days of open opposition than do any fresh thinking. They posed little threat to church order, even though they occasionally produced flurries of repression from the ecclesiastical machine.

A similar fate befell the Hussites, though they were to cause considerably more trouble to the established authorities before they could be put down. Wyclif's views aroused great interest in the central European kingdom of Bohemia (roughly the modern Czechoslovakia), where indeed a great many Wyclifite manuscripts survive today; contact had come after the marriage of the King of Bohemia's daughter to King Richard II of England. In particular, Wyclif's thought much excited the Dean of the Philosophical Faculty in the University of Prague, a priest called Jan Hus. Hus's zeal for church reform was expressed in a series of increasingly outspoken sermons which lost him the support which he had originally enjoyed from the reformist Archbishop of Prague; soon his attacks on the church were linked with growing Bohemian nationalism and the Czech nobility's resentment at what they saw as church interference in their affairs, and he was on the way to becoming a national hero. In 1412, by now the Rector of the University, he was excommunicated by one of the three Popes, and he appealed to a General Council. This Council, held at Constance in 1414–15, was the one which ended the papal schism, but it also condemned Hus, and broke the promise of safe conduct which he had been given. He was burnt as a heretic in 1415.

In burning Hus the institutional church had shown once more that it was no longer capable of dealing constructively with a movement of reform. The effect of his death was to turn him into a Czech martyr; the unrest in Bohemia exploded into a national uprising which effectively established an independent Bohemian church at first supported by the King and the Czech nobility. Pressure from both the Holy Roman Emperor and the Pope led the Bohemian establishment to abandon much of this experiment in 1419, but this in turn sparked off popular fury at the betrayal of Hus's memory. The campaign to save the Hussite church became tangled up with a bitter class struggle as the aristocracy, now thoroughly alarmed at what was happening, tried to suppress the movement; in reaction some Hussites grew ever more radical, with some priests leading their followers to found communist settlements to await an imminent Second Coming. Like the extreme Spirituals before them, they were rejecting every institution of medieval society.

Moderate Hussites were by now merely demanding that they should have the right to receive Holy Communion in both kinds (bread and wine) instead of the usual medieval custom of reserving wine to the clergy, and they determined to wipe out this radical challenge; they joined with supporters of the Pope in a long and viciously-fought campaign to destroy the settlements. They were largely successful by 1452, and only a remnant survived of the radicals; these lost all their violent revolutionary character, surviving as a wholly pacifist group which would later find its main centre in the province of Moravia, coming to be known as the Moravian Brethren. It was a curious turn of history that these Moravian Brethren, whose hero Hus had taken his inspiration from the writings of one great English Christian, should after three centuries have a great influence on another Englishman: John Wesley (see Chapter Fourteen below).

Humanism

While central Europe was thus being torn apart by the Hussite civil wars, and while the church in England was busy robbing the Lollards of any power or influence, a very different movement of thought was gathering strength in southern Europe and particularly Italy: humanism. The humanists despised the scholastic arguments of nominalists and Thomists. Such disputes were for them just irrelevant games in logic; the humanists were the first to make fun of scholastics by picturing them disputing about the number of angels who could stand on the head of a pin. For them, people should have a different priority, and that should be to explore human experience with the aid of literature. It is this concentration on the human condition which led nineteenth-century writers to invent the word 'humanism'. The literature which excited the humanists was that of the classical past of Greece and Rome.

Why did humanism start in Italy? Probably it has a lot to do with the political conditions of the Italian peninsula in the fourteenth century; it consisted of a bewildering variety of states large and small, with very varied systems of government and a higher proportion of important and wealthy cities than anywhere else in Europe. These cities sheltered populations which tended to be better educated than elsewhere, and which were caught up in the constant political struggles which disfigured life in Italy. Thus a wide cross-section of people was involved in politics, keenly aware that human beings have devised all sorts of different ways to organize their affairs. It was this variety which humanists were obsessed with exploring, and it was natural for Italians in this energetic, inquisitive society to look back to the ruins of ancient Rome in their midst. The first great humanist writer, Francis Petrarch, had a profound love for ancient Rome; he saw it as having been ruined by the barbarians and never recovering until his own age. He marvelled at the insights which Cicero, the great Roman writer of the second century BC, could give him on the workings of human society, but he was also convinced that now his own predecessor the poet Dante had produced an epic poem (the *Divine Comedy*) which surpassed anything the ancients had written. Petrarch saw this as a 'rebirth' of literature. It is from this idea that later historians took the use of the word 'Renaissance' ('rebirth') to describe the revolution in thought and practice which the humanists brought about.

What was so special about the work of the humanists? To us it might seem rather dull, for at the heart of it was a patient process of gathering together manuscripts of classical texts, editing the best version of them possible and then sucking them dry of ideas to apply to modern society. We have in any case already talked about two 'Renaissances' of classical literature, in the time of Charlemagne (ninth century) and in the twelfth century, so what makes this fourteenth to sixteenth century Renaissance so different? Partly we can point to the final conquest of Constantinople by the Turks in 1453; the loss of this last fragment of the Byzantine Empire brought Greek scholars fleeing west with a hoard of classical manuscripts previously unknown in the West. However, the single most significant difference is the new speed in communication which the humanist Renaissance involved; ideas spread much more rapidly than in any previous age because of a technological breakthrough in communication. This was the combination of the introduction of paper manufacture from the Near East and the adoption of an old Chinese idea, printing texts in moveable type. Once this double technology was adopted, the laborious process of producing *vellum* from animal skins and then writing on it by hand to produce one manuscript copy of a work became just an old-fashioned luxury. Multiple copies of texts could be printed at a fraction of the old cost; printing presses were quite cheap to set up and could quite easily be carted from place to place. Suddenly there was plenty to read, and more people were prepared to acquire the skills with which they could read.

This would be a vital fact in altering the church's position in Western society. Through the early medieval period and perhaps as late as the thirteenth century, very few laypeople could read, and fewer still could write. This meant that books were virtually a monopoly of the clergy, and it was comparatively easy for the official church to control ideas as its leaders wished. Now the technological revolution of printing ended this near-monopoly, just at the time when the humanists were changing the way in which thinking people looked at the world.

We must be careful not to be misled by the way in which the word 'humanist' is used in the modern world; very few Renaissance humanists abandoned Christianity. A few were so enthusiastic about the classical world that they tried to revive ancient religious systems like neo-Platonism; this was an eccentric minority. Fewer still went so far as becoming atheists, for it was very difficult before the intellectual changes of the seventeenth and eighteenth centuries to make the great leap of the imagination which atheist convictions would involve. Most humanists were sincere Christians who wished to apply the exciting lessons which they found in literature to explain their faith in a new way. Nevertheless, their work was bound to undermine the structures of authority which the medieval church had so painstakingly built up.

To begin with, the humanists' enthusiasm for the classical past painted it in ever brighter colours. They made the medieval world look dull and limited; their language studies, for instance, showed how much more stylish and elegant was the Latin of such ancient writers as Cicero than the Latin of the Middle Ages. It became the ambition of every bright young boy to write just like Cicero; so this meant that every humanist actually talked a different sort of Latin from his scholastic opponents – as different, say, as the English of Charles Dickens is from the English of Groucho Marx. Moreover, as the humanists eagerly looked at their classical texts, they could immediately see that they were looking at a different world, a different culture; they were reminded that societies can change profoundly over time. This had been a truth which had been very easy to forget in the High Middle Ages. Nothing is more helpful to established authority than a general belief that things have always been as they are now, but the humanists were showing that things had not always been the same. They were also looking at a culture where the Christian church had been marginal or had not existed at all. Some of their classical authors, like the Jewish historian Josephus, for example, actually dealt with events mentioned in the Bible, but dealt with them in an entirely different way. This must threaten the teachings of the church.

This was serious enough, but there was something more serious still in the humanists' work of editing texts. If one set of texts, classical authors, could be carefully edited by comparing all the newly available manuscripts and seeing which gave the best reading, then the method was surely worth applying to the most important of all texts, the Bible. During the fifteenth century, the humanists got to work on the writings of St Paul and the Gospels, and found that exactly the same sort of corrections were needed to the Latin Vulgate version (first established by Jerome eleven hundred years before) as were needed by any other text. This was inevitable when the text had been copied over and over again by hand: try yourself at copying out a long text, and you will probably find that you make one or two errors on every page, plus one or two which you will never notice! Some humanists were very outspoken in condemning the corruption of the existing Vulgate texts; they were self-confident, their prestige was high, and they were receiving patronage from some of the greatest and wealthiest people of the time. Ironically, many of these patrons were leading churchmen.

This new attitude to accurate texts meant an end to the attitude which had allowed forgery to flourish in the early medieval period. The Italian priest and humanist scholar Lorenzo Valla was responsible for exposing the most influential of the earlier forgeries, the Donation of Constantine (see above, Chapter Nine), by using his skills as a textual critic; in so doing, he was destroying one of the foundation documents of the medieval papacy's claims. The humanists were setting up a new standard of truth; it should be measured by their own individual judgments rather than by the authority and teaching of the church. In doing this, the gentlest, most retiring humanist scholar was being subversive whether he liked it or not.

The 'Devotio Moderna' and Erasmus

During the fourteenth and fifteenth centuries, then, we have seen the development of a church hierarchy which was not flexible enough to sort out the many serious defects which it developed, and which also found it difficult to cope with much of the most lively religion of its day except through unimaginative repression. Yet we must not think that there was no life in the late medieval church, or that it was doomed to fall apart as it actually did during the sixteenth century. In fact the explosion of popular lay piety which had been so marked in the eleventh and twelfth centuries went on producing religious energies which could be absorbed by the system, and which made the fifteenth century a time of intense devotion and spiritual liveliness within the Western church. Piety nevertheless remained decisively shaped by the patterns of life which twelfth-century monasteries had developed. This becomes clear if we consider the very influential movement which took its roots in the northern Netherlands at the end of the fourteenth century and which as it spread throughout northern Europe, came to be known as 'the Modern Devotion' (*Devotio Moderna* in Latin).

The *Devotio* was designed to reform the lives of clergy and laity alike, but the way in which it set out to do this was still at heart monastic, owing much to the unspectacular piety of the

Augustinians. Spiritual leaders of the *Devotio* set up an ideal of an austere, simple life filled with prayer and frequent acts of worship; there was little place in this for the more extravagant emphases of late medieval piety, little place for pilgrimages and relics. They founded new monastic communities or took over and transformed old ones, particularly in Augustinian congregations which imitated the life of their main house at Windesheim in Holland; simultaneously the laity were encouraged to set up informal communities where they could live together as 'Brothers and Sisters of the Common Life' side by side with ordinary non-monastic priests. The English dissenting tradition or Methodism might find much to admire in their personal, almost Puritan spirituality, and indeed John Wesley was a great lover of one of the most significant writings produced by the *Devotio*, the pattern for spiritual life entitled *The Imitation of Christ*, by the German Augustinian Thomas à Kempis.

Yet even if the *Devotio* made the laity live like monks, the converse was also true; this lay devotion was a statement that the laity could be as good Christians as monks. This was something which the clergy-centred church of the Middle Ages was in danger of forgetting. Although followers of the *Devotio* offered little obvious challenge to the hierarchy, and indeed won much admiration from clergy, their spread owed little to the church's institutions. We have already noted that their emphasis on personal contemplation of God and on individual experience appealed to nominalists, but it also attracted many humanists, who saw this as part of their own attempt to explore human experience. As humanism spread among thinking people of northern Europe from its Italian homeland, the two movements became increasingly linked, which had grave implications for all established church authority.

One man in particular symbolizes the potential which both humanism and the *Devotio* had for Western Christianity, and also the painful dilemmas with which they would be presented: Desiderius Erasmus. He is representative in so many ways: he was a devoted editor of texts, and the author of the first bestseller in the age of printing, a book called the *Adages* which in frequently-expanded editions, presented the best of Christian humanist learning to an eager lay public by collecting and commenting on classical and Christian proverbs. He was born at Gouda in the heart of the Dutch territories which had produced the *Devotio*, and he was much influenced by this simple, personal devotional style. Yet when he found himself overtaken by the storm of the Reformation, he was to draw back and show that he was prepared only to suggest reforms and not to destroy the structure of the Western church. He had no inkling that his own work would fuel a revolution; his life symbolizes both the glory and the tragedy of the Christian humanist.

Erasmus's life was dominated by his unhappy early experiences as a monk in a reformed Augustinian house. Although it was here that his lifelong love of the classics and his association with *Devotio* piety began, he hated being a monk, and spent the rest of his life escaping from monastic life and ridiculing monasteries. Humanist Latin was the escape route for him, when his expertise in communication got him the job of secretary to the Bishop of Cambrai; this was just the first stage in a brilliant career in the humanist world of northern Europe. His early university days in Paris were poverty-stricken, and left him with the further goal in life of living comfortably; Paris also led him not merely to despise monks but also the scholastic thinkers who still formed the University's Establishment there. A year at Oxford from 1499 encouraged a shift in the direction of his enthusiasm; from his fascination with classical literature, he became increasingly drawn to theology, and convinced that if he was to make any real progress in it, he must go beyond the normal world of Latin in which the theological thought of the West was expressed: he must learn Greek.

The painful effort which Erasmus put into this proved the most important success of his life. Now he could come face to face with the earliest writers of the church's history, and in particular with St Paul, talking in their own language. He worked away at new editions of the Greek and Latin Fathers, and from about 1513 these rolled off the press in a series of beautifully-produced editions which were the fruit of his friendship with a brilliant Swiss printer, Johan Froben. Great printers in those days were not just craftsmen; they were cultivated men who combined into one all the functions of a modern publishing house. It was Froben who encouraged Erasmus to begin his most important work, an edition of the Greek New Testament, with Erasmus's own humanistic Latin translation alongside it in parallel columns.

If we pick up a copy of one of Froben's handsome editions of the Erasmus New Testament today, it is difficult for us to recapture the excitement which the work caused among educated people in the early sixteenth century. If the sixteenth-century Reformation hinged on the idea of the central place of the Bible as the Word of God, it was Erasmus's Bible to which the Reformers turned as they struggled to find the meaning of the Word and present it in new ways to Western Europe, translating from Erasmus's Greek and Latin to languages which everyone could understand. It was a gift to the world from one scholar, not from the church; and from a scholar who had precious little affection for the church hierarchy. To Erasmus, smarting from the memory of his miserable time in the monastery as a sensitive and emotionally tortured young man, the established church structures were little more than a meal ticket for life. In books which pious people read with glee all over educated Europe, he used all the savage wit which he could command to ridicule the faults of the structure, even publishing an anonymous satire which showed the deceased Pope Julius II failing to persuade St Peter to let him through the gates of Heaven.

Yet the paradox of Erasmus is that when the storm of the Reformation broke, he stayed with the old church. At first desperately avoiding taking sides, he was drawn into fierce controversy with Martin Luther, a man of very different temperament. After fleeing places where he might be identified with one extreme or the other, he ended his days in a house looking on to the Cathedral square in the little Catholic city of Freiburg im Breisgau. Increasingly he was drawn to seek stability in the tradition of the church – a tradition which his satires had done much to discredit and on which his achievement of biblical translation had cast so much doubt. As the Reformation struggles grew ever more bitter, the gentle tolerant spirit of his beloved humanism would largely be forgotten by both sides.

Chronology for Chapter Eleven

Chapter Eleven

The Second Reformation
(1500 to 1600)

We have reviewed the troubles and weaknesses of the Western church's organization in the late Middle Ages, and the challenge to its authority from Lollards, Hussites and humanists. Especially after Erasmus had ridiculed the church's faults, nearly every educated person acknowledged that there were things seriously wrong which needed sorting out. Yet virtually no one in 1500 could have imagined that within a century, Western Europe would be split between mutually exclusive versions of Christianity, and they would have been horrified and bewildered if they could have known. By 1500, after all, the church had succeeded in defeating the bulk of those who dissented from it, and the wave of criticism which now rose from all sides was mainly saying that churchmen did not live up to the high standards which they set themselves. Few said that these standards were wrong.

In particular, few people wished to challenge the close association which the church had made between the Mass and the doctrine of Purgatory. Purgatory had been one of the great success stories of medieval thought; it had helped to satisfy the spiritual hunger of most of Europe for five centuries. As the Mass came to be seen more and more as a form of prayer which would guarantee the relief of souls in Purgatory, speeding them on their way to eternal bliss, the function of priesthood became more centred on the priest's ability to perform the sequence of words and actions which transformed bread and wine into the body and blood of Christ. The priest was a man who did things rather than a man who preached things; he needed little training to learn this central ritual, and even his worthiness or unworthiness as a human being could hardly affect his ability to perform it. There would be obvious problems for the credibility of the priesthood if priests became too unworthy; the church authorities did their best to control clerical quality, but the laity's demand for mass-priests made the task well-nigh impossible. Beyond the ranks of the parish clergy, who generally commanded popular respect and did their job of pastoral care with reasonable efficiency, there was an army of poverty-stricken clerical drudges who had no hope of a parish at any stage of their careers and existed as the casual labour of the ecclesiastical world. This was as much a cause of scandal as the more spectacular misdeeds of churchmen at the very top of the system.

The laity's craving for the benefits of the mass had shifted their interest and the direction of their funding from monasteries to their parish churches. If you look at a medieval parish church building anywhere in Europe, you will probably soon realize that it was not designed as a single congregational space, but was split up into an often straggly collection of chapels, each for the saying of mass. Such churches were the centres of a vigorous parish life and were clearly much loved, if the constant stream of legacies to them in wills is anything to go by. The paradox was that laypeople might cherish their church buildings and show every sign of devotion while vigorously criticizing the clergy who staffed the churches; but this is not unknown even today!

Everywhere the Western church of 1500 showed an enormous variety of standards. Part depended on the region, with sharp contrasts even in neighbouring states. The church in England, for example, was generally well if not very imaginatively organized, while in the kingdom of Scotland the picture was one of confusion and decay, and while in Ireland the various orders of friars struggled with some success to restore spiritual vitality to a highly unstable country. In Spain a vigorous programme of spiritual renewal was being directed from above; in the patchwork of states which made up Germany and central Europe, the aristocracy were making a thoroughgoing job of taking over wealthy church posts which did not demand much work, such as places in the numerous rich monasteries, or canonries in cathedrals. It was noticeable that when the German peasantry rose in revolt against the nobility and the church in 1524–5, their destructive fury was quite selectively directed against such nests of idle aristocrats in abbeys, college churches and cathedrals, rather than against the relatively hard-working bishops or parish clergy. Here again, it was the defects of the system rather than the system itself which provoked their anger.

If there was any part of the structure of salvation centred on purgatory or the mass which caused thoughtful people unease, it was the growth of indulgences. We have seen how in the early Middle Ages, the prayers of monks might be used as a way of carrying out penances for sin; similarly the indulgence was a means of avoiding the pains of purgatory. It was based on the idea that the unbounded merits of Christ and the merits of the Virgin Mary and the other saints formed a treasury of merit, a spiritual deposit account on which the official church had the right to draw for the benefit of anyone it chose. In its early stages, the indulgence had been linked with the enthusiasm of the Crusades, when Popes had used their guardianship of the treasury of merit to proclaim immediate entry into heaven for all crusaders who died in a state of penitence and confession.

Gradually the conditions for the issue of indulgences loosened up; one can see that this was a combination of genuine pastoral concern on the part of the Papacy that its treasury of merit should be used generously, with the insatiable pressure of consumer demand from the laity. Frequently indulgences came to be issued to mark some particular sacred occasion, such as the dedication of a new church, but the fatal step came in the early fourteenth century, when the Papacy allowed people to buy indulgences. By the end of the fifteenth century this traffic in indulgences had reached the proportions of an industry, which employed professional salesmen. Pious followers of the *Devotio Moderna* despised such heartless trafficking in souls; humanist scholars like Erasmus ridiculed it. Most crucially, it was to spark off a bitter reaction in the spiritual struggles of a young university lecturer, Martin Luther, which (without his intending it) would lead to the destruction of the united Western church.

Luther

Luther was the son of a miner, from a long line of free peasants. In all his years in study, he never forgot how ordinary people thought and talked, and he always remained a man who felt rather than thought. To look for a coherent intellectual system in his brilliant outpouring of writing is a vain task; even more than with the great Augustine of Hippo whom he so much admired, his career was a series of reactions to the varied crises in which he found himself. The first reaction which set him on the road into the ministry was his impulsive vow to enter a monastery when he survived a terrifying thunderstorm; up to that moment in 1505 he had been studying at the University of Erfurt with a legal career planned out for him by his father.

The monastery he entered at Erfurt was the best sort of reformed Augustinian house, and Luther was a good monk, trusted by his superiors. He was one of an important delegation to Rome in 1510 (like most visitors from across the Alps, he was shocked by the extravagant life of the city); already in 1508 he had been sent to continue his studies at the University of Wittenberg in the Electorate of Saxony. Wittenberg, Saxony and its successive Electors would become inseparable from his career. The title 'Elector' needs a little explanation: in the system of the Holy Roman Empire, each Emperor did not hold his title by hereditary right, but had to be chosen from a field of candidates by a college of only seven electors, of whom the Elector of Saxony was one. The Elector of Saxony was therefore in a good position to protect anyone he felt like from the emperor's wrath, and this would later be very useful to Luther in his troubles, when the Elector Frederic (nicknamed the Wise) would stand loyally by him. It had been Frederic who in his fondness for the town of Wittenberg had founded a new university there; another aspect of his affection was his remarkable collection of relics of the saints with which he hoped to make the Castle church in Wittenberg a major centre of pilgrimage: a rather unexpected side to the man who would be such a support for Luther against the ecclesiastical hierarchy.

As Luther went on studying and lecturing, he became increasingly tortured by inward anxieties and guilt. He became filled with the vision of an angry God, whom no sinner could escape; and none of the standard escape-routes provided by the contemporary church were any use – his own conscientious monastic life, the round of masses which satisfied so many, least of all the indulgence. He came to see all these as mere works of humankind, and as he pondered Erasmus's presentation of the New Testament message, he found a new resolution of the problem of salvation which brought him peace. His nominalist training had taught him to emphasize the will of God and the helplessness of the human will before it; but now he rejected the nominalist idea that part of the process of salvation consisted in human good works done at the prompting of God. Works are not necessary to salvation; Christ's atonement is enough. The just shall live by their faith alone.

Even before Luther had seen the Erasmus New Testament, he expressed all this in a course of lectures on the Epistle to the Romans in 1515. Further lectures continued an emphasis on the authority of the Bible alone, rather than on the opinions of the medieval masters of theology, and also began attacking the abuses in the institutional church. At this stage, it was only the abuses of the system, not the system itself, which raised Luther's criticisms. A new direction was to be forced on him as he reacted in anger to an especially scandalous campaign to sell indulgences.

The occasion of this campaign was the coincidence of the Pope's desperate need for money to complete the monumental rebuilding of St Peter's Basilica in Rome with the ambitions of a young German nobleman, Albrecht of Brandenburg. Albrecht was a typical example of the aristocrat turned churchman to further his own interests; in the course of his career, he had already become Archbishop of Magdeburg, but now he wanted to become Archbishop of Mainz as well. This was not simply because Mainz was a very wealthy see: the Archbishopric of Mainz carried the right to be one of the seven imperial Electors. The attractions for Albrecht were obvious. However, to hold two archbishoprics at the same time was such an exceptional and indeed deplorable event that it would need a special dispensation from Rome, and a dispensation of such seriousness needed massive fees payable to the Pope. The Pope and Albrecht therefore agreed to do a deal; Albrecht would back a campaign to sell indulgences in Germany to pay for St Peter's rebuilding, and would split the profits with the Pope. They employed a Dominican friar, Johann Tetzel, to act as sales director, and in 1517 the campaign got off to a flying start.

Tetzel's flamboyant activities annoyed the Augustinians, who were traditional rivals of the Dominicans; they annoyed the Elector Frederic, who feared for the attendance figures of pilgrims to his own prized collection of relics, but above all they infuriated Luther. Indulgences were a blatant contradiction to the theology of justification which had caused him so much turmoil and in the end such joy. A series of sermons attacking the whole principle of indulgences led on to his announcing a university disputation on the subject (to be conducted, of course, in Latin); the traditional story of his nailing the ninety-five theses for disputation to the door of the Wittenberg Castle church is probably true. This announcement might not have led to anything, but what pushed the issue disastrously further was the fury of the Dominicans at this attack on their colleague Tetzel. From this moment on, Luther and his conservative opponents in the church hierarchy were on a collision course from which neither side seemed able to escape. Luther, utterly sure of his own rightness and orthodoxy, brought popular opinion into his case. One might even say that he created public opinion in Germany for the first time, for in an energetic rush of printed pamphlets, pictures and broadsides, he presented his arguments not just in academic Latin, but in vigorous German. This was heard delightedly among all classes throughout central Europe, and naturally it caused even more alarm among his opponents. Worst of all, after fruitless meetings with papal representatives, in 1518 he appealed to a General Council of the church.

By 1519 the church authorities themselves were forcing Luther into a corner: Dr Johann Eck, one of the cleverest theologians of his day, pushed Luther into admitting in open debate that some of the disgraced propositions of Jan Hus should not have been condemned. By 1520 Pope Leo X had condemned Luther's works in their turn as heretical in the Bull *Exsurge Domine*; Luther's reply was to burn the Bull and write further works which explicitly and systematically, in Latin and in German, described the church and the German nation as made prisoner in thought and action by a Roman papal plot. With this, the monk who had only sought to state what he thought was pure Catholic doctrine, had broken with the centre of the medieval Catholic system. Next came a break with the other great institution of the medieval world, the Holy Roman Empire. The young and piously Catholic Emperor Charles V summoned Luther before the Imperial Diet (Assembly) in the city of Worms in 1521, but Luther refused to change his stated views. He probably never said the famous words 'Here I stand; God help me, I cannot do other', but if he did not, he ought to have done. This assertion that in the end it is the individual who stands answerable to God is one of the most precious bequests of Protestantism to the universal Christian church.

To his lasting credit, Charles V honoured the safe conduct which
he had promised Luther, and let him go. Later the Emperor
bitterly regretted doing so, and one can understand why. In effect,
Germany was split for good, and every certainty within the church
was shattered. Luther himself, who spent the next eight months in
hiding, studying and creating a version of the Bible in majestic
German, was horrified on his return to Wittenberg to find how far
his followers had gone to destroy the past and overthrow authority;
now, in co-operation with the secular authorities, he would have
no choice but to build an entire new church in place of the
Catholicism which seemed to be collapsing throughout Germany.
Although he would reject the idea of a mediating priesthood,
which he saw as part of the corruption of the medieval institution,
he would institute a separated ministry to celebrate the sacraments
and to preach the word of God, and in 1542 he would take it upon
himself to consecrate a Bishop for the city of Naumburg.

This consecration was part of Luther's search for authority
within his new structure. The problem had confronted him acutely
when there had been a general revolt of the German peasantry
against their social superiors in 1524. Their worries about the way
in which the nobility were whittling away their prosperity and
privileges had combined with the excitement of the Lutheran
upheaval to suggest that the last days of the world were at hand,
and that injustice should be overthrown: Catholics had some
justice in accusing Luther of being responsible for this popular
explosion. It was perhaps natural that Luther reacted to such
accusations by seeking to distance himself as far as possible from
the peasants' actions; in a savage pamphlet against the peasantry,
he gave full backing to the aristocracy's vicious revenge on the
rebels. He was in an impossible position: totally reliant on German
princes like Frederic the Wise for support in defending his reformed church against the Emperor and the Pope. Since he had
overthrown the entire structure of church authority which had
Rome as its centre, where else could he turn but to the princes? It
was, indeed, the princes who had given the new movement the
name of 'Protestantism', after Luther's supporters among them
had issued a solemn 'Protestation' against the decisions of the
Catholic-dominated Imperial Diet at Speyer in 1529.

The chastening experience of pastoral care over a whole church,
and the terrible lessons of the Peasants' Revolt, added to Luther's

pessimism about human affairs. He needed the sword of the prince to discipline unruly people, and he needed to believe that the sword had been given the prince by God himself. The Lutheran church was soon marked out as a disciplined body, obeying the powers-that-be, and even retaining many of the pre-Reformation forms in its church worship. Soon after Luther's death in 1546, it ceased to be the most dynamic or aggressive force within the new reforming movement, though it would come to be the state religion through Scandinavia and much of Germany. There was nothing that the Emperor Charles V could do to stop this process, particularly with his constant worries about the Turks who were threatening his eastern borders and who had already swallowed up the once-powerful and sophisticated Christian kingdom of Hungary. In 1548 Charles resigned himself at least to temporary toleration of the Lutheran presence (much to the Pope's fury) with a doctrinal compromise known as the Interim, and in 1555 he gave permanent recognition to the Lutherans by the Peace of Augsburg. This established the principle that the religious preference of each ruler within the Empire should decide whether the ruler's subjects should be Catholic or Lutheran: the principle of *cuius regio eius religio*.

The Radical Reformation

Many of those who gleefully followed Luther into rebellion against the church in his early days became bitterly hostile to the way in which he had reconciled himself with the stable forces in German states and had founded yet another state-supported church system. They wanted to go much further: they wanted the church to reject an association with the world which they regarded as a perversion of the Christian gospel particularly caused by the church's alliance with the Emperor Constantine. Churches should be an association of saints, gathered by consciously confessing biblical truth. Collectively we can call these people the 'Radical Reformation', differentiating it from the varieties of Reformation spearheaded by Reformers like Luther, Zwingli, Calvin or Cranmer; but this label conceals the immense variety of radical Reform.

There were radical groups which were influenced by certain sorts of medieval mysticism and by old heretical groups like the

Brethren of the Free Spirit; they stressed that their vision of God came from an 'Inner Light', that is, personal inward experience of God's saving power, rather than the message of the Bible. Other groups were much more concerned to stress the authority of scripture; some were led by this to deny that the doctrine of the Trinity was scriptural, and the first Unitarian groups began to emerge. Others sought to found a body of Christian believers which would be as much as possible like the church of the New Testament. Such a church should be new and apostolic in every generation, so there could be no question of baptizing helpless and ignorant infants into the faith. These groups therefore rejected the idea of infant baptism and rebaptized all those who believed in their creed; the nickname which they were given of 'Anabaptists' (from Greek words meaning 'rebaptizers') has continued to be used for them.

Various leaders of Anabaptist movements appeared in different parts of north and central Europe. Most saw their rejection of the world as meaning that they should avoid all contact with government, for instance as officials or soldiers; these Anabaptists were therefore pacifists. One section of the movement, however, were so convinced that all existing human institutions were of the Devil that they sought to overthrow them with a wild militancy which recalls the fanaticism of the Khmer Rouge regime of Pol Pot in Kampuchea. In particular they intervened in the internal struggles of the German city of Münster, which had been governed by a Catholic prince-bishop; in 1533 they seized power from the Lutheran clique which had taken over the city, and with leadership from two Dutchmen, turned it into a revolutionary kingdom of the saints. When the Catholic bishop and the Lutherans forgot their differences and jointly besieged the city, the Anabaptists inside constructed a society which grew steadily more bizarre and horrific. Their handsome young leader John of Leyden grew into a megalomaniac, introducing polygamy and living in insane luxury while his besieged people starved; eventually, after a year's siege, they were massacred as the forces of law and order burst in. The memory of Münster would be a nightmare haunting both Catholics and mainstream Protestants for the rest of the century; both religious sides ruthlessly hunted down Anabaptists, militants and pacifists alike, to crush any new threat to the *status quo*.

The Swiss Reformation: Zwingli and Calvin

However, even the mainstream Reformers were not destined to remain a united force against Rome. While Luther was finding to his astonishment that he had created a new church in Germany, another impulse of Reformation was gathering support in Switzerland, then a very loose collection of independent cities and miniature states. The first Swiss Protestant leader was a priest called Huldreich (or Ulrich) Zwingli, a very different character from the impulsive, emotional, warm-hearted Luther; Zwingli's turning to Reformation had no drama about it, no moment of crisis. Seldom can a great religious leader have had less sparkle about him; his conviction that the church needed drastic reformation seems to have come from his humanist training and his careful reading of Erasmus's New Testament. Nevertheless, if he lacked Luther's fire, he also lacked his respect for the past and the love of beauty which made Luther cherish images, traditional church music and Latin in services; he was also much more radical in his view about the nature of the eucharist. Luther continued to believe in a real presence of Christ in the consecrated bread and wine of the eucharist, but for Zwingli, the bread and wine were no more than memorials of a sacrifice of Christ once offered and never to be repeated. It was on this issue that the two Reformers bitterly and permanently disagreed. Lutheran princes tried to bring them together and achieve a compromise at a conference ('Colloquy' in the language of the day) at Marburg in 1529, but it did not succeed.

Nevertheless the Swiss Reformation pioneered by Zwingli in his stronghold at Zurich was destined to be very important. After Zwingli's death in a rather pointless little Swiss civil war in 1531, his successor as chief pastor at Zurich, Johann Heinrich Bullinger, became very influential among the leading Reformers in England, making many friendships and keeping up long correspondences with them, besides providing refuge for many of them when they became refugees from the Catholic Queen Mary I of England. Bullinger's thinking would be very influential on Archbishop Thomas Cranmer when Cranmer formulated a new liturgy for the reformed Church of England. Moreover, without the foundations laid by Zwingli, it is unlikely that Jean Calvin would have gained the base in Switzerland from which he so decisively influenced the future of the Protestant Reformation.

Calvin was not Swiss but French, brought up in the northern French cathedral city of Noyon. Like Luther's father, Calvin's father intended to set him on a legal career, but in the same way, events turned out very differently. Calvin was starting out with some worthy but unspectacular work as a humanist scholar when in 1533 a political and religious crisis erupted in France. Lutheran ideas had been steadily infiltrating French university circles, and in this year, a major row broke out between religious conservatives and reformers. After a year of indecision, the French king Francis I was prompted in 1534 to come down on the side of the conservatives, frightened by a militant campaign of poster propaganda attacking the Mass; Protestants seemed a threat to national security. Calvin was by now identified as a member of the reformist group and fled France, ending up in Basel by 1535.

Calvin's Protestant conversion was slow and unspectacular; there was none of the drama or heartsearching which accompanied Luther's change of direction, or if there was, Calvin was always reticent about it. This was characteristic of his controlled, systematic approach to religion; although he could be very emotional if he was crossed, the lessons he had learnt in his early training as a lawyer never left him, and he was able to give a shape and an apparent consistency to Protestant faith in a way which Luther never could. It was in Basel that he produced the first version of the *Institutes of the Christian Religion*, which was a work of the highest influence in Protestantism outside the Lutheran world. Over the next few years he greatly expanded it, but the basic outlines remained unaltered. It provided something to which Protestants could turn to confront the remaining monolithic structure of the Roman church.

In the *Institutes*, Calvin's concern, just like Luther's, was to assert the Catholic unity of the Western church. It was the Roman Catholics, not the Protestants, who had betrayed the faith of the early church, not simply the early church of the Apostles, but the whole of the faith down to the decisions of the Council of Chalcedon. Here was an answer to the favourite Catholic jibe against the Protestants: 'Where was your church before Luther?' Calvin's teaching was based firmly on Augustine of Hippo, although this ignored the fact that, in many ways, Augustine's formulations had been novel, and had not been typical of the writings of the Early Fathers.

As in Augustine, the central premise of his work was the majesty of God and humankind's helplessness before him. This reduces our free will virtually to nothing. Luther had also taken up this characteristically Augustinian theme, but Calvin gave it a new force, asking the question which must trouble any Christian carrying the message of the gospel to others: why do some believe and others not when they hear the good news? For Calvin, this discrepancy was the consequence of sin. Humankind is utterly fallen, and any faith we have is entirely by the gift of God. But when did God take the decision to instil faith through grace? Before the foundation of the world, according to Eph. 1.4; God is consistent, so such a decision can never be revoked. There is both selection and rejection involved; predestination is thus double, both to salvation and to damnation. Although Christ died for all, he intercedes with the Father only for the elect, the chosen who are supplied with faith.

Calvin maintained that those thus blessed with faith might have personal assurance of salvation. For those who had such assurance, predestination was a very comfortable doctrine; it produced a sense of crusading purpose and a willingness to tear through any existing structures which opposed the plans of the elect. It was a frighteningly logical scheme of doctrine, and its destructive power was enough to make the people of the northern Netherlands succeed in throwing off the control of their lord the King of Spain, for the godly Calvinists of Scotland to overthrow their Catholic Queen Mary, and for the Protestants of France nearly to succeed in transforming their kingdom's religion and government. In England it profoundly influenced the establishment Protestantism of Elizabeth I's church, where it became orthodoxy for three generations of devout Englishmen up to the 1630s; later, it would be the ideological fuel which lay behind the temporary overthrow of the English monarchy and the Anglican Church during the 1640s and 1650s.

All this began in Basel, but it was completed in Geneva. Calvin's arrival in Geneva in 1536 was an accident, for he had intended to find refuge in the safe free city of Strasbourg; however, while staying in Geneva, he was seized on by the minister Guillaume Farel to organize a reformation which had already begun. A series of struggles against opponents both inside and outside the city left Calvin supreme from the 1550s until his death in 1564, free to make reality from his vision of the church in a form which was to have wide influence. The Genevan church became much more tightly structured than the medieval church, but like the medieval church, it was an institution alongside the state, not subordinate to it as in the Lutheran system. Calvin's vision of the church was of an independent corporation, which maintained its own life and which was entitled to criticize and encourage correction within the state if this proved necessary. There was no place in this church for the apostolic succession of bishops; government was by a carefully-ordered set of assemblies (presbyteries) with a majority of laypeople. Despite its doctrine of predestination, it claimed to exercise discipline over the entire population.

So the church was still making claims on the whole of society; worship was designed as a means of presenting the faith to everybody in word and sacrament. As in Luther's church, congregational music became very important; everyone was given a chance to sing the psalms, set to tunes in metre which to begin with were borrowed from the popular music of the time, or set to similar tunes. The eucharistic sacrament was given a high place; no longer was it the key to purgatory, involving a repetition of Christ's sacrifice, but Calvin had no time for Zwingli's memorialist ideas. The eucharist was a place to meet the real presence of God; however, it must be paired with an equally high view of the place of preaching and instruction. A sermon was equally part of the word made flesh, and Calvin said that in preaching, a congregation 'heard the very words pronounced by God himself'. In the pre-industrial world, societies which emphasized preaching to this extent were presenting ordinary people with a constant diet of abstract ideas which encouraged them to acquire education to understand them and become articulate themselves; hence the high value placed on education in traditional Calvinist societies like Scotland or the Netherlands. When the Calvinist apparatus of coercion broke down, this high level of education might begin to be put to other uses than those of religion.

Coercion was a feature of the sort of society which Calvin created in Geneva, and it is the image of his city which has remained most celebrated. He was just as concerned to regulate the minds of people as any medieval churchman; it was Calvin's Geneva which in 1553 burnt the Unitarian thinker Michael Servetus, already condemned by the Roman Catholic Church authorities in his absence. The only modification Calvin was prepared to see was his unsuccessful effort to get Servetus's sentence commuted to beheading, but in any case, Servetus's death did Calvin's reputation no harm at the time. As at Münster, both sides could combine to destroy religious radicalism, although Protestants were uneasy with the term heresy, so associated with Catholic persecution, and they preferred to accuse their radical enemies of blasphemy.

By the time of Calvin's death, Geneva had become the intellectual power-house for Protestantism; the University or Academy which he had brought into being attracted an international clientele and staff. Calvin's followers had hardened into yet another branch of the church, although like Luther, he had only sought to purify the single Western Catholic church. Now no dealings with Rome were possible, and even with Lutherans, the personality clash between Luther and Calvin continued to divide their followers after the deaths of these two great leaders. Western Christendom, already institutionally separated from the East for half a millennium, was now itself irredeemably split.

The English Reformation

The Reformation in England was such a peculiar affair that it needs separate treatment from the developments on the Continent. The English church before the Reformation was an unusually well-run part of the Western church; its people were famed for their enthusiasm for devotional life and for their respect for the Pope (admittedly a conveniently distant figure to them). Many senior English churchmen were keenly interested in humanism, and were well aware that church structures could do with drastic overhaul, although most bishops were too sensitive to the Lollard past to listen to even minor criticisms of the existing set-up. During the 1520s many students and young lecturers in the two universities began exploring the new ideas which were filtering in from the Lutheran upheavals in Germany, but neither they nor the surviving Lollards were responsible for the break with Rome when it came. It was the political concerns of King Henry VIII which were uppermost.

Henry was uncomfortably aware that in the previous century, problems about the succession to the throne had plunged his country into political chaos. By his pious first wife Katherine of Aragon he had a daughter, Mary, but there had not been a woman on the English throne since a disastrous experience in the twelfth century; he had no legitimate male heir. By the late 1520s Katherine was past child-bearing, and Henry's previous fondness for her had cooled to the point of loathing, while his love for a young lady-in-waiting, Anne Boleyn, reached fever-point. He determined to end his marriage to Katherine, and convinced himself that in any case he had a moral duty to do so since she had previously been married to his deceased elder brother. One cannot understand Henry's obsessive search for a divorce without understanding that it assumed the proportions of a moral crusade for this self-righteous and ruthless man.

Katherine, who was a Spanish princess with her own pride and obstinacy, stoutly resisted any attempt to get her to agree to a divorce, and in this she could count on the support of her nephew, the Holy Roman Emperor Charles V. The only person who could grant Henry a divorce was the Pope (Clement VII), and he was caught in the complications of European diplomacy which during 1527 saw him a helpless spectator while Imperial troops systematically sacked the holy city of Rome itself. Roman diplomats endlessly spun out the divorce negotiations until Henry could wait no longer. Between 1529 and 1531 he conceived the revolutionary idea of breaking with the Pope and declaring that England had always been an 'empire' in which the King had no superior other than God himself. Then he could get his divorce in England.

Scholars have long argued whether it was Henry himself who had the courage and the imagination to take this drastic step, but it is clear that he was saying this sort of thing many years before the divorce crisis gave it a particular usefulness. Probably Henry was encouraged to give shape to his existing ideas by the new chief minister who emerged out of the political confusion at the end of the 1520s: Thomas Cromwell. Cromwell made his fortune in Henry's service by the administrative gifts, the boldness and the attention to detail which enabled him to turn Henry's grandiose dream of a break with Rome into reality. He was so useful to Henry, a fundamentally lazy man, that the King probably never realized just how thoroughgoing was Cromwell's commitment to Lutheran reform in the church – luckily for Cromwell, for the King detested Luther. Cromwell used the wide powers which Henry gave him in the English church to begin sweeping reforms, and to promote an official version of an English Bible, ironically using a translation produced by the condemned heretic William Tyndale which itself drew heavily on Luther's biblical work. He even adroitly escaped the consequences of Henry's bitter disappointment when the King secured his divorce from Katherine and his marriage to Anne Boleyn, only to find that Anne in her turn produced a girl and not a male heir. However, in 1540, Cromwell's enemies among the conservative aristocracy managed to poison the King's mind against him and hastily had him executed; Henry soon deeply regretted his action, but it was too late.

The English church after Cromwell's fall reflected Henry's confused state of thinking on what he had done in breaking with Rome. He himself remained doctrinally Catholic, upholding the theology of the Mass and doing nothing to change his church further in a Protestant direction. Although he had allowed Cromwell to carry out a highly efficient programme of dissolving every monastic house in England, thereby producing a vast windfall for the royal treasury, he never explicitly condemned the monastic life, and he upheld the rule of celibacy for all the clergy, even refusing to dispense the dispossessed monks and nuns from their vows of chastity. By agreement with the Pope, his brother monarch Francis I of France had been able to secure almost as great independence within the French church as Henry had seized for himself unilaterally in England, and it would have been possible for Henry to negotiate his way back into communion with Rome.

In the event the King did not; probably his monstrous egoism meant that he would never relinquish the title of Supreme Head of the Church which his Parliament had confirmed to him. Instead, as the King sank into increasingly bad health during the 1540s, the delicate balance between religious conservatives and Protestants among his advisers began tilting decisively in favour of relatives of the third of Henry's six wives, Jane Seymour; they were convinced Protestants. On Henry's death, Edward Seymour, Earl of Hertford, engineered a palace revolution which left him with supreme control to run the kingdom during the minority of Henry's son Edward, the male heir whom Henry had finally gained by the Seymour marriage. As the boy king grew up under devoutly Protestant tuition, Seymour (who now took the title Duke of

Somerset) got Parliament to abolish the old laws against heresy and to legalize clerical marriage; he left the leading Protestant clergy to revolutionize the doctrine and practice of the English church. The chief figure among them was Thomas Cranmer, whom Henry had forced the Pope to appoint as Archbishop of Canterbury in 1533, and who had promptly repudiated the papal allegiance in order to grant Henry his divorce from Katherine. A fair-minded and moderate man who had managed to retain Henry's affection through all the tortuous changes in royal policy, Cranmer had now reached the point where he was a convinced Protestant much influenced by Swiss eucharistic theology, and it was with these convictions that he set out to create a new English liturgy for Edward's church.

Cranmer's first Prayer Book of 1549 kept much of the old Catholic forms, yet its underlying theology was moving away from medieval orthodoxy. Probably Cranmer only intended it for a temporary measure, and when he was given greater freedom of manoeuvre by the changing political situation, his second Prayer Book of 1552 was much more explicitly Swiss in the memorialist language which it used about the eucharist. Already in 1550 the ordination service which he and his like-minded colleagues had produced left out any reference to the idea of eucharistic sacrifice in its description of clerical functions; its intention was to produce Protestant ministers of word and sacrament rather than the medieval pattern of priests who offered a sacrifice to mediate between God and his people.

All this proved shortlived, because Edward's childhood good health gave way to tuberculosis, killing him during 1553. His lawful heir was his Catholic sister Mary, daughter of the unfortunate Katherine of Aragon; despite the Edwardian regime's desperate attempts to follow the boy-king's wishes and alter the succession away from her to a Protestant relative, Mary came to power on a wave of national enthusiasm for Henry VIII's daughter. Mary (not to be confused with the other Catholic Mary Queen of Scots) sadly misread the popular fervour which had put her on the throne; she thought that it meant that the kingdom would gladly support her dearest wish to return England to obedience to Rome. In this she was mistaken; probably most people were happy when she restored the sort of Catholic observances to the church which had existed in Henry VIII's last years, but after twenty years of anti-papal propaganda by the English government, few had much enthusiasm for a return to papal overlordship. By now there was a party of convinced Protestant laypeople, particularly in the south of England; Mary's impulse was to try and destroy their morale by a programme of show trials and public burnings, and she did not have the sense to see that this campaign produced widespread public sympathy for those who died. Disastrous blunders in foreign policy also made her government increasingly unpopular.

Nevertheless, if Mary had survived as long as the younger sister who succeeded her on the throne, she would have probably succeeded in re-establishing Catholicism as the permanent religion of England. Instead, she died of cancer after only five years in which she hardly had time to sort out the chaos which two decades of constant religious change had caused in the life of the church, and she had made little attempt to bring to England the new life which was beginning to rebuild Catholic morale on the continent (see Chapter Twelve). Her sister Elizabeth, who came to the throne in 1558, was the daughter of Henry VIII by Anne Boleyn, and as such a symbol of the Protestant cause. She and her team of ministers immediately broke with Rome and instituted a programme of Protestant restoration; Cranmer's 1552 Prayer-Book was brought back with little alteration. However, the Settlement of Religion which the government pushed through Parliament in 1559 was carefully balanced so as not to upset the powerful section of the nation which was still suspicious of Protestantism; the Queen was named Supreme Governor of the Church rather than Supreme Head, to prevent the general scandal which might be felt at a woman heading the church, and the Catholic structure of bishop, priest and deacon was retained for the ministry.

What theology would dominate this new church? Rather to Elizabeth's disappointment, not even the more moderate among Mary's senior clergy were prepared to accept the Settlement, so she would have no choice but to turn to the Protestant clergy who had survived Mary's persecution; many of them had been much influenced by their exile in Switzerland and other Continental Protestant strongholds. Nevertheless, Elizabeth clung on obstinately to the Settlement over which she had presided in 1559, allowing no major concessions to the influential body among the clergy and laity who found the Catholic survivals in it offensive and who wished the English church to look more like the Protestant churches of the Continent. The church she produced had a Protestant theology which sat rather awkwardly like a cuckoo in the nest of a Catholic, almost unreformed structure. The contradictions between the two have gone on conspiring to create a Church of England which is never quite sure whether or not it belongs to the family of churches of the mainstream Reformation.

Chronology for Chapter Twelve

1415	Portuguese capture Ceuta in north Africa
1444	First known Portuguese contact with mouth of River Senegal
1474	Kingdoms of Aragon and Castile united by marriage
1479	Spanish Inquisition set up
1492	Granada conquered by Spanish. Christopher Columbus reaches America
1494	Pope Alexander VI arbitrates between Spain and Portugal in America
1495	Ximenes de Cisneros becomes Archbishop of Toledo
1497	Vasco da Gama starts Portuguese voyage which reaches India
1521	Ignatius Loyola finds a living Christian faith
1523	Bartolomé de Las Casas becomes a Dominican
1527	Francisco de Vitoria begins lectures on international law
1529	Matteo di Bassi founds Capuchins
1534	Ignatius Loyola founds Society of Jesus (Jesuits). Pope Paul III elected
1537	Paul III appoints Commission *De Emendenda Ecclesia*
1540	Paul III approves Jesuits
1541	Colloquy of Ratisbon between Roman Catholics and Protestants fails
1542	Roman Inquisition set up. Francis Xavier arrives in India
1545–7	First session of Council of Trent
1549	Francis Xavier arrives in Japan
1551–2	Second session of Council of Trent
1553–8	Roman Catholic reaction in England under Mary I
1555	Giovanni Caraffa becomes Pope
1557	Papal Index set up. New English policy of colonizing Ireland begins
1558	Elizabeth becomes Queen of England
1562–3	Third session of Council of Trent
1564	Spanish settlement in the Philippines begins
1576	Stefan Bathory becomes King of Poland
1580	Spanish and Portuguese monarchies united
1582	Prince-Archbishop of Magdeburg (Lutheran) forced to withdraw from Imperial Diet
1583	Matteo Ricci enters Chinese Empire
1587	Vatican printing press founded
1590	Tokugawa family achieves supreme power in Japan: beginning of the end for Christian missions
1598	Edict of Nantes in France
1604	Robert de Nobili arrives in India
1607	First permanent English North American colony: Virginia
1609–11	Spanish Inquisition declares its scepticism about witches
1610	Dutch establish trading station at Batavia in East Indies

Chapter Twelve

The Expansion of Europe (1500 to 1700)

The sixteenth century saw the first large-scale moves in the process which has brought Western European culture to affect the whole of the planet: a process which is probably not yet complete. The Vikings, an adventurous and resourceful people of Scandinavia, had indeed taken their culture across oceans and founded overseas colonies as early as the ninth century, but since many of their settlements outside Europe, particularly in the New World, did not enjoy long-term success, this outward expansion had little effect on the rest of Europe. It was the conquests in the New World beginning in the last decades of the fifteenth century which were permanently to change the relationship of Western Europe to all other world cultures. Moreover, these conquests were to mean that when the Western church first established a substantial presence outside its home base, the form it would take would be that of the Catholicism which kept its links with Rome.

It is this fact which makes it impossible to separate the expansion of Europe from the sixteenth-century movement of recovery within the Roman church which has come to be known as the Counter-Reformation. It is very easy, especially for Protestants, to take a cue from the name 'Counter-Reformation' and to assume that what happened was just a reaction to the shockwaves caused by the actions of Luther, Zwingli, Calvin, Henry VIII and the radicals. This is not so, because to find the roots of the Counter-Reformation, we must go back beyond the Reformation, and look at what was happening in the kingdoms of Spain and Portugal. The whole of the Iberian peninsula contained much land so barren that it produced little return for farmers, and Spain and Portugal were in any case on the edge of the Mediterranean world in which most of the wealth of medieval Europe was concentrated. It was therefore natural for Spaniards and Portuguese to seek their fortunes elsewhere: to turn their attention to the expanses of the Atlantic Ocean and beyond. The Portuguese, with the whole of their barren kingdom facing on to the Atlantic, were the first to make a move; they began exploring the coast of west Africa, setting up a line of trading posts and eventually establishing a route to India round the Cape of Good Hope.

Although the Portuguese achievement in Africa and Asia was astonishing, it was still within the known world of the ancients. The next move, however, was to discover an entire new continent to the west, and here the initiative came from the newly-united kingdom of Spain. For centuries Spanish politics, a bewilderingly tangled story, had been dominated by the efforts of the various Spanish kingdoms to get rid of the Islamic states which had been established there during the eighth century. The last Islamic stronghold fell when the city of Granada was conquered in 1492 by the armies of Ferdinand and Isabella, joint monarchs of the kingdoms of Aragon and Castile. In the same year, Ferdinand and Isabella sponsored the voyage of a Genoese sailor, Christopher Columbus. Columbus had decided to take advantage of the common assumption among contemporary sailors that the world was a sphere, rather than the flat disc which was the picture presented by most classical geographers, and try to find yet another way of reaching the wealth of Asia by sailing due west. In fact he produced not a new route to China and India, but the first contact with the continent which Europeans soon came to name North and South America, although they went on naming the native peoples whom they found 'Indians'.

Here was a surprise for theologians and a potential challenge to the authority of scripture: a whole continent which had received no mention in the Bible. What is puzzling is that this discovery was not more disruptive. One way of coping with it was to search for the lost Ten Tribes of Israel in the Americas, and this quest, which was pursued by Catholic and Protestant alike well into the seventeenth century, seems to have diverted most people from the destructive implications of the New World. Within two years of Columbus's discovery, Pope Alexander VI showed that in the short term at least he could adjust to it, when in 1494 he acted as arbitrator between the rival claims of Spain and Portugal in the new lands. He drew a north-south line on the map to give them different spheres of influence, but in the uncertain state of contemporary geography, this gave the Portuguese much more of a foothold in South America than was expected; they came to develop settlements in what is now Brazil, while the Spaniards set to work annexing everything else that they could.

The Iberian powers were not coming into an empty continent. Very soon they made contact with empires in Central and Southern America which despite their Stone Age technology were sophisticated and powerful and which had ready access to abundant supplies of precious metals. Partly because of European greed for gold and silver, initial friendly relations quickly soured and resulted in Spanish attacks which utterly destroyed the central organizations of the native states and established a vast territorial Empire for the Spanish monarchy. However, with the conquerors ('Conquistadores' in Spanish), with the settlers and colonial administrators, came priests. They quickly started turning their attention to bringing the light of the gospel to the native peoples, and in their pastoral concern for these new flocks, the churchmen began asking awkward questions about the conquest. By what right did the Spanish attack and destroy great empires which had offered them no injury and which had to begin with offered them no resistance? It was true that the papal arbitration of 1493–4 had given the Iberian powers the right to rule all the new lands, but not all good Catholics before the Reformation accepted the Pope's claims to universal temporal sovereignty which lay behind the arbitration. What about the legal title of the native rulers?

One could sidestep the issue by appealing to the rhetoric of the Crusades, saying that the conquests had brought the Christian faith to new lands; certainly Queen Isabella looked on the conquest in this light. However, for many missionaries in the field and academics back home, this was not good enough; a fierce political and philosophical debate began. Prominent in the New World were the writings of a Dominican called Bartolomé de Las Casas, who before becoming a friar had been a lawyer, and had been stimulated to think about the treatment of the natives when his confessor had refused to give him absolution in the confessional because of his involvement in colonial exploitation. He brought his legal skills to a series of pamphlets bitterly protesting against the exploitation of Indians, with detailed facts and figures to support his complaints. Although he was thus a pioneer of the discussion of human rights, his zeal for the Indians led him to encourage the importation of African slaves to America as cheap labour; a sad irony. Las Casas's failure to see this inconsistency was symbolic of one of the darkest sides of Europe's first expansion: the systematic exploitation of Africa over three centuries to provide labour for the New World. Not just the Iberian powers would be involved; France and Britain would take up the system with enthusiasm.

Despite this fatal flaw, the church went on pondering the questions raised by the New World conquests. In Spain, another Dominican who lectured at various Spanish universities, Francisco de Vitoria, brooded on the problems of international relations which were posed by the Spanish aggression in America, and in these early discussions of international law, he did much to undermine Christian arguments for Crusades and to limit the development of theories which would extend the justification for wars. Such thinkers as Las Casas and Vitoria were predictably unpopular with the Spanish colonists, and although the Spanish government did its best to protect the legal rights of its 'Indian' subjects, that did not prevent it consolidating its empire in the New World. During the sixteenth century it built up the greatest international empire which Europe had so far known, and when the Portuguese monarchy was for the time being united with that of Spain in 1580, the widely-scattered Portuguese possessions were added as well.

Meanwhile, the Iberian kingdoms and their empires had resisted any penetration by Protestantism, except in the outlying territory of the northern Netherlands. What was the reason for this total failure by the Protestants? Part of the answer was that the Spanish monarchy in particular had carried out its own Reformation before the Reformation had ever happened; and this was a Reformation loyal to Rome.

The church in medieval Spain was a more aggressive force than elsewhere in Europe because medieval Spanish Christian civilization was more aggressive, gaining its ground steadily against the Muslims. The church, which as elsewhere was immensely rich and powerful, came increasingly under the control of the Spanish kings, particularly when Aragon and Castile were united. Part of the deal with the Pope over the Americas was to leave the development of the church and the missionary effort there entirely under the control of the monarchy; the Pope was virtually excluded. This continued throughout the dominions of the King of Spain long beyond the sixteenth century, so we have the paradox that in the lands where Protestantism had practically no success against Catholicism, the Pope was in effect powerless.

The sense of mission continued in the Spanish church back home long after the defeat of the Muslims. The main driving force in reforming abuses came from the Cardinal Archbishop of Toledo, Ximenes de Cisneros, who amid his energetic work in church, state and biblical scholarship, brought drastic reforms to the Franciscan Order which made it one of the most powerful and vigorous forces of the religious life throughout the Empire and beyond. At the same time, the work of the Spanish Inquisition, directed by the Spanish monarchy and not by Rome, concentrated first on seeking out secret Muslim and Jewish resistance to Christianity, and as the Reformation began to develop elsewhere, made sure that it would not affect Spain.

The Spanish Inquisition has had a bad press from history; its reputation is not altogether justified, and it certainly did not turn Spain into a police state. It has been blamed for excluding humanism, particularly in the form which Erasmus popularized, from Spanish Catholicism, but this was more probably the result of the native vigour and local character of Spanish religion; Erasmian humanism seemed an irrelevance. The Inquisition certainly did encourage one of the most unattractive features of Spanish Catholicism in this age, an obsessive concern with racial purity and with rooting out Jews and Moors (that is, Muslims); its fears that these groups included many who merely made a show of Christianity and really wished to destroy Catholic Spain were justified by the rebellions which did occur, but that hardly makes the Inquisition's conduct towards racial minorities any more acceptable to modern eyes.

The Spanish church was therefore already something of a success-story at least in terms of institutional reform before the Lutheran explosion. However, even in Italy, there were attempts to do something about the spirituality of the church, attempts which took the usual medieval form of new religious communities. Rather as in the *Devotio Moderna* of northern Europe, groups of Christians started getting together in the 1490s to improve their own lives and to carry out works of charity. They formed 'oratories', which is perhaps best translated as 'prayer-cells'; among the young men who joined these Italian oratories were to be found some of the people who would be most significant in the Counter-Reformation. Other more formal religious orders were set up, often merely breaking away from what they saw as the corruption of an existing order; thus the order known as the Capuchins (from the special shape of their hood) was a branch of the Franciscans, and proved very successful even when its leader Bernardo Ochino turned Protestant in 1542. However, the greatest of all sixteenth-century religious orders, and one which was to be crucial to the future of the Roman church, was an offshoot of the Spanish piety which we have already examined: the Society of Jesus, often called the Jesuits.

The Jesuits, the Counter-Reformation and the Council of Trent

The founder of the Jesuits was a Spanish soldier, Ignatius Loyola. While convalescing from a serious battle injury in 1521, out of sheer boredom he started reading devotional books, and was fired to embrace the religious life. His problem was the same as Luther's: how best to reach out to God — yet his answer to the problem was precisely the reverse: to rely on the unity and authority of the institutional church. When he came to found a new religious order, obedience, a truly military discipline, would be its keynote, and he went about this task with a good soldier's efficiency. With six university friends in Paris he took vows with the aim of going on pilgrimage to Jerusalem; it was sheer accident that delays prevented them from going there, and Ignatius's attention was turned to a wider field. The accident would have spectacular results; from the original seven, who got solemn papal approval for their vows in 1540, there were more than a thousand members of the Society by the 1550s.

Jesuit training became long and rigorous, centred on the austere 'military handbook' of the inner life, the *Spiritual Exercises*, which Loyola himself composed; the aim was to produce intellectuals who would be gifted in passing on the Christian faith. The Society wore no distinctive religious habit; it also abandoned the usual medieval way of life for a religious order in that it had no regular daily communal services. This gave the Jesuits a unique flexibility in carrying out the work of the order as individuals, while they remained subject to a firm central discipline. Even at the time, their rapid success won them a sinister reputation, which was promoted as much by the jealousy of rival religious orders as by Protestants. With its sense of driving purpose, its militancy and its tight organization, the Society of Jesus has been likened to the Presbyterianism of Calvin's Geneva, and it is a curious coincidence that Calvin and Loyola had been studying at the University of Paris at the same time. It is perhaps just as well that they seem never to have met.

Ignatius was thus preparing an army for the Pope in the 1530s, but it was an army which seemed to lack a Pope to use it. The change came with the election of Paul III as Pope in 1534. In many ways, Paul was a typical Pope of the late medieval type, a representative of the great Italian family the Farnese, who nevertheless realized that the chaos which the Protestant Reformers were bringing to the Western church must be answered with some radical attempts at reform. So while his creation of two of his teenage grandsons as Cardinals was little surprise to observers, it was much more of a surprise that Paul also created as Cardinals leading churchmen who had been much involved in the oratory movement: for instance, Gasparo Contarini and Giampetro Caraffa, who had been associated with the oratories in Venice and Rome respectively. In 1537 he also appointed these men to a commission to consider what needed reforming. The report on this commission *De Emendenda Ecclesia* ('on reforming the church') was so outspoken that the Lutherans published it as propaganda, but here was the unprecedented and refreshing sight of members of the hierarchy laying into the system on which their own positions rested.

Among the senior churchmen who thirsted for reform in Rome, there were two approaches. 'Liberals' like Contarini took their cue from the humanist reformism of Erasmus and wanted to find some way of meeting the Lutherans so that they could reunite the church; Contarini was particularly sympathetic to Luther's idea of justification by faith. Their opponents, led by Caraffa, regarded Contarini and his colleagues as little better than heretics; Caraffa, a ruthless and savagely austere man, sought a vigorous purification of the church and was especially hostile to the idea of a General Council to bring about reforms. The last real attempt at an agreement came at a Colloquy (conference) at Ratisbon, the modern

Regensburg, in 1541. This was a failure for Contarini; the delegates produced a formula on justification which satisfied both sides, but which was then condemned by Luther. The Colloquy did not get round to discussing the most contentious issue, the position of the papacy. Within a year Contarini was dead; the Erasmian side of the Counter-Reformation was gradually losing ground.

The change in direction was further symbolized in 1542 by the foundation of the Roman Inquisition on the initiative of Caraffa. This took its cue from the massive success of the Spanish Inquisition, with the difference that Caraffa's organization was entirely under the control of the Papacy. Catholic monarchs disliked its interference, so it only had influence in Italy; however, with Caraffa in charge, its work was savage and highly damaging to Italian culture. The Index of prohibited books which he pioneered in 1557 extended even to works by Erasmus, and he burnt books on a huge scale. Caraffa became Pope Paul IV in 1555, and this meant that conservatives were in full control of the Vatican administrative machine; The Erasmians were in full retreat. This was particularly significant because it was only in the 1540s that moves were made to hold a General Council to reform the state of the church; this meant that there would be no attempt at conciliating Protestants, and that reunion on any other terms but their total surrender would be impossible.

The calling of a Council had been delayed at least in part by the mutual suspicions of great Catholic powers like the King of France and the Holy Roman Emperor; the Germans wanted it to be held on German soil, while the French wanted to postpone it as long as possible in case it sorted out too many German problems and so might give the Emperor a freer hand against France. The compromise solution was to meet at the little town of Trent, which conveniently for the Pope was in north Italy, but also formed part of the Holy Roman Empire and could thus be claimed by the Germans to be on German soil. The delegates at last assembled in 1545, and from then on there were three groups of sessions: 1545–7, 1551–2 and 1562–3. The Latin name for Trent was *Tridentum*, from which comes the adjective 'Tridentine', particularly used to describe the uniform rite of the Mass which the Council would produce in the place of a whole variety of medieval rites.

This Council was crucial for the future shape of the Roman church, but it was hardly representative of it: about seven hundred bishops would have had the right to attend, but the average attendance was not more than one hundred; the King of France forbade French bishops to go, and it was therefore dominated by Italians. This would decide the general tone of the Council; it turned out that few of the Italians made much attempt to revive Conciliarist ideas, and the Pope would take the initiative in deciding the direction of policy. The main concern of successive Popes was to define Catholic doctrine, and to the anguish of the Emperor Charles V, still seeking compromise with his German Protestant subjects, they did this in an aggressively medieval fashion. Thus by 8 April 1546, a keynote statement rejected the Protestant assertion that sole reliance could be placed on God's word in the Bible; salvation was therefore completely dependent on the Catholic Church and the traditions and interpretations of scripture which it sanctioned. The sacraments were reaffirmed to be seven in number, all instituted by Christ, and the second group of sessions similarly made explicit denials of any Reformation restatements of the nature of sacraments.

Despite this emphatic rejection of any doctrinal change, there were no further sessions of the Council while Paul IV was alive; he had never believed that holding a General Council would do any good. However, his successor Pius IV was faced with a continuing crisis of Catholicism, which he was convinced would only be solved by recalling the Council. Now there was something of a reaction against Paul IV's extremism; the chief influence in steering what the Pope wanted through the tangled politics of the Council was Cardinal Giovanni Morone, who had been prominent in the moderate group seeking reconciliation with the Protestants, and who had been harassed to the point of imprisonment by Paul IV.

However, the Jesuits were by now a major force in Rome, and so although the Council would turn its mind to thoroughgoing structural reform, there would be no concessions to the Reformers in what it did. The settlement was essentially conservative, dealing with the faults of the medieval system as it failed to live up to its own ideals, rather than taking a radical look at the system itself. It clearly implied that humankind could only find salvation through the institutions of the established church, and within that church, the Pope was supreme. It also confirmed the Italian mould of leadership within the Roman church; from 1523 to 1978 all the Popes were Italian by birth. They presided over a central organization which increasingly regained self-confidence, financial stability and effectiveness. In 1587, surprisingly late, the Vatican acquired its own printing press to engage in ideological warfare with Protestants, and also for this purpose it founded the department which gives us our modern word 'propaganda', from its title *De propaganda fide*: 'for spreading the faith'.

The Counter-Reformation in action: Europe

However, the church which emerged from the defensive and reconstructive activities of the Council of Trent was no mere empty bureaucracy, or it would not have been so successful in regaining much of the ground previously lost to Protestants. A brief tour of Europe will reveal this. Spain we have already dealt with; it continued on its vigorously individual path, still keeping the Pope at arms' length, with the paradoxical result that the Jesuit Order founded by a Spaniard long played a very secondary role in the King of Spain's dominions, because the King saw it as a dangerous extension of papal influence.

France also became a success story for Roman Catholic revival. During the 1560s, provincial aristocrats and some town élites became very influenced by Protestantism and increasingly cast their reformist ideas in the mould of Calvin's Geneva; these were the *Huguenots*. For decades it was a possibility that they might combine their religious zeal with their enthusiasm to reduce the power of central government in France, and end up by overthrowing Catholicism altogether; France was torn apart by civil war, which only ended when in 1598 King Henry IV, a diplomatic convert from Protestantism to Catholicism, secured a compromise known as the Edict of Nantes. This gave the Huguenots a guaranteed existence in France, but gave the Catholic Church such a leading role that with royal encouragement it gradually whittled away Protestant advantages.

In England, the story was quite opposite. Elizabeth I was firm in imposing Protestantism through her country after 1558, although she did so in a deliberately untidy fashion, rarely driving Catholic sympathizers among her subjects to the point where they got desperate enough to rebel against her rule. In fact most of them proved conspicuously loyal to her, and the result was that although English Catholics put a heroic effort into training new Catholic priests abroad and sending them to England to face certain death if the government caught them, all this effort only succeeded in keeping a minority of Englishmen, mainly gentry and their tenantry, loyal to Rome. The priests found themselves acting as chaplains to a semi-secret community rather than starting an aggressive campaign of missionary work. As so often in sixteenth-century Europe, it was the attitude of the monarch which made all the difference to large-scale success or failure in the future of English religion.

This can be seen if we look at the very different situation in Germany. In 1557 the Venetian Ambassador to the Holy Roman Emperor reported to his government that nine-tenths of Germany was Protestant, and although this was probably an exaggeration, the odds were on all Germany being lost to Rome. However, in the next few decades, most of south and central Germany was won back by a combination of Jesuit effort and military force. The Jesuits specialized in providing good education; its excellence attracted the upper classes, and had a dramatic effect on German universities. Equally, the Jesuits impressed ordinary folk with the reminder that Catholics could have as pure and vigorous a faith as Protestants. At the same time, the Dukes of Bavaria, the Wittelsbach dynasty, gave powerful support to the Holy Roman Emperor in backing Catholicism; they combined devout Catholicism with considerable dynastic ambition which was not blind to the advantages of reducing the power of their Lutheran nobility. Wherever possible, they sent in their troops to enforce the Counter-Reformation, and this was of particular importance in stopping the *cuius regio eius religio* principle being used to further Protestant advantage. When the Imperial Elector the Prince-Archbishop of Magdeburg converted to Protestantism, the Emperor and the Bavarians insisted that he withdraw from the Imperial Diet and surrender power. It was the beginning of a whole series of counter-revolutions in bishoprics and abbeys which had steadily been turning Protestant.

The greatest Catholic success was in Poland, which in contrast to the German situation, shows that Counter-Reformation Catholicism was capable of making its own way even without much official pressure. We are so used to thinking of Poland as an overwhelmingly Roman Catholic country that we forget how odd this is, in northern Europe where most states have become largely

Protestant. In fact in the mid sixteenth century, most impartial observers would have said that Poland was much more likely to become a stronghold of Protestantism than was Mary I's England. The Polish kingdom had a very weak central government, and so it was easy for all sorts of religious dissent to flourish; Poland was one of the most tolerant states in Europe. Hussite influence remained strong, and Unitarians were organized enough to dominate some towns, and have their own synods and a university college. King Stefan Bathory (1576–86) infuriated many Catholics by saying that they should promote their beliefs 'not by violence, fire and the sword, but by instruction and good example'. In fact this policy paid rich dividends. The Catholic Church energetically reformed its faults, and once more the Jesuits gradually won the support of the nobility by offering first class educational institutions. Protestantism slowly went into decline, but largely without bloodshed or pressure.

Ireland provides another Catholic success-story, this time unusually in the face of deep government hostility. This was the other kingdom of the English Crown, which throughout the sixteenth century tried a variety of policies aimed at imposing real central control and English-speaking institutions on the mainly Gaelic population. Part of this drive went into providing a version of the English Protestant established Church for Ireland, but here the effort was half-hearted and was seen by both the Gaelic Irish and the descendants of earlier English settlers as part of the frequently ruthless and unjust efforts of the government to exploit Ireland as an English colony. Instead, the lively piety which the energies of the friars had established in the half century before the Reformation formed the basis for a great work of mission on behalf of Rome. Roman Catholicism became increasingly identified with the struggle to preserve the old (and highly confused) structures of Ireland against an English and Scots takeover; the religious divide which still exists was already well-formed by the mid seventeenth century.

All over the regions of Europe where the Roman church painfully won back its old power, the next two centuries saw a long process of putting into practice the vision of an organized and highly-structured church which Trent had set out; the work was only interrupted by the French Revolution of 1789. The church waged a constant struggle to produce a clergy which would be as worthy of respect as any Protestant minister; one of the main thrusts of the Counter-Reformation was to aim for the first comprehensive system of seminaries (theological colleges) in the history of the church, a task which was still not complete in 1789. The agendas of both Catholic and Protestant clergy and the problems facing them were surprisingly similar: they wanted to bring order and discipline to a population which was perpetually resentful of the attempt and which took a lot of taming.

The Catholics probably had the advantage, in that they found it much easier to absorb the rich variety of medieval custom, such as the ancient traditions of local saints and pilgrimages, which they merely had to make a little more decorous. Protestants were handicapped by their emphasis on preaching the Word and understanding God's message in the Bible. Although this had been a great liberation for many in the first phases of the Reformation, and it continued to be a delight and a way of life for instructed laypeople, it did demand a level of literacy and a capacity to understand abstract ideas which remained beyond the grasp of a great proportion of the population. Protestant societies tended to develop a great divide between people of the godly world, comparatively well-educated, decent and sober in their everyday lives and appreciative of what the clergy might teach them, and those in a world beyond, whose loyalty was still owed to the more earthy life of the alehouse and to a jumble of custom and magic whose origins lay well before the Reformation. The divide between the churched and the unchurched was no new feature of Europe after the Industrial Revolution.

One of the oddest ways in which there was a common experience across the religious divide of the Reformation was in the obsessive fear of witches which affected Catholic and Protestant alike. There has been no complete explanation for this fear, which resulted in the deaths of thousands of people between about 1550 and 1650, on a scale which had no precedent in the medieval world. Perhaps the general sense that all religious landmarks had been swept away by the religious struggles of the time led to an attempt to find a scapegoat for the fears created by this sudden loss of old certainties; this made people look for agents of the Devil. Some scholars have argued that the pursuit of witches was part of the Catholic and Protestant Churches' attempts to establish a new discipline at local level, controlling people's minds by emphasizing the lures of Satan. It is to the credit of the much-maligned Spanish Inquisition that after a little hesitation, it came down firmly against the search for witches; thanks to its healthy scepticism, Spain was the only part of Europe which remained unaffected by this ugly hysteria.

The Counter-Reformation in action: the world mission

We have already seen that Spain and Portugal began the spread of Western Christianity outside Europe when they founded their seaborne empires. Since they continued loyal to the Pope (after a fashion), this meant that the first great expansion of Western faith was directed by the agents of the Counter-Reformation. The Protestants did very little missionary work by comparison; they were still busy fighting for their existence in Europe during the sixteenth century. At the end of the century, the newly-independent Protestant Dutch began building up a trading empire in the East Indies and elsewhere, but they seem to have been more concerned with earning money through their contacts with other races than with converting them to Calvinist Christianity. Similarly, when the English started establishing colonies along the North American seaboard during the early seventeenth century, the colonists were mainly preoccupied with setting up their own variants on the ideal of godly life in England, and very few of them showed much interest in converting the native Indians. Apart from some early eighteenth-century stirrings, the main energy of Protestant missionary work would not appear until the nineteenth century.

Meanwhile, Counter-Reformation Catholicism was performing spectacular if not always well-rewarded feats of missionary exploration in America and Asia. In America, of course, Christianity could rely on official backing from the colonial governments of Spain and Portugal, subject to the hundred and one other concerns of colonial administrators; this was not so in Asia. Here the Portuguese were the main European Catholic power, and their empire was always run on a shoestring, a series of trading posts dotted along the coasts of Africa, India, Malaysia and China where the hapless colonial governors were usually reduced to wild improvisations in order to defend their territories or to avoid bankruptcy. In other words, there would be little or no military backing for Christianity, particularly against the far stronger native empires which ruled in India and China. Christianity would have to make its own way on its merits.

This posed considerable problems for the missionaries, who were usually Jesuits or friars of various orders. In Asia they were facing people with age-old and subtle cultures, full of self-confidence and likely to be profoundly sceptical that these Westerners could teach them anything of value. There was already a small and ancient Christian church in India deriving from Nestorian Syrian roots, but the Portuguese contempt for these schismatics did nothing to impress the Hindu establishment with Christian brotherly love. The perennial problem in India, which the missionaries did not at first appreciate, was that converts to Christianity automatically lost caste; it was not surprising that the missionaries' main early success was with the lowest peoples in the caste system. Only when the Jesuits began building up their strength after the arrival of Francis Xavier in 1542 was any effort made to understand Indian culture or even language. The most interesting and bold experiment was made by an Italian Jesuit, Robert de Nobili, who took the logical but unprecedented step of working in the same way as a high-caste Indian and adopting Indian dress. The Portuguese fiercely opposed Nobili's work, but finally lost their case against him in Rome in 1623. Whatever success the church had in the Tamil country of South India was entirely thanks to Nobili and his Italian successors, but their work would suffer from severe Muslim persecution during the eighteenth century.

China was a similar case to India. The Chinese were not interested in large-scale contacts with foreign countries, not even for trade. The Jesuits, with their usual flexibility and imagination, quickly took the decision that missionaries must adopt themselves to Chinese customs, but such was their ignorance of the country that their first great missionary, the Italian Matteo Ricci, began by wearing the dress of a *bonze* (Buddhist priest) without realizing that the *bonzes* were little esteemed in China. The Chinese upper class was impressed with the Jesuits' knowledge of mathematics, astronomy and geography, and the Society gained an honoured place at the imperial court through these skills; however, as in India, the sheer scale of the task before them, with inadequate resources of money and men, meant that their impact through the country was tiny.

To make matters worse, the Portuguese authorities outside China were suspicious of the majority of the Jesuits who were not Portuguese, and rival religious orders, the Dominicans and Franciscans, launched bitter attacks on them. The friars completely disagreed with the Jesuits in their attitude to the Chinese way of life, particularly traditional rites in honour of Confucius and the family; they even publicly asserted that deceased Emperors were burning in Hell. They took their complaints against the Jesuits as far as Rome itself, and after a long struggle, they won condemnations of the Chinese rites from successive Popes in 1704 and 1715. It was not surprising that after this, Christianity's first effort to understand and accommodate itself to another culture had ended in failure.

Christian work in Japan was a story of spectacular success followed by almost total defeat, with in each case the pace being set by the internal politics of Japan. Francis Xavier and the Jesuits arrived as early as 1549, at a time when Japan was split between rival feudal lords. Many of these saw Christianity as a useful way of attracting Portuguese trade and also of furthering their own political aims: particularly the powerful Tokugawa family. By the end of the century there were perhaps as many as 300,000 converts in Japan, but by now the Tokugawa had eliminated all their rivals, and Christianity seemed a nuisance rather than a convenience. In the early seventeenth century they expelled Europeans, and launched one of the most savage persecutions in the history of Christianity, reducing the church to a tiny and half-instructed remnant which would struggle to maintain any sort of existence until Europeans were again allowed free access to the country in the 1850s. The Japanese persecution is a standing argument against the old idea that the blood of the martyrs is the seed of the church.

Only in the Philippine Islands, which were a Spanish colony named after King Philip II of Spain, did Christianity secure a substantial foothold among ordinary people, as the church's powerful backing of a coup d'etat in 1986 demonstrated; but here, as in America, the church could rely on backing from the colonial authorities. In fact, in a bizarre link-up, the bishopric of Manila in the Philippines was first ranked as a part of the archdiocese of the Spanish colony in Mexico, thousands of miles across the Pacific! The perpetual trouble in all these mission fields was the European reluctance to accept the native peoples on equal terms; perhaps only the Vikings among all the conquering imperial powers in Western European history have not shown racial prejudice in their dealings with those they conquered. This meant that the missionaries were reluctant to create native priests on a large scale or with equal authority to themselves; even where efforts were made, as in the Portuguese settlements in west Africa and India, the native clergy were treated as inferiors and very rarely became bishops. In South America, the same attitude led even the Jesuits to treat their Indian converts almost as children, organizing them into villages to protect them against the greed and exploitation of the other colonists, but always in a benevolent European dictatorship. When the Jesuits were forcibly dissolved as a result of European politics in 1773, they left their Indians without any experience of leadership, and their carefully-structured Indian communities quickly collapsed.

Part of the reason for the troubles which this first Western Christian missionary enterprise faced in the later seventeenth and eighteenth centuries was the increasing weakness of the Spanish and Portuguese empires. It had been a marvellous achievement for these comparatively ill-endowed Iberian countries to put together world empires in the first place, but they faced mounting problems and increasing interference from other European powers, at first the Dutch, and later Britain and France. With their decline, the Catholic missionary impulse suffered a great setback. Meanwhile, in seventeenth-century Europe, a new series of destructive wars was further shaping the Protestant churches.

Chronology for Chapter Thirteen

1540	Jesuits receive papal approval
1555	Peace of Augsburg
1559	Calvinist Academy of Geneva founded
1560	Presbyterian system set up in Scotland
1562	Civil War breaks out in France
1566	Revolt of the Netherlands against Spain begins
1603	James VI of Scotland succeeds Elizabeth I on English throne
1607	First English North American colony: Virginia
1609	Evangelical Union of German Protestant princes
1610	Frederic succeeds as Elector Palatine
1618–19	Synod of Dort
1618	Thirty Years War begins with Bohemian crisis
1620	Battle of the White Mountain: Frederic driven from the Bohemian throne. Massachusetts founded
1625	Charles I succeeds to English/Scottish thrones
1628	Huguenots lose main stronghold of La Rochelle
1632	Lord Baltimore founds colony of Maryland
1633	William Laud becomes Archbishop of Canterbury
1635	Roger Williams founds colony of Rhode Island
1637	Prayer Book imposed on Scotland by royal decree. War breaks out with England
1641	Catholic rebellion in Ireland against English government
1642	First English Civil War begins
1643	Westminster Assembly begins
1648	Peace of Westphalia ends Thirty Years War. Westminster Confession formulated
1649	Charles I of England executed
1656	Meeting of General Baptists in London
1658	Savoy Confession of Faith (Independents)
1660	Charles II restored to English/Scottish thrones
1662	New Book of Common Prayer published in England. Many clergy ejected from Church of England
1676–9	Peace of Nijmegen negotiated face-to-face between Catholics and Protestants
1682	Colony of Pennsylvania gets royal charter
1688	King James of England/Scotland deposed
1689	English Act of Toleration for Protestant Dissenters
1690	James fails to win back British thrones thanks to defeat at the Boyne
1700	War of the Spanish Succession begins

Chapter Thirteen

Wars and the Future of Protestantism (1550 to 1700)

By 1600 Europe was not simply divided between Catholic and Protestant, but at least four ways: Roman Catholic, Lutheran, Calvinist and the ambiguous 'Anglicanism' of the established Churches of England and Wales and Ireland. Often Calvinists and Lutherans could be as bitterly hostile to each other as to Catholics, while the Civil Wars which ripped Britain apart in the mid seventeenth century were another reminder that Protestants could not agree on how their religion should be expressed. Even within these broad confessional divisions, there was generally little attempt to create coherent international organizations which would unite confessions across national boundaries; the nearest thing which international Calvinism got to a General Council, for instance, was the single meeting around the Synod of the Dutch church at Dort in 1618–19.

How would Europe divide between these four groupings? It was quite clear that the south, the Mediterranean countries, were decisively committed to continuing Roman obedience, particularly as Protestantism in the south of France went into steep decline after the capture of the great Huguenot stronghold La Rochelle by the Catholic central government in 1628. It was equally clear that the far north, the Scandinavian countries, the northern Netherlands and most of the British Isles, were committed to Protestantism. The area of uncertainty was central Europe, and it would be this dangerously unstable area which sparked off the continent-wide warfare of the first half of the century: the series of wars between 1618 and 1648 which have become known as the Thirty Years War. It took in all a century of wars between 1550 and

1650 to create some sort of permanent confessional division in Europe, the divisions which survive on the European religious map to the present day.

There was an uneasy peace in Germany through the later sixteenth century, while major religious wars were deciding the future of France and the Low Countries (the modern Netherlands and Belgium). In Germany, the princes of the Empire were steadily consolidating their power: so were the Habsburg family, which since 1438 had supplied all the Holy Roman Emperors elected by the seven members of the Imperial College. Quite apart from the Imperial title, the Habsburgs enjoyed vast lands both inside and outside the boundaries of the Empire, and there was bound to be a clash between their interests in gaining further power and the interests of the princes. However, the religious situation made matters worse. The Habsburgs remained firm supporters of Rome, but by the Peace of Augsburg of 1555, they had accepted the existence of Lutheranism. The trouble was that in 1555 two vital groups had not yet appeared in the Empire: on the one hand, the Jesuits, and on the other the Calvinists. Both brought their own aggressive ideology to disturb the situation afresh.

In 1600 all the leading princes were still Lutherans, content to go along with the Peace of Augsburg despite their increasing worries about the Counter-Reformation being sponsored by the Habsburgs, the Bavarians and the Jesuits. The situation was transformed by Frederic V, the Elector Palatine (called Palatine because his remote predecessors had once held office in the Imperial Palace), whose main territories lay in the Rhineland. One of the previous Electors Palatine had converted from Lutheranism to Calvinism, but this had been reversed on his death; now Frederic once more made the move into Calvinism, and in addition to enforcing it illegally in his own dominions, he encouraged Calvinists to paralyse the work of the Imperial Diet. Already in 1609 the Prostestant princes had created a defensive league, the Protestant Evangelical Union. On the Habsburg side, the leading member of the family was the Archduke Ferdinand, a fiercely devout Roman Catholic with a Jesuit education and Jesuit advisors.

Matters came to a head in 1618 with a new crisis in Bohemia. There were all sorts of tensions in this kingdom, which had fallen under Habsburg control in 1526 – Catholic versus Protestant,

Czech versus German, aristocracy versus peasantry, among others – and all these tensions exploded into open revolt when the Archduke Ferdinand became King of Bohemia. The Czech nobility rebelled in an attempt both to regain their long-lost independence, and to stop Ferdinand backing a thoroughgoing Counter-Reformation as he had done in his other Danubian possessions. They offered the throne to the Calvinist Elector Palatine, hoping that his contacts with other European Protestant powers (he was the King of England's son-in-law) would protect them from Habsburg wrath. In this they were sadly mistaken. Quite apart from any consideration of prestige, the Habsburgs could not lose Bohemia because its King was an Imperial elector, and of the seven members of the electoral College, three of the others were Catholic archbishops and three were Protestant princes. To keep the electoral balance in their favour, the Habsburgs threw all their resources into defeating Frederic; within two years they had smashed the Bohemian armies and driven him into permanent exile.

This defeat had transformed the situation in favour of the Habsburgs. It was catastrophic from the point of view not only of Protestant princes throughout central and northern Europe, but also for the Catholic king of France, who had long been fearful of any increase in the influence of the twin Habsburg great powers of Spain and the Holy Roman Empire. So it was a combination of religious defensiveness and plain fear of Habsburg ambition which led various European powers to intervene against the Habsburgs and to turn this Bohemian dispute into a sequence of European-wide wars; most of the Emperor's enemies paid lip-service to the idea of restoring poor Frederic, but in practice he was largely forgotten, and he was destined to languish with his exiled Court in the Hague.

Much of the war was intensely destructive within Germany; there were moments when the fortunes of Counter-Reformation Catholicism as represented by the Emperor and his allies were higher than they had ever been or would be again. However, the end-result was the compromise peace of Westphalia in 1648. This ended the prospect that the Holy Roman Empire would ever be a reality again, so one of the foundation institutions of medieval Europe had gone the same way as the single unified Western church under the Pope. The Peace of Augsburg was largely restored, with the addition of recognition for Calvinists, and religious allegiances of territories were frozen along the lines which both sides held in 1624. This established the principle of peaceful co-existence between different brands of official Christianity. It took the exhaustion of thirty years of warfare to produce this mood, so different from the religious passions which had started the wars; a symptom of it was the extraordinary provision of the treaty for an alternation of Catholic and Protestant bishops in the diocese of Osnabruck. As a way of settling German affairs, the Peace was to prove a remarkable success.

The fact that Catholic France had fought the Catholic Empire for its own interests during the Thirty Years War was prophetic of the future shape of European wars. After 1648, naked power politics increasingly replaced the divisions of the Reformation as a reason for going to war. In 1676–9 a peace congress to end the war between the Dutch and the French was held at Nijmegen in the Netherlands; it is historic in being the first time that Catholics and Protestants negotiated together face to face. By the end of the century, another world war, the War of the Spanish Succession, was entirely about the balance of dynastic power within Europe, with no suggestion of religious motives in the line-up of forces on each side. Although at this stage, no religious body abandoned its claim to be the best way of coming to the truth, the dream of recreating the religious unity of Europe by military force was shown to be impractical. This was yet another step away from the medieval world – one might say, the first faltering and unconscious step towards an age of Christian ecumenism.

The British Civil Wars

The three kingdoms in the British Isles ruled by the Stuart dynasty kept out of the Thirty Years War, much to the grief of many devoutly Protestant Englishmen and Scotsmen who wanted to show international solidarity with the Protestant cause; however, Britain in its turn was involved in a series of civil wars between 1642 and 1660 in which religion played a vital part. The rest of the chapter discusses these wars in more detail than elsewhere in this book, because without some knowledge of the complexities of the period, it is difficult to understand some of the most important features of the modern Protestant world. All varieties of Protestantism of British descent have been shaped by those turbulent years.

Not all the problems which faced early seventeenth-century England were religious. Elizabeth I had been dragged into a world war against Spain and also into an endless Irish guerrilla war without any major revision of England's antiquated tax system, and with all sorts of unresolved tensions between the wishes of her central government and of the local landed élites who were the government's only source of administrators. Any regime would have to sort out these serious financial and social problems after her forty-five year reign, but King James VI of Scotland, who came peacefully to take the English throne by hereditary right as James I in 1603, found himself frustrated from taking radical action partly by his subjects' conservative suspicions of change and partly by his own administrative laziness.

James's son Charles I (King from 1625) began to make the necessary reforms, but completely ruined his own efforts by a mixture of tactlessness, bad communications and an attempt at a religious revolution within his two churches of England and Scotland. In Chapter Eleven I briefly sketched the 'cuckoo in the nest' character of the English church after the Reformation; Elizabeth had allowed its Catholic and fairly unreformed structures to be run by churchmen whose Protestant theology was of the Swiss Reformed varieties centred on Bullinger's Zurich and Calvin's Geneva. By dominating the two universities, these clerics had solidly based their support among the gentry and nobility who were educated there, and the result was that by the end of Elizabeth's reign in 1603, the church was run by a Calvinist lay and clerical establishment. This persuaded nearly all Protestant zealots that for all the church's faults, it was a suitable instrument for setting forth a pure reformed faith throughout the kingdom.

This was to change dramatically during Charles's reign. Perhaps inevitably, the Catholic structure of the church began to exert its own emotional pull, especially from the 1580s on a small group of intellectuals in Oxford and Cambridge. They began looking beyond the Reformation once more, to value the church's past, taking particular delight in rediscovering the theology of the early Fathers. They began emphasizing the positive value of the apostolic succession of bishops (preserved more by luck than judgment in 1559), and stressing that this meant that although the Church of England had rejected medieval Romish abuses, it should see itself as a part of the Catholic Church rather than as a branch of Protestantism. By the 1620s this group had grown in assertiveness and self-confidence, and its opponents had begun labelling it 'Arminian' in allusion to Arminius, a Dutch theologian of the previous few decades who had opposed strict Calvinism in the Netherlands. Soon it captured the imagination of King Charles, who to the fury and puzzlement of the older church establishment, began promoting 'Arminians'. The leader among the group, William Laud, was appointed Archbishop of Canterbury in 1633.

In effect Charles was embarking on a revolution in the Church of England against the landowning and clerical establishment which had been in control for at least sixty years. He was doing so with the minimum of explanation or tact. Even so, he might have got away with this, and also succeeded in his plans for reform in English government, had he and Laud not indulged in lunatic religious adventuring in his other kingdom of Scotland. Scotland's Reformation had been later and much more thoroughgoing than England's, starting in 1560 and increasingly becoming dominated not just by Calvinists but by doctrinaire believers in the presbyterian church system set up in Geneva. King James, who understood his Scottish subjects much better than he did his English, had proved a masterly operator in reintroducing bishops to Scotland alongside this presbyterian system; once he came to the English throne, he further manoeuvred the Scots church by a clever mixture of bullying and genial persuasion into accepting other modifications which would bring it more into line with the English religious set-up.

James's system was producing happy if rather confused results in Scotland – a church which was becoming both presbyterian and episcopal – when Charles blundered into the situation. Knowing nothing and apparently caring less about Scottish opinion, he listened only to a few Arminian sympathizers among the Scottish bishops, and in 1637 imposed on Scotland a version of the English Prayer Book modified in a Catholic direction. There had been no consultation with the people who mattered in Scotland, and the kingdom exploded with indignation; in two successive wars, the Scots leadership showed its rejection not only of the Prayer Book but also of the bishops who had collaborated with its introduction, and in the process they totally defeated two royal armies sent from England.

Charles's critics in England were now able to unite the whole nation in rage against him; yet as they imposed a drastic settlement of their religious and political grievances on their King, many within the establishment began to be worried by their radicalism. It was all very well to get rid of Charles's Arminian bishops and his ministers, but now many of his Parliamentary opponents seemed to be intent on the destruction of all bishops and the Church of England as well. At the same time, in 1642 a major national rebellion broke out in Ireland, and England was split down the middle as to whether the King could be trusted with an army to defeat it. It was around this issue that the first English Civil War broke out in 1641, with the King now able to pose as the defender rather than the subverter of the Church of England for many Englishmen. A whole series of civil wars followed in the three kingdoms of England, Scotland and Ireland right up to 1660.

One of the major issues to be fought between the King's supporters and the opposition leadership who ruled in Parliament from Westminster was what should happen to the Church of England. Increasingly the whole Elizabethan Settlement of the church was identified with the King's cause. On the Parliamentarian side, a split developed between Presbyterians, who were prepared to follow the Scots line and set up an English Presbyterian Church, and the Independents, who were suspicious of Parliament's Scots allies and wanted a much more loose system which would have the minimum of central organization for the religious life of England. The Presbyterians had their strength in the Westminster Parliament, and it was Parliament which set up a synod in 1643 to reform the church in England. Not surprisingly, this 'Westminster Assembly', which came to include Scots representatives, produced a Confession of Faith which was Calvinist and Presbyterian in form.

This Westminster Confession of 1648 still retains an honoured place in the doctrinal standards of the Church of Scotland, but paradoxically enough, it was destined to have a much lesser place in English religious life. The reason was that the Independents had their power-base in the army which Parliament had built up to fight the King, and as the army became ever more successful against Charles, its leaders started making up their own minds on the future of the nation. The total defeat of the King in 1646 only made matters worse, because Parliament and the Army now quarrelled about what to do with him as well as about the future shape of national religion. A military *coup d'état* ousted the Presbyterian leadership and resulted in the King's execution in 1649; the army's leading general, Oliver Cromwell, was now faced with the task of working out a new structure of government for the whole of the British Isles. It proved a hopeless task; Cromwell experimented with a variety of new national assemblies but was eventually forced to set up a military-backed dictatorship which looked more and more like the old monarchy. When he died in 1658 there was no one of similar standing to take his place, and in desperation, after two years of mounting confusion, one of the army leaders led a successful move to restore the old monarchy with the exiled Prince Charles, son of the executed Charles I. The experiment in 'Commonwealth' was over; the 'Interregnum' (time between two reigns) was at an end.

Results of the Civil Wars (1): 'Old Dissent'

It was during this period that the English Dissenting bodies older than the Methodists can be recognized as taking permanent shape; they are known as 'Old Dissent' to distinguish them from the later movement of Methodism. There had been small congregations of English Protestants who approximated to these later groups during the reign of Elizabeth I; some can be traced back to areas which had been affected by pre-Reformation Lollardy, while some were probably affected by the radical Reformation on the Continent. They should be distinguished from the much larger minority of the clergy and gentry who had become so dissatisfied with Elizabeth's church settlement in the middle of her reign that they had pressed for a fully presbyterian system; this impulse had died down in the 1590s in the face of government repression and of the unmistakably Protestant convictions of the church hierarchy. Those who were thus discontented, often labelled Puritans, would not take their unhappiness to the point of separating from the establishment, and they despised and feared the few who did, terming them separatists or sectaries.

However, there was a considerable change when Parliament destroyed the episcopal structure of the Anglican Church in the Civil War of 1642–6, and government control faltered. Parliament's army was particularly affected by religious radicalism, for in it men were fighting for a godly cause and were free of any control from the traditional parish system. In all branches of religious life there was a feeling that the Last Days predicted in the Bible were about to come, especially when the King was executed, and this millenarian excitement spawned many sects who wished to play the part of the faithful remnant before God's throne. Some tried to overthrow all previous society, and all established customs: the Diggers tried to dig up common land to establish and maintain communes, while the Ranters expressed their freedom of all worldly and spiritual laws by ecstatic blasphemy and running naked down the street.

Similarly disruptive and wild was the group which centred on George Fox, an exponent of the old doctrine of the 'Inner Light' (see above, Chapter Eleven); simply calling themselves the Friends, they gained the nickname Quakers. One of the strangest things about this sect was that almost alone among the weirder groups of the Civil War period, they survived and transformed their character into a peaceable, self-restrained people who even though they still reject all sacramental forms in their worship, seem almost like a contemplative religious order in the universal church. Their present-day association with peace, disarmament and ecological movements is a quiet return to their original commitment to questioning all established authority.

Such groups as these terrified the mainstream supporters of Parliament, most of whom had fought Charles I to preserve the old England as they understood it. Parliamentarian leaders like Oliver Cromwell were torn between their desire to establish a truly godly state in England which would be a new Jerusalem, and their wish to restore the stability of the past; usually conservatism won out, and the radicals found themselves forced out of positions of power in Cromwell's army and government. However, Cromwell was committed, against the Presbyterians whom he had defeated in Parliament, to establishing a truly comprehensive Protestantism as the religion of England. Under his guidance, the English church became more widely-based than it ever would be again, and while he proved himself a brutally thorough enemy to Irish Roman Catholicism, in England he encouraged an unprecedented toleration. The Roman Catholic minority found itself less persecuted in the Interregnum than under the monarchy, despite its support for the King in the Civil War. The gentry minority who remained loyal to Anglican episcopalianism were left alone as long as they caused no trouble, and Cromwell even allowed the Jews back into England after an official expulsion which had lasted three and a half centuries.

In this new situation, the church in England became a vast federation of parishes with virtually no central structure apart from a committee known as the Triers, set up to examine candidates for the ministry and drawn from all shades of mainstream Protestant opinion. As a result, parishes could go their own way, which usually meant a personal adaptation of the (supposedly illegal) Book of Common Prayer in a Protestant direction, or an equally selective use of its lawful Parliamentary replacement, the Directory of Public Worship. In some areas, Presbyterian ministers managed to set up a local Presbyterian structure, but also groups emerged alongside the parish system who wished to worship as a gathered congregation of those who were moved to join together. Such groups grew out of the separatist churches which had begun to take shape in Elizabeth's reign.

The broad division in the 'Gathered Churches' was between those who accepted infant baptism (the Independents) and those who rejected it (the Baptists); however, the differences within this division were many, especially between the 'Particular' Baptists who still held to a Calvinist belief in predestination, and a growing group of 'General' Baptists who rejected that doctrine. Each grouping began developing structures so that they could associate with like-minded Christians: regional organizations for the Particular Baptists, and national meetings which drew up policy guidelines for the General Baptists and the Independents. The General Baptists met in London in 1656 to decide matters of doctrine and the attitude of their congregations to the state. The Independents met also in London at the old Savoy Palace in 1658 to draw up a Confession of Faith which was closely akin to the 1648 Westminster Confession, but which declared the value and necessity of independence for every individual congregation: hence their alternative and later more usual name of Congregationalists.

The Restoration of Charles II in 1660 brought the Interregnum experiments to an abrupt end. Much to its astonishment, the Presbyterian leadership which had been prominent in inviting back Charles found its mass support swept away in a wave of nostalgic enthusiasm for the martyred King Charles I, the old ways of

Cranmer's Prayer Book and the episcopal structure of the church. The leading Anglican clergy waiting in the wings made full use of this mood, completely outmanoeuvring the Presbyterians in setting up a new church and a liturgy which was a very slightly revised version of Cranmer's Book: the Prayer Book of 1662. The Church of England now re-established would be much more exclusive in its doctrine, with its back now largely turned on Calvinism: the new boundaries were symbolized by the departure of nearly three thousand clergy who could not fit into the new system. By their hard-line stance, the Anglicans had created 'Old Dissent'. English Protestantism was fractured in a way which has yet to be healed, and the reign of Charles II saw the main groupings of the Interregnum, the Presbyterians, the Independents and the Baptists, putting up a desperate struggle to survive against often severe persecution from the Anglican authorities in church and state.

Yet survive they did. James II succeeded his brother Charles as King in 1685, and in three years managed to throw away the very considerable advantages in political and military power which his brother's political skill had built up. A convert to Roman Catholicism, he tried to improve the position of his fellow-Catholics in such an inept way that he aroused the fears of both the Anglican establishment and the Dissenters. His overthrow in 1688 was virtually bloodless because the whole political establishment stood by and let it happen, earning it the name of the 'Glorious Revolution'. James's efforts to regain his throne by rebellions in Scotland and Ireland were a good deal more bloody, and the final defeat of his Catholic Irish forces at the Battle of the Boyne in 1690 remains one of the most explosive memories in the unhappy history of Irish Catholic/Protestant relations.

In England, however, James's defeat brought relief to the Dissenters. Neither the new King, James's Dutch son-in-law William of Orange, nor the Anglican establishment could ignore the memory or the future usefulness of the united Protestant front against James, and some leading churchmen tried to find ways of bringing Dissent back into the Church of England. In the event, political circumstances meant that there was a much more illogical compromise: Dissenting bodies were given the opportunity to worship legally alongside the Anglican parochial system on certain conditions, laid down in a Toleration Act in 1689. Hardline

Anglicans repeatedly tried to put the clock back during the early eighteenth century, but in fact this was only the beginning in a long process of granting full civil rights to those outside the established British churches which was eventually to be completed during the nineteenth century.

The Act of Toleration was an event of great significance, for like the outcome of the Thirty Years War it was another uncertain step in allowing Christians of opposing views to live side by side. Whatever its official claims, the Church of England had now surrendered in its attempt to represent the only Christianity which could have a true existence in the kingdom; alongside the now officially established Presbyterianism of the Church of Scotland and the Presbyterianism of Scots settlers in Ireland, there would be several different faces of English Protestantism which were each destined to become the centre of worldwide families of churches.

Results of the Civil Wars (2): religion in North America

Another result of Charles I's religious policies was to give a distinctive shape to Protestantism in North America. The English had started taking an interest in the wealth of America during the sixteenth century, and from the 1580s they made a series of efforts to rival the Spanish success by founding their own colonies to the north of the Spanish empire. The first colony to survive was Virginia, named after the lately deceased Virgin Queen Elizabeth; here the settlers brought with them an Anglican clergyman, and the colony remained Anglican in its leadership. However, those who found the Anglican Church structure too flawed to regard it as God's church began to look elsewhere in the new lands of America for a place where they could build a purer community in which to worship God. Virginia was too Anglican for them, so they made their venture far to the north up the Atlantic coast, in an area which they named New England.

Although the New England settlers made their colony much less like old England than Virginia was, the majority of them were not separatists but Puritans; they wanted a truer form of an established church. Their first colony, Plymouth, Massachusetts, was founded in 1620 well before the group round William Laud had achieved power in England, but during the 1630s the radical religious changes brought about by Charles I's regime encouraged many people to uproot themselves and try the hazards of a long Atlantic voyage. In that decade perhaps as many as 20,000 emigrated to the New World – rather more than the entire contemporary population of Norwich, the second largest city in early Stuart England. They included a number of university-trained ministers ejected from or not prepared to serve in Laud's church, and as early as 1636 they founded a university college to train up new clergy. The form that their church took was the paradoxical one of a Congregationalist structure with established status. In 1631 the Massachusetts Bay Company ceased to be an open corporation; the franchise for the colony's assembly was limited to church members. The elect, the 'Saints', were in charge of the commonwealth; they were a minority of the population. Technically this was not a theocracy, a state run by the church, but the church's government ran side by side with secular government.

This state, self-consciously a protest against the King's church, itself in turn produced dissent. Roger Williams, a strict separatist minister, wanted complete religious toleration, and after fleeing the colony to escape arrest in 1635, founded a new settlement called Rhode Island, where he was joined by Baptist groups in 1639. Williams was one of the few colonists to preach among the native Indians. Further religious experiments would be made, linking with the burst of religious energy in the England of the Civil Wars and Interregnum. Roman Catholic aristocrats friendly with the King sponsored a colony which they named Maryland after Charles's wife Henrietta Maria (1632); in fact the royalists' defeat in the Civil Wars meant that Catholics did not take the leading role in Maryland, but in 1649 they were given a unique freedom to practise their religion by a guarantee of complete toleration for all those who believed in Jesus Christ. Rhode Island and Maryland had arrived at a similar result by opposite routes. Another product of the Civil Wars was the arrival of the Quakers, determined to spread their ecstatic message of freedom. The Congregationalist governments in New England detested them, and even hanged four of them for missionary activities between 1659 and 1661. This caused a sharp reaction of protest both in New England and in the home country; Charles II ordered the executions to stop, though he too had little time for the Quakers. It was ironical that a royal regime so like the one from which the Puritan settlers had fled should now restrain their zeal for persecution.

A new chance for the Quakers came when William Penn became interested in founding a refuge for them in the New World. A Quaker himself, he was also the son of an Admiral and friendly with the Catholic future king, James II, and with these useful connections, he got a royal charter in 1682 for a new colony to be called Pennsylvania. His plan was bold and imaginative: he renounced the use of coercion in religion, granted free exercise of religion to all monotheists of whatever views who wished to seek refuge in his colony, and tried to maintain friendly relations with the Indians. Soon Pennsylvania came to have a rich mix not simply of English Protestant expression, but also Scots Presbyterians and the descendants of radical Reformation groups of the Continent like the Anabaptists. All this diversity proved fatal to Penn's original vision of a community run according to Quaker ideals (and good relations with the Indians also proved sadly difficult to maintain).

Nevertheless Pennsylvania set a notable example. No one religious group could claim official status, unlike the other colonies where certain groups continued to claim official advantages even if they were a minority. This was the first state to evolve the characteristic pattern of religion which survives to the present day in the United States of America: a pattern of religious denominations, none claiming the exclusive status of the church, but rather making up the slices of a Protestant 'cake' which together adds up to a church. This was the beginning of a different ideal from the seventeenth-century development of religious toleration as we have seen it in Europe or in England; now religious liberty was developing. Toleration is a grudging concession granted by one body from a position of strength; liberty provides a situation in which all religious groups are competing on an equal basis.

Anglicanism did strengthen its position in the English American colonies after the restoration of Charles II, gaining established status in some of them. However, the origins of so many colonies in religious protest against the Anglican system guaranteed that it would never be as dominant as it was in England, and the circumstances of the American colonies' successful rebellion against the mother country in 1776–83 ended any chance that it had of general establishment. Anglicanism had always been hampered in its

American work by not having any bishops to direct it on the spot, and it took until 1784 to acquire them. American Anglicans then got round the embarrassing link between English Anglican bishops and the English monarchy by having their first bishops consecrated by Scots Episcopalian bishops, who were themselves members of a church disestablished after the Glorious Revolution of 1688. Even then, the new Protestant Episcopal Church of the United States was slow to find ways of following other Protestant denominations in the work of evangelizing the vast new lands opening up to settlers in the west of the old colonies; it remained little affected by the revivals which stemmed from the eighteenth-century Great Awakenings (see below, Chapter Fourteen). Anglicanism is still a comparatively small if disproportionately influential part of the American religious scene.

The consequences of the British civil wars were therefore wholly out of scale with what could have been expected in the seventeenth century from a marginal, second-rank European power; the United States of America was destined to lead one of the twentieth century's two main power systems, and because it retained its Protestant and English-speaking character, it is the American varieties of English Protestantism which are the most character-istic forms of Protestant Christianity today. This is a Christianity which has been shaped by a very different historical experience from that of Western Europe, and the similarities in language and confessional background may mislead us into missing the deep contrasts.

The American success was an ironical outcome of the collapse of Puritan power in England after Charles II's Restoration. The triumph of Laudian or 'High Church' Anglicanism in 1660–2 was to some extent an illusion, not simply because of what was to happen in America, or because of the coming of Puritanism in a new guise in the eighteenth-century Evangelical Movement, but also because of other profound changes in the Western European world. Society would be transformed by an Industrial Revolution starting in England, and besides this, a revolution was taking place in the basic assumptions and preoccupations of Europeans which would make the disagreements between Puritans and Arminians seem a minor family squabble.

Part III

New Worlds

Chronology for Chapter Fourteen

1543	Copernicus publishes full version of his astronomical theories. Koran published in Latin
1621	Francis Bacon's political career ends in disgrace
1629	René Descartes settles in the Netherlands
1642–6	First English Civil War
1651	Paul Gerhardt begins public ministry in Mittelwalde
1662	Charles II of England gives a charter to Royal Society
1663	Philipp Jakob Spener begins public ministry in Strasbourg
1686	Beginning of Turks' expulsion from Hungary
1687	Isaac Newton, *Principia Mathematica* published
1694	University of Halle founded
1695	John Locke, *The Reasonableness of Christianity* published
1720	Theodorus J. Freylinghausen starts pastoral work in New Jersey
1722	Nikolaus von Zinzendorf organizes community on his estate
1727	Jonathan Edwards experiences conversion
1735–7	John Wesley working in Georgia
1736	George Whitefield begins open air preaching
1738	John Wesley's Aldersgate experience
1739	George Whitefield begins preaching in America. John Wesley begins open air preaching
1748	David Hume, *Philosophical Essays Concerning Human Understanding* published
1751	*Encyclopédie* begins publication
1755	First Separate Baptist work begins in American South. Immanuel Kant appointed lecturer in Königsberg University
1758	Voltaire retires to estate at Ferney
1761	Jean-Jacques Rousseau has his first novel published
1776	American Revolution breaks out
1783	Charles Simeon appointed Vicar of Holy Trinity, Cambridge
1784	John Wesley ordains Thomas Coke for American work. Scots bishops consecrate bishop for American Episcopalians
1787	English Wesleyan chapels licensed under laws for dissenting meeting houses
1797	First significant secession from Wesleyan Methodism (Methodist New Connexion)
1807	William Wilberforce secures abolition of slave trade
1815	Henry Ryder (Evangelical) appointed Bishop of Gloucester
1833	William Wilberforce secures abolition of slavery in British Empire

Chapter Fourteen

Science and Sin (1600 to 1800)

Up to the sixteenth century, culture and knowledge in Western Europe had been dominated by the work of the past: the writers of classical antiquity, the greatest of whom were Plato and Aristotle, or the thinkers of the Middle Ages who themselves built on this classical heritage. Knowledge was largely contained within the manuscripts so laboriously preserved by the Carolingian Renaissance or discovered after that: each new discovery had much the same effect as the opening-up of a new oilfield in the oil-hungry world of the 1970s. However, by 1550, the supply of hitherto unknown manuscripts was running low; Western European culture was developing the equivalent of an energy crisis. The only answer, as today, was to explore new sources of energy: instead of looking to the past, to rely more on new concepts and to discover the full potential of humankind for thinking afresh. This would produce a new and very different world from anything which had gone before; the result is that much more separates our thoughts and assumptions from people in Tudor England than separates their thoughts and assumptions from people in ancient Rome.

Throughout the Middle Ages, the highest intellectual achievements and energies of Western European society had been concentrated on religion and theology; this was part of Europe's legacy from the ancient world. Theology was called the Queen of the Sciences, and this was no mere courtesy title. During the sixteenth-century Reformation, which was really the swansong of the old priorities and assumptions, questions of theology were still capable of splitting Europe down the middle and causing a century of warfare, as we have seen. Yet by 1650, it was as if theology had argued itself to a standstill; the old arguments continued, but they no longer covered fresh ground, and they no longer occupied the centre of the stage. More and more importance was coming to be attached to scientific discovery: to affirming the value of the things of this world rather than the next. There had indeed been much scientific enquiry and technological advance during the Middle Ages: the invention of the windmill, the mechanical clock or the magnetic compass were major fruits of medieval society's restless ingenuity. However, this was subordinate to the higher concerns of a God-centred universe.

The shift towards an emphasis on science started, perhaps inevitably, with further examination of the past. Part of this examination simply took the scientific legacy of the classical world and with a great effort of the imagination, looked at it afresh: thus one of the most disturbing achievements of sixteenth-century thought, the Polish astronomer Copernicus's theoretical demonstration that the earth moves round the sun, was entirely based on a reworking of well-known data systematized by the second-century Roman astronomer Ptolemy. However, Renaissance humanism might also encourage scientific advance by its interest in the most mystic and other-worldly side of ancient philosophy.

As proof of this, one of the most surprising things to emerge from recent research on the so-called 'Scientific Revolution' of the sixteenth to eighteenth centuries is how much it was bound up with mysticism and the occult. Neo-Platonism came into this heady brew, especially in the form of Hermeticism, a revival of interest in the mystical classical writings attributed to a mythical figure called Hermes Trismegistus. These ancient works presented a form of gnosticism, in which humankind could reach divine status through knowledge; so increasingly divine status would be gained by research into the secrets of nature. It is easy to see how this might lead on to scientific exploration. A deep belief in the truth of astrology might come from considering the writings of Plato on the cosmos, but in turn, an astrologer's quest to get horoscopes as accurate and useful as possible might lead him into exact and independent observation of the heavens: the basis of practical experimental work in astronomy. Many important sixteenth-century astronomers like Johann Kepler and Tycho Brahe had strong links with mysticism.

There is certainly more than one element in the origins of modern preoccupations with science. Some scholars have pointed to other sources besides the humanist interest in classical mysticism; some stress the millenarian excitement which we noted in Chapter Thirteen as disturbing Civil War England, suggesting that English intellectuals were affected by the prophecies in the Book of Daniel that in the Last Days, knowledge will increase. Others prefer to point to practical advances such as the art of navigation developed in the age of the first seaborne empires, which led people to place a greater value on practical experiment for practical advances.

Bacon and English Empiricism

One of the most important figures to make new attitudes to science respectable was the English politician and writer Francis Bacon. Throughout a long public career, which ended in disaster with disgrace and impeachment engineered by his enemies, Bacon was fascinated by the problems of advancing human knowledge; he was rigidly hostile to any system of thought from the past which seemed to him an obstacle to such advance. He especially hated the effects of ancient philosophy, which in good Protestant fashion he saw as having been perpetuated through the Middle Ages by superstitious and ignorant monks. This led him to exalt practical experiment as the only way to test out ideas, and he published elaborate schemes of method by which scientific work should proceed.

Critics said that Bacon 'wrote philosophy like a Lord Chancellor', but that may be part of the reason for his success in seventeenth-century England; the English have more respect for Lord Chancellors than they do for philosophers. After he died in 1626, his writings gained particularly wide circulation once the English official censorship broke down in 1640, and his enthusiasm for experimentation produced many groups of followers during the years of new possibilities in the Interregnum. Even when Charles II was restored, the impulse to experiment continued to flourish, and was given royal patronage with the granting of a charter to the Royal Society in 1662. Here many of the members were no more than gentlemen amateurs interested in science, but once more, this snob value did the cause of experimentation more good than harm in English society. The scientific experiment would permanently replace a reliance on a knowledge of what ancient writers had said.

There were serious drawbacks to Bacon's attitudes and methods. First, they were wildly optimistic; Bacon thought that by using experimental methods similar to the ones which he proposed, all knowledge would be available to the human race in a few generations. Moreover, in his rejection of ancient wisdom, and his emphasis that the only useful facts were those which were proved by experiment (the view known as 'Empiricism'), he ignored the role which theory might have to play in advancing human knowledge; for instance, he undervalued Copernicus's astronomical work, resenting his use of advanced mathematics, which Bacon simply did not understand. Perhaps more alarmingly, the increasing emphasis on experimental fact meant that scientific truth was being pulled apart from the truths offered by religion. Bacon deliberately encouraged this process in order to free science from the restrictions which the church might place on it. He himself was a conventional if fairly critical member of England's established church, but he did not let this spill over into his scientific thought; he said that knowledge of God could only come from divine revelation, and so theology could be neatly separated from scientific enquiry as on a different level of truth. Scientists following this principle could ignore the problems of theology in their work, even if they remained mainstream Christians. If they did not so remain, then the scientific fact derived from experiment would rule the Western world alone and supreme.

The changing place of science in English life was taken a stage further by the advances in mathematics and physics made by Sir Isaac Newton. Like many sensitive minds of the seventeenth century, Newton seems a figure poised between a former age and an age newly emerging: in the phrase of the contemporary writer Sir Thomas Browne, living in 'divided and distinguished worlds'. Newton shared all the seventeenth-century fascination with millennial ideas, writing extensively on the Book of Revelation; he remained a deeply devout if unorthodox Christian. Yet at the same time his scientific work was creating a world-view which hardly had need for the traditional Christian picture of God. His exposition of the principles of gravity suggested a universe running on certain physical laws which humankind had the capacity to discover and to express in mathematically measurable terms. Although God had created and ordered this universe and continued to prevent it disappearing back into chaos and non-existence, it would be trivializing his majesty to suppose that he went on actively intervening in its affairs.

God's glory was therefore to be proved by natural not supernatural wonders: half a century before, Francis Bacon had already observed that 'God never wrought miracle to convince atheism, because his ordinary works convince it'. Such a view could be seen as a very comforting integration of the Christian faith with scientific advance, but in the long term it would suggest that there was no need to consider God at all. Theology was yielding its central place in human thought to physics.

Descartes and Locke

The increasing emphasis on a universe running by observable physical laws was bound to have repercussions in philosophy, and its impact is particularly seen in the thought of René Descartes. With Descartes we see another symbolically divided figure: a Catholic veteran of the Thirty Years War who never quarrelled with the Catholic hierarchy, yet chose to settle in Amsterdam, the largest city of the Protestant and exceptionally tolerant Dutch Republic: some of his work was published in the traditional language of international scholarship, Latin, but some in his native French. In his thought he brought his training and experience in mathematics to bear on philosophy; no one had used a mathematical approach to philosophy in quite this way before, and Descartes believed that this would enable him to avoid misleading preconceptions about the nature of being and thought. This was to approach the problem of knowledge from precisely the opposite direction from Bacon's English empiricism; whereas Bacon made deductions by gathering individual pieces of data to find a general pattern. Descartes started from his own consciousness of himself: the famous maxim, 'I think, therefore I am'.

With this argument from consciousness, Descartes could construct what he regarded as an unanswerable and scientific proof of the existence of God. However, he came up against the problem which worried many seventeenth-century thinkers contemplating the new exposure of a machine-like universe: how did the physical matter which could be measured, felt and seen relate to the world of consciousness, of the mind, which was the starting-point of his philosophy? Descartes found it easier to define this problem than to solve it: he emphasized that there was a fundamental divide within creation, between what he called 'extension' (that is, matter) and 'thought' (that is, spirit). Taking its name from him, this division has been termed 'Cartesian dualism', a very different dualism from the ancient dualism of the Gnostics. They had given a moral quality to the divide: spirit was infinitely superior to matter. In this new dualism, there was no morality: the two states of being were simply different.

Thus despite their very different approaches, the English Empiricists and the Cartesians were both making a fundamental division within knowledge and being, and they were robbing the universe of the morality which had been the life blood of the God-centred world-pictures of earlier centuries. There was little that the older world-pictures could do to resist the process; although the clash between old and new produced happy confusions and inconclusive results for many people, the sheer weight of new information which the interest in science was releasing was bound to overwhelm the earlier systems. In the long seesaw contest within Christianity between faith and reason, it was now reason which seemed to have the decisive advantage, for it was through reason that the new scientific truth could be harvested.

This emphasis on reason was strongly reinforced in Christianity by the European-wide impact of the thought of the Englishman John Locke. Besides pleading for toleration within church structures and providing an argued defence for the existence of the regime which overthrew King James II of England in 1688, Locke followed Descartes in affirming that God's existence could be proved; Christian belief was therefore not so much a matter of faith as of rational assent to something which was obviously reasonable. After this central belief, there was little need for further dogmas of faith, for few of them were so self-evident or provable as the central fact of God's existence: hence Locke's plea for the toleration of variety in Christian opinion. Such a Christian belief should be reflected in the world in good conduct, which should bring its own rewards – and Locke felt that there was nothing wrong in looking for such rewards.

Such comfortable and attractively moderate ideas proved extremely popular throughout the thinking world of Western Europe, even penetrating from its Protestant to its Catholic half. At their most extreme, they might take the form of deism, which was a type of belief in God which denied any place to divine revelation or the supernatural: God was merely the creator of the world, with no further active interest in it (in another famous image, the watchmaker who makes and then winds up and leaves the watch). Even in more moderate forms, Locke's outlook led people to deplore the stress on dogma, which after all, had produced such horrific results in the wars of the Reformation. Many felt the doctrine of the Trinity to be unreasonable as well as having little basis in scripture, so the late seventeenth century saw a new emergence of Unitarianism. Where there were no strict doctrinal formulae or strong central authorities to stop this trend, for instance among some of the wealthier and more intellectually alert congregations of English Old Dissent, an increasing number of Christians made the decision to abandon Trinitarian belief and become Unitarians.

The mood of Europe as it entered the eighteenth century was therefore one of increasing optimism and faith in the capacity of humankind to master all that needed to be mastered by the use of reason. Reason and its products had quite clearly surpassed the wisdom of the ancients, so the deep-seated European sense of inferiority to the classical past was at last at an end. Contacts with the outside world reinforced this outlook. It was during the seventeenth century that Western Europe finally ceased to be on the defensive against Islam; after a last desperate and unsuccessful push by the Turks as far west as Vienna in 1683, the Habsburgs began the long task of rolling back the Turkish Empire out of Europe, with the recapture of the kingdom of Hungary.

At the same time Europeans were beginning to assess the results of their contacts with the great civilizations of the East, all of which had been brought into European consciousness by the mid-seventeenth century. Perhaps the secret of the massive success of Western European culture in the world has been this interest in penetrating the inner life of other cultures, first seen in Europe in the Renaissance. No other civilization has shown such a desire to compare itself with unfamiliar societies until the rise of a similar mood among the Japanese in the nineteenth century. The first Koran was printed in Latin translation in the same year that Copernicus published his work on the earth and the sun, 1543; by the end of the seventeenth century, even Confucian literature was beginning to reach Europe from China. The readers were impressed: here was wisdom to equal that to be found in the Christian scriptures, reinforcing the mood that the universal power of human reason was a better basis for religious belief than scriptural revelation.

Such emphasis on progress and human capacity was in direct contrast to the pessimism of much traditional Christian belief, particularly in the form which Augustine's genius had created: its stress on the fatal character of Adam's Fall, and on the consequent overwhelming nature of original sin. A rejection of Christian pessimism would lead in turn to a lessened attention to the place of Christ's death on the cross as an atonement for humankind's sin; for if there is no Fall, there is no need for an atonement to undo it. One of the themes in the history of Christian theology is another seesaw conflict, this time between emphases on the two bounds of Jesus Christ's earthly life: his incarnation and his atoning death on the cross. In Chapter Ten we noted how the late medieval period and the Reformation had stressed the sufferings of Christ on the cross and the atonement: in the eighteenth century we see the opposite emphasis on the incarnation of Christ as a gift of God to the created world, a reflection of the dignity of humankind.

The Evangelical Revival: Methodism

It was not surprising that when a religious reaction came against the reasonable Christianity of eighteenth-century Europe, it should produce a faith which once more laid especial stress on the atonement. This reaction emerged in England and its thirteen north American colonies, but also on the Continent, producing movements which were linked but not identical. Let us consider the English movement first; this was what came to be described as the Evangelical Revival, an impulse which in part found a home within the Church of England. However, it also revitalized Old Dissent and produced a new religious body which more by accident than design found itself outside the established church: Methodism.

The leading figure in this movement was John Wesley, an Anglican clergyman. When considering Wesley's background, Methodists have tended to place a large emphasis on the spirituality of his maternal grandfather, a clergyman ejected from the established church in the Anglican reaction of Charles II's reign; probably we would hear less of this link with Old Dissent if Methodism had not severed its links with Anglicanism. In fact, both Wesley's parents were strongly attached to the High Church Anglicanism which William Laud had pioneered under Charles I, which had triumphed in Charles II's restoration, but which had found itself increasingly left aside after the fall of James II because of the new regime's suspicion that its first loyalty continued to lie with the exiled King. The Anglican Church which Wesley knew as a young man was dominated by the very different religious style of the 'Latitudinarians', so nicknamed because of their willingness to tolerate a wide latitude of religious belief within a broadly tolerant national church. As a result, Wesley started his clerical career with a High Church religious viewpoint out of step with the establishment of his church, particularly as he found his second home in Oxford University, still an obstinate stronghold of the embattled High Church party. Already while at Oxford, he gathered a group of friends to join together in devotion and good works; their ordered lifestyle and High Church piety earned them the initially mocking title of 'Methodists'.

However, there were to be wider influences on the religious make-up of this remarkable man. A further element was added by what seemed to be a discouraging and negative experience: Wesley's attempt to work as a missionary for the High Church organization the Society for the Propagation of the Gospel, in the newly-founded English American colony of Georgia. This ended in disaster, mainly because of his own pastoral clumsiness; however, while travelling out to Georgia in 1735, he was much impressed by the piety and courage of a group of German Moravian Brethren, spiritual descendants of the Hussites (see Chapter Ten), and one of the few groups in European Protestantism at the time to attach much importance to missionary work. On his return from Georgia, his self-confidence severely damaged, he was much comforted by the Moravians, and he found a new excitement and a new depth of faith when in 1738 he attended a Moravian meeting in Aldersgate Street in London. As Methodists are reminded every year, this 'Aldersgate experience' was a turning-point for him, and the trigger was hearing a reading from one of the key documents of the sixteenth-century German Reformation, Luther's preface to the Epistle to the Romans. So a Protestant

Evangelical fire was added to the Anglican Catholicism of his youth.

With a new conviction that he must not simply seek personal holiness but spread the message of salvation as far as he could, Wesley now embarked on a lifetime's mission throughout the British Isles. He saw that the structures of the established church were unequal to this challenge; its ancient distribution of parishes was exceedingly difficult to amend and update, yet the distribution of population, particularly in England, was beginning dramatically to change. How could the new population centres be given an effective picture of God's Word, or receive the pastoral care which they deserved? Wesley's answer was disconcertingly unconventional for a High Church Anglican: in 1739 he followed his friend George Whitefield (at first rather nervously) in preaching in the open air like the early friars, and he was astonished at the dramatic results which followed. Crowds were gripped by mass emotion and a sense of their own sin; soon he was building up societies who found peace, personal dignity and a new reality in the Christian message. These took on the Oxford nickname of 'Methodists'.

All this irregular activity was very worrying to the church authorities; many parish clergy also felt that their own efforts were being belittled by the work of Wesley and his associates. Faced with much hostility, Wesley had no choice in some places but to continue with his open air preaching, or even to forget his Anglican principles and accept the hospitality of a pulpit in a Dissenting meeting house. Not only that, but he quickly built headquarters to organize his work, starting in London and Bristol in 1739. Soon his societies of believers were following this by putting up buildings for themselves all over the country. It was these buildings which provided one of the two forces posing the question of identity for Wesley's new movement. Was he simply founding a society to bring new life to the Anglican Church? What about his congregations in Presbyterian Scotland, if this was so? And how did his buildings stand in the eyes of the law? The only legal way in which he could sustain them was to declare them to be dissenting chapels and to get them registered as the law demanded. Much against his will, in 1787 Wesley was forced to advise his societies that this must be done.

However, a second force was even more serious in pushing Wesley's movement away from the Church of England which he loved so much. Wesley's followers began very successful work in the British American colonies. Like the Anglicans over there, they found their efforts seriously affected by the American Revolution which broke out in the thirteen colonies in 1776; with the withdrawal of many Anglican clergy, there was virtually no one to whom Wesley's American followers could go to receive Holy Communion. Wesley was a firm believer that the eucharist should be at the centre of the Christian life, and this seemed to him to be a desperate situation; he could not persuade any English bishop to ordain men to fill the gap.

Accordingly in 1784 Wesley took his stand on his own rights as an ordained priest of the church to ordain men on his own initiative – ironically, in the same year as American Anglicans solved the same dilemma by going to Scottish Episcopalian bishops to get their bishops consecrated (see above, Chapter Thirteen). Although his brother Charles, also an Anglican clergyman, deplored the move, John obstinately refused to recognize that he had done anything decisive, even though he went on to ordain men for areas within the British Isles and elsewhere where he thought this emergency measure justified. With further inconsistency, he was furious when the leaders of the American Methodists allowed themselves to be called Bishops; ever since then, the American tradition of Methodism has been episcopal in organization, although without any doctrine of episcopal apostolic succession.

For all John Wesley's insistence that he lived and died a member of the Church of England, it was probably inevitable in eighteenth-century conditions that his movement of Methodists should separate from Anglicanism. Many of his followers had been so remote from active contact with the church before Methodism affected their lives that they had little of Wesley's feelings for Anglicanism. Perhaps if he had been born in a different time and place, he could have sustained a movement of piety like some of the great religious Orders of the Middle Ages, but the Anglican Church had set its face against monasticism at the Reformation, and could not cope with this form of religious expression. Wesley's deliberate avoidance of the full consequences of his actions meant that he left a host of problems for the structure of preachers and societies which he had created; on his death in 1791, his successors had to grapple with the questions of identity and the balance of authority within their movement which his immense personal prestige had postponed. There were many different answers to these questions, and often the quarrels over them were extremely bitter. Although it grew in numbers and influence, British Methodism was characterized by constant internal splits during its first century of existence from 1791, and it is only in the twentieth century that most of its main divisions have come together in a single Methodist Church. In the process of union, a sense of Methodist identity has been much sustained by Methodism's shared love for the hymns of John Wesley's brother Charles, one of the greatest of all Christian hymn writers.

Not all leading figures of the Evangelical Revival were swept into Wesley's movement. His early associate George Whitefield deeply disagreed with Wesley's rejection of Calvinist predestination, and founded his own associations of Calvinist congregations, markedly less influential than the Methodists except in Wales. Many Evangelicals managed to avoid the separation from the Church of England into which Wesley's and Whitefield's followers were forced; while Wesley boldly said that the world was his parish, they turned their evangelical faith into using the existing parish structure of the Church of England. Through their energies, certain areas and parishes within the church became strongholds of Evangelical work, so that by the end of the eighteenth century, there was a recognizable Evangelical party among the clergy and gentry.

The Anglican clerical establishment looked on the movement with considerable suspicion well into the nineteenth century, but with the appointment of a definite Evangelical as Bishop of Gloucester in 1815, it was clear that their established place in the church was secure. Partly this was achieved by a steady build-up of support among the clergy; the Evangelicals greatly affected the views of young men preparing for the church's ministry in the University of Cambridge through the long-lived personal influence of the Cambridge clergyman Charles Simeon. Some Evangelical laymen were influential enough to play a role in the British Parliament and work out their piety in practical action; their most celebrated triumph was the parliamentary abolition of slavery in the British Empire, achieved in 1833 after decades of struggle by the MP William Wilberforce. This was a vital stage in a movement of opinion within Christianity against slavery which by the twentieth century meant that for the first time in Christian history, the church consistently and universally condemned the enslavement of human beings.

The Great Awakenings and German Pietism

Two further reactions against 'reasonable religion' had developed in North America and in Germany. In the American colonies this took the name of the 'Great Awakenings', a series of outbursts of religious energy which in varying degrees affected the different components of the Protestant religious life rooted in colonial society. The Awakenings emerged at a time when the leaderships of many American churches were beginning to feel that the dreams of the founding fathers had been betrayed; the church establishments in several colonies represented only a minority of the population, and many people had no church contacts at all. In contrast to Wesley's movement in England, the main thrust of the Awakenings in the northern colonies was Calvinist, and one of their earliest stirrings came in the 1720s as the result of the dissatisfaction of a newly-arrived Dutch Calvinist minister, Theodorus Freylinghausen, at what he saw as the formality of the Dutch Reformed Church in New Jersey. Freylinghausen probably did more to stir up trouble than to bring new life, but the patterns of the Awakening which he stimulated would remain important features of American religion to the present day: a constant appeal to the need for 'revival' within the church, and a tension between those who advocated revival and those who did not find this a useful method of advancing the work of the church.

During the 1730s a similar excitement, and a similar backlash, appeared in Presbyterian churches, stimulated in particular by the electrifying preaching of the Englishman George Whitefield. Whitefield used the method of open-air preaching here to dramatic effect, although he deplored and tried to control the more emotional preaching of the revival which he found in America. Equally influential alongside Whitefield was an American Congregational minister, Jonathan Edwards; Edwards combined an academic rigour which came from his deep interest in philosophy with an uncompromising attachment to Calvinism, reinforced by his experience of conversion in 1727. Like Whitefield, he was concerned to curb the excesses of the Awakenings in order to defend them from their critics within the churches.

Edwards was working in his native New England, in the strong-hold of established Congregationalism; in the colonies to the south, it was largely in the Baptist churches, mostly unsympathetic to Calvinism, and among the non-Calvinist Methodists, that the Awakenings had their chief impact. In the south, the denomination of the Separate Baptists was virtually created by the Awakenings, while rather late, in the 1770s and after, the Methodists also took up the mechanism of revival and flourished as a result. Two of the most influential strands within American Protestantism thus owe their prominence to the first Awakenings period. Moreover, the sense of common American heritage among different Protestant denominations was much strengthened by this common experience of eighteenth-century ferment: the Awakenings helped to create an American identity for what had been offshoots of European churches.

Socially, the Awakenings produced a new concern with the education and evangelizing of the native 'Indian' population, although this did not stop its continuing exploitation and gradual decline in numbers as the American frontier expanded westwards. Politically, the energies of the movement helped to unite the thirteen British colonies, spreading a common sense of purpose; often this purpose fed off continuing excitement over the idea of the millennium, still a potent legacy of seventeenth-century Protestantism. Just as it had done in England in the Civil Wars, millennial interest produced a sense that there was a special destiny for the new lands, particularly since they were an untamed wilderness unsullied by ancient European sins. In this feeling we can glimpse the beginning of the 'American Dream' which even the traumas of the Vietnam War and the Watergate Scandal in recent decades do not seem to have destroyed.

Rather earlier than the movements which we have so far discussed, from the 1670s, Pietism became a new force within German Lutheranism; like them, it sprang from an unease at the spiritual inadequacies of the established church. The pioneer in it was the minister Philipp Jakob Spener, who in his pastoral work in Strasbourg and Frankfurt was concerned to work through the existing structures of church life to bring back a more personal religion to the Lutheran world, to restore or complete Luther's vision. Services should be given new directness and life, partly by abandoning the Latin which still played a large part in Lutheran liturgy; sermons should become more directed towards encouraging devotional life. The laity should be encouraged to form devotional societies (*collegia pietatis*) for prayer and study, like the *Devotio Moderna* or the oratories of pre-Reformation Europe, or the Methodist class meetings of later years. Just as Methodism was to base much of its power and sense of identity on the hymns of Charles Wesley, so Spener's movement was much helped by the hymn-writing genius of Paul Gerhardt, a man of broad sympathies who like Luther himself was as capable of being moved by the medieval Catholic mystical tradition as by his strong Protestant faith.

Pietism attracted much opposition, but in the end it was much more successful than Methodism in gaining a central place within the church establishment, and much less prone than the Great Awakenings to produce institutional splits. It found a base in the new University of Halle, which would train thousands of pastors besides the majority of officials administering the increasingly influential north German state of Prussia. One separated group had an influence out of all proportion to its size. A nobleman and civil servant from the state of Saxony, Nikolaus von Zinzendorf, was inspired by his pietist faith (he was Spener's godson) to organize some remnants of the Moravian community into a settlement on his estates at Herrnhut, which became the centre of Moravian work all over the world. It was these Moravians who were so influential on John Wesley, who visited Herrnhut and translated some of their hymns for his own societies' use.

With its secure base inside the Lutheran establishment, Pietism powerfully and permanently affected German life; both in its Moravian form and in Lutheranism, it brought a new enthusiasm for missionary work which gave a wider vision to the Lutheran world. It has had many critics, who complain that its emphasis on personal religion has led to passivity: an inward-looking faith which distrusts both worldly concern and any intellectual enquiry. Undoubtedly by the mid-eighteenth century it was beginning in turn to develop into a formal and legalistic system. Yet for many Germans, its stress on the possibility of overcoming human limitations by the experience of conversion would prove as liberating a doctrine as it would for Wesley's Methodists.

Enlightenment

The Pietists, the Methodists, the Evangelicals and the preachers of the Great Awakenings sought to recall Western Europe and North America to a sense of human sin, and to the Augustinian idea of humankind's dependence on God. Yet the boundless optimism and trust in human capacity of Bacon and Descartes were not so easily crushed; indeed, during the eighteenth century, this mood reached its high point at the very time when the movements which we have just described were putting down roots. The eighteenth century was an age in which educated people consciously saw themselves as being blessed with greater understanding than their superstitious, blinkered predecessors; they described their time as the Enlightenment. In France, such thinkers (*philosophes* in French) showed their debt to Francis Bacon's vision of a universal collection of knowledge by compiling and publishing the *Encyclopédie*. In this pioneering Encyclopedia was a collection of knowledge, arranged now in no hierarchy of being, but in the fashionable alphabetical style: the eighteenth century's answer to the systems and classifications of Aristotle and Thomas Aquinas. The tone was Deist, and despite official French censorship, the assumptions behind the *Encyclopédie* were those of natural religion: in the Baconian manner, hard facts were hard facts.

Thinkers of the Enlightenment, whether French, German or British, despised revelation and the supernatural; they detested, for example, what they saw as the mystical obscurities of Pietism. The most influential exponent of this world-outlook was the French writer Francois-Marie Arouet, usually known by his pen-name as Voltaire. For Voltaire, the philosophy of Locke and the mechanical universe of Newton had banished mystery from human affairs, and he waged a lifelong campaign against the Roman Catholic Church, which he saw as a self-interested conspiracy to perpetuate this mystery. His was an elitist view of enlightenment; although he spoke out bravely against injustices perpetuated by the Roman Catholic authorities, he was capable of advising King Frederic the Great of Prussia to destroy Christianity among the enlightened minority, but not among the 'rabble' who are 'apt for every yoke'. It was the church's irrational power, and its capacity to interfere with the minds of the intelligent, which he detested; all over Europe those with pretensions to being part of the world of

the *philosophes* read him with delight, and looked at the traditional life of the church with contempt.

The effect of Voltaire's verbal attacks on organized religion was
to deny any meaningful place to God in the scheme of things. If
there was a force called God which guided the affairs of people, it
tended to become impersonal, a mere abstraction: the world became a cold and empty place. The writer Jean-Jacques Rousseau
tried to remedy this by devising a 'natural religion' based on the
Christian Gospels while attempting to avoid what he saw as the
unhealthy dogmatism disfiguring traditional Christian belief. Like
so many of these post-Baconian systems, Rousseau's ideas were
based on an optimistic view of humankind's potential: we are born
good, not bad, and it is the fault of society's institutions that we are
pushed towards vice and selfishness. So although Rousseau looked
back to a golden age, like traditional Christianity, his Fall was
merely a wrong turning, a mistake, rather than the humanly-
generated catastrophe of Augustine's theology. The force of love,
and a right ordering of human affairs, would put right the mistakes
of the past. There was a warmth of feeling and a romantic enthusiasm in Rousseau's writing – much of his ideas was expressed in
what are avowedly romantic novels – which made his thought very
attractive to those seeking new ideals, particularly after the revolutionary explosion of 1789.

However, perhaps more radical than any of the French *philosophes* was the work of the German philosopher Immanuel Kant. A
gentle, retiring university lecturer at Königsberg, Kant nevertheless revolutionized Western European thought, building on the
foundations provided by Bacon and the science of Sir Isaac
Newton to shape the way the West has thought in the nineteenth
and twentieth centuries. The effect of his work was to reduce still
further the place that a historical Christian faith and the institutions which support it might have in the concerns of Western
culture.

Kant was much more concerned to work on from the tradition of
Newton than that of Descartes, but like Descartes, he argued from
the existence of individual consciousness rather than from the
givenness of a God found in revelation. However, following questions already posed by the Scottish philosopher David Hume, he
denied that even individual consciousness ('I think, therefore I
am') was enough to prove the existence of the self. He could say

that the mind orders everything which it experiences, and that somehow it has a set of rules by which it can judge these experiences. These rules enable the mind to order the information which it receives about space and time within the universe, yet the rules themselves come before any actual experience of space and time. Moreover, it is impossible to prove that these rules are true. All that can be said is that they are absolutely necessary to ordering what we perceive and giving it a quality which we can label objectivity.

Kant was therefore standing previous philosophies on their heads; usually they had suggested that each individual mind gives a picture of structures in a real world which lies outside that mind. Now Kant was saying that the mind orders the world by the way in which it interprets experience. There are vital 'Ideas' which are beyond the possibility of experience, and therefore beyond any traditional proof: Kant called these God, Freedom and Immortality. Although these are not accessible through reason, being beyond experience, they can be reached by the conscience within the individual, a conscience which forces us to regulate our affairs according to its dictates. This is a new sort of faith to meet the battle between faith and reason: indeed, in a famous phrase, Kant said 'I had to remove knowledge to make room for faith'.

There is thus a God in Kant's system, a God which is the ultimate goal to which the individual stretches out, hoping to meet this goal in the immortality which stretches out beyond our imperfect world. Yet this is a God whose existence cannot be proved; who needs no revelation, needs no Christ to enter the world and suffer on a cross, no Bible but the inner voice of conscience calling us towards the distant image of God. Ethics, considerations of right conduct, have dethroned dogmatic theology in the Kantian world-view. The science which had started with the mystical humanists of the Renaissance, and which in the seventeenth century had left this mysticism behind to create a machine-like universe stripped of morality, had now created its own agenda for religion. What would happen to the Christianity which had forged its image in a world shaped by Plato and Aristotle? Nor was this the only challenge which the Western church faced as the eighteenth century drew to its close. England and France were producing two contrasting revolutions which in combination would prove devastating to the religious structures built up in Europe since the time of Constantine.

Chronology for Chapter Fifteen

1694	Bank of England founded
1708	Abraham Darby founds Coalbrookdale Company, Shropshire
1714	Queen Anne is dead
1755	Robert Clive defeats Bengali allies of French, Battle of Plassey
1759	First large-scale canal for transport, Worsley to Manchester
1772	'Enlightened Despots' make first Partition of Poland
1773	Jesuit Order dissolved by Pope Clement XIV
1778	Iron Bridge built near Coalbrookdale by Darbys
1787	French government bankrupt
1788	First permanent European settlement, Australia
1789	Elements of French Estates declare themselves the National Assembly
1790	French Civil Constitution of the Clergy passed
1791	Louis XVI of France arrested. French Republic declared
1792	France declares war on Holy Roman Emperor
1793	Execution of Louis XVI and family; height of the 'Terror'
1795	London Missionary Society (at first interdenominational) founded
1799	Napoleon Bonaparte's *coup d'état*
1801	Concordat between Napoleon and Pope Pius VII
1815	Napoleon's final defeat at Battle of Waterloo
1825	First steam-powered passenger railway, Stockton to Darlington
1839	Louis Blanc, *The Organization of Labour* published
1842	Chinese Empire first forced to make concessions to Europeans
1848	Communist Manifesto published
1854	US Commodore Perry makes contact with Japanese government
1864	First Socialist International meets
1866	Transatlantic telegraph cable laid
1885	Murder of General Charles Gordon, Khartoum: sensation in Britain
1896	Abyssinians defeat Italians, Battle of Adowa
1905	End of Russo-Japanese War with Japanese victory
1911	Chinese Empire replaced by Republic
1914	First World War breaks out
1917	Russian Empire collapses. Bolshevik (Communist) regime eventually replaces Social Democratic Republic
1921	Bolsheviks win civil war in Russia
1935	Mussolini invades and conquers Abyssinia
1942	Japanese capture Singapore from British
1949	Mainland China taken over by Communists
1957	First European African colony to achieve independence: Ghana (Gold Coast)

Chapter Fifteen

Two Secular Revolutions (1700 to 1900)

The first meaning of the word 'revolution' was the one which has survived in modern engineering: a complete circle of motion, or an event in which circumstances went round full circle to where they had begun. During the eighteenth century this meaning shifted when it referred to human affairs, and a 'revolution' became an event or series of events which totally and permanently changed a situation. This certainly fits two great events of the eighteenth century which both guaranteed that things could never be the same again in Europe: the first Industrial Revolution, which took its origins in England, and the Revolution of 1789 in France.

The English Industrial Revolution is not a single event and is not especially easy to pin down. We probably all have a vague picture in our minds of 'dark satanic mills', and we might have been to Ironbridge in Shropshire to see a scatter of factories and settlements in a superb valley site which calls itself 'the cradle of the Industrial Revolution'. We can say about these events that the Industrial Revolution involved a shift in the source of national wealth from farm produce to manufactured goods, as long as we remember that long before the Industrial Revolution, much of England's wealth came from the large-scale manufacture of cloth. We can point to the new importance in the manufacturing economy of machines with moving parts, which meant that production became concentrated in factory units to make it possible to use such machines on a large scale. Here, too, we have to be careful. The process of mechanization was a slow one, and for well over a century from 1700 it only applied in certain industries: pumping mines free of water, for instance, or in the spinning of thread for the textile industries. Outside these processes it might remain just as economical to use traditional hand-craft skills in production, and there might be no good alternative in any case: a mechanized process like the spinning of thread might well give a boost to a traditional craft like handloom weaving. The trees and farms of Ironbridge are a symbol of the fact that industry did not always generate great industrial towns, while England's greatest city, London, had very few factories up to 1900. To show how slowly the 'dark satanic mills' developed in the Industrial Revolution, it is worth noting that as late as 1838, less than half a million out of a total English labour force of seven million worked in factories.

A more straightforward criterion for tracking down the Industrial Revolution would be to look at the sources of power for productivity. The Revolution involved the use of energy sources in new ways: first, a much more systematic use of the power of running water to drive mills for industry, and then, a realization of the enormous possibilities for using the steam of boiling water to drive machines. Using these two sources of power also meant new opportunities to improve transport both of material and of people: water could be used in constructing artificial rivers (canals) to transport heavy goods beyond the range of the natural river system, while by the early nineteenth century, successful experiments were being made with steam-powered engines which could move from their fixed site. Combining these with the older idea of running vehicles on rails proved one of the most important features of Western civilization in the nineteenth century; railways were built everywhere. Steam power became the dominant force of the first Industrial Revolution; coal was its lifeblood, just as oil became the lifeblood of the second Industrial Revolution of the twentieth century.

If there are problems in defining the Industrial Revolution, there are also difficulties and unresolved problems in explaining why it started in England in the eighteenth century. It is clear that by the end of the seventeenth century, England enjoyed a resourceful and imaginative system of farming for profit which was able to produce enough food to banish the threat of widespread famine from the kingdom: a most unusual achievement in Europe at the time, which encouraged population growth. This in turn both enlarged the home market and created a pool of cheap labour. It also meant that there was considerable surplus wealth to invest in production, and this was aided by the fact that before any other major competitor, England had developed a proper banking system able to provide credit for large-scale enterprise: a by-product of the English government's desperate need for money during the 1690s because of its heavy involvement in Continental wars.

The result was that well before the building of factories or the deployment of steam power became widespread, in fact during the early eighteenth century, England's manufacturing output began rising, and this rise became dramatic from about 1750. This led to a further rise in population: not because more children were surviving infancy or people were living longer, but because the new prosperity encouraged people to take the financial risk of getting married earlier in their lives and thus of having larger families. Normally such population rises brought their own auto-matic checks as food prices rose and made people poorer once more: one of the great remaining puzzles about late eighteenth-century England is how its economy had gained the resilience to keep food prices down as the population mushroomed, and how it could therefore escape the ancient poverty cycle to rush on with yet more population growth.

Whatever the explanation, once this had happened, England's growth in productivity through the nineteenth century would have the sure backing of cheap labour and high consumer demand. However terrible conditions might be in factories and industrial towns, the plain fact is that English people were taller, healthier, better fed and probably therefore happier in 1850 than in 1750. It was not surprising that English society was so self-confident and optimistic in this era. Where England showed the way, the rest of Europe and its satellites followed. Similar processes are percept-ible in France and the eastern United States from the 1830s, in Germany dramatically fast from the 1870s, and elsewhere in southern and eastern Europe much more patchily from around the same decade.

It has been necessary to give this rather lengthy explanation of the secular background to get a proper idea of the change which now confronted Christianity. It hardly mattered whether the new industrial society grew through the factory system or through the expansion of household-based production; the vastly-increased scale of production meant that the church was now faced with many more towns than it had ever had to cope with since the fall of the Western Roman Empire. The medieval and post-Reformation church had never shown itself well able to cope with large towns; the parish system perfected by Gregory VII's Reformation had been least effective in its efforts to contain urban dissent. In the short term, the benefit in the English Industrial Revolution went to the Dissenting bodies and the new structures of Methodism, which could create effective networks of preaching and pastoral care without the legal obstacles which the established Churches of England and Scotland faced in improving their response. In due course the established churches put their houses in order during the nineteenth century, and began to catch up.

However, although all churches continued to grow in numbers throughout the century, it was apparent from the 1880s in Britain that this growth was not keeping in step with population growth. The proportion of those having little or no contact with church life, already significant before the Industrial Revolution, began remorselessly to increase. Similar patterns emerged in most parts of industrialized Europe. What is puzzling is that in Europe's North American offshoot, the United States of America, the pattern was precisely the reverse, despite the fact that America's Industrial Revolution was much more quickly based on factories and large urban centres than was Britain's. When the English thirteen colonies successfully rebelled against the mother country in 1776–83, it has been calculated that no more than ten per cent of the American population were full members of the various churches: a figure not that different from church membership in Britain at the present day. Yet throughout the nineteenth century, European immigration and a constant return to the 'Great Awakenings' mechanism of revival resulted in a steady rise of corporate Christian practice, which actually accelerated in the twentieth century after the Second World War. By 1960 American church membership was around seventy per cent, and even after the national anxieties and upheavals of the 1960s, it remains at a far higher level than in industrialized northern Europe.

The world expansion of the industrial West

The new resources of power, speed and productivity within the Western world gave it an unprecedented advantage over every other world culture; this was not an advantage which was destined to last more than a century and a half from 1800, but while it did, the effects were devastating. When this advantage was translated into an advantage in military technology, no other world power could beat a Western army unless the Westerners displayed extreme incompetence. This was a crushing psychological blow to the non-Christian civilizations. Islam, whose story of world expansion had been continuous since its seventh-century foundation (with the hard-fought exception of medieval and early modern Europe), now entered a phase of stagnation and defensiveness which did not end until the late twentieth century. China, whose ancient civilization had always been able to afford a serene lack of curiosity about the rest of the world, found from about 1800 that it was incapable of resisting outside interference in its affairs; its Empire was reduced to a plaything of rival European interests, and was eventually so discredited among its own people as to be overthrown in 1911. The Confucian and Buddhist traditions which upheld Chinese society have yet to make a full recovery. Buddhist and Hindu culture in India suffered similarly from the eighteenth- and nineteenth-century British takeover. It was the Japanese, with a traditional curiosity about aliens wholly exceptional among their neighbours, who were first to see that their unusually abrupt and complete humiliation at the hands of Westerners was best remedied by a vigorous imitation of the industry which lay behind Western success.

Part of the urge to expand Western European dominance in the world took the form of building up land empires over subject peoples overseas: a fairly brief episode in the history of Western development, lasting about two centuries from 1750, but one of profound significance. Previously no Western state had tried to conquer new lands on a large scale unless it wished to send its people there to make a new home: this had been the pattern with the Spanish and Portuguese empires in South America and the English and French empires in North America. Now a new move came, largely thanks to a French commander in India, Joseph Francois Dupleix. In the early eighteenth century, Dupleix realized that the Indian states which apparently menaced the survival of the small European coastal strongholds were much weaker than they looked, and that with improving European weaponry it might be possible actually to take them over and rule them in European interests. His idea was filched and used with brilliant success by the British general Robert Clive, so India became an overwhelmingly British colonial possession. However, this eighteenth-century initiative was followed up by all the major European states except the internally troubled Austro-Hungarian monarchy during the nineteenth century. Russia simply continued its long march eastward into Asia; the French put down roots in Indochina and Algeria, the British followed up their Indian success by starting new settler colonies in Australia and New Zealand.

Africa generally came rather late in the order of European expansion. The main powers already there, Britain and Portugal, were at first reluctant to expand their existing trading stations, and the chief initiative for Britain came from one individual, Cecil Rhodes, who pressed British interests northwards from Cape Colony in the hope of creating a continuous band of British territory right through the Continent up to Egypt. In the 1880s British public opinion swung strongly in favour of African conquests after the heroic absurdities of General Charles Gordon's exploits and eventual murder in the Sudan, and after this no British government dared to do much to resist the urge to acquisition. The French story was equally strange: a huge French African empire was created from the 1880s by a military clique of dissatisfied royalists who were hungry to serve their country but hated the Republican regime back home; once their military adventures had shown spectacular success, the Republican government had to back their efforts to avoid being upstaged.

At much the same time, the newly-created nation-states of Italy and Germany demanded a share of the colonial cake as a proof of their national status, while even little Belgium acquired an enormous empire in the Congo by an accident: the private enterprise of the Belgian king which led to a colonial regime so spectacularly inefficient and brutal that the Belgian government was forced to take it over. The older empires of the Spanish, the Portuguese and the Dutch imitated these moves by expanding out from their previously-held colonial outposts. By the end of the nineteenth century, only the empire of Abyssinia (Ethiopia), with its own ancient and very Africanized form of Monophysite Christianity, had successfully defended itself against European colonial interference.

The mid-eighteenth-century change in the mood of the secular powers of Europe was quickly followed by a change in the mood of the churches. Roman Catholic missionary work ran out of steam during the eighteenth century, particularly after the early blow of the Jesuit defeat in the controversy over traditional rites (see above, Chapter Twelve) and the later complete dissolution of the Jesuit Order in 1773. Under the impulse of the Evangelical Revival, Protestantism began renewing the European effort in its own way; many of the main missionary societies in England and the United States date from the turn of the eighteenth and nineteenth centuries, while eventually the Presbyterian Church of Scotland overcame its Calvinist doubts about the relationship between predestination and overseas missions, and put its own effort into the work. Evangelical enthusiasm was stimulated by the French revolutionary wars of the 1790s, which many saw as a sign of the Last Days; so it became an urgent task to preach the Good News. Others, with a sudden consciousness of guilt at the Christian West's part in the slave trade, felt that they must make amends by preaching the gospel. Roman Catholicism also recovered its morale in the early nineteenth century; as the relationship with the older Catholic colonial powers became less significant, the Catholic Church was less hampered in the mission field by the traditional restrictions which these governments had imposed for reasons of state.

One can see behind this new missionary energy a reflection of the boundless energy and confidence of the early generations of Industrial Revolution society. Missionaries tended to see the new marvels of Western ingenuity as a gift from God intended to bring happiness and freedom from want to the whole world. After all, the results were there for all to see in Western Europe; and no one could deny that nineteenth-century extensions of the Industrial Revolution like the steam-ship and the electric telegraph made the organization and sustaining of missionary effort a good deal easier. It was notable that the countries most affected by the Industrial Revolution were also those most active in the mission field: Britain, the United States, France, Belgium, north Germany, north Italy. The missionaries' work tended to begin before the European territorial empires were created, particularly in Africa, but they generally encouraged the arrival of European military protection and usually benefited from the establishment of colonial regimes. Most colonial governments saw the work of the missionaries as a cheap way of bringing the culture of the mother country to native peoples; so anti-clerical French Republican governments were happy to see royalist monks working in west Africa, if they brought French civilization to their flocks. In fairness, it should be said that many colonial administrators were also sincerely convinced of the need of their subject peoples to hear of the saving power of the gospel.

The great historian of missionary effort K.S. Latourette called the period 1800–1914 'the Great Century' for Christian mission. It was a time of much heroism and solid achievement, and although the missionaries repeated many of the mistakes of the Counter-Reformation missions, as they got to know and love their people, they began to realize that Western European culture might not necessarily be superior to the cultures which it met: that Western European culture was not necessarily to be identified with Christianity. This adjustment would have to be made, since by the beginning of the twentieth century, non-European perceptions of Europe began to change.

Feelings of helplessness in the face of European superiority were transformed by the shattering defeat which the Japanese were able to inflict on the Russian Empire in a war of 1904–5; Westerners were not invincible after all. Then in 1914, all the major European powers became involved in fighting each other, and they spread this conflict throughout their colonial empires, even using armies drawn from their non-European subjects to fight in Europe. The horrific waste of the war in lives, property and human happiness made it very difficult to believe that the supposedly Christian civilization of Industrial Europe had much superior virtue to any other culture. In addition, ironically, a new Western interest in Asian religion brought back self-confidence to the East: for instance in Sri Lanka (the British colony of Ceylon), it was American and British enthusiasts for Buddhism who helped to restore the shattered morale of the Buddhists against the nineteenth-century Christian missions.

European prestige suffered further. In both Africa and America, black opinion was outraged when the Western democracies made no more than token efforts to oppose Mussolini's Italian Fascist invasion of Abyssinia in 1935. The rapid Japanese success against the British and Dutch in the Second World War was another blow; in their conquests, the Japanese deliberately appealed to Asian nationalism against European interference. Although they failed in their greatest goal of overthrowing the British power in India, and they were eventually defeated in 1945 with American help, within three decades of the end of the Second World War, nearly all European powers had dismantled the formal apparatus of rule in their overseas colonies: a startingly rapid end to a system of power.

Now the Asian territories of Russia and the detached bastion of white rule in South Africa are the only substantial survivals of empire, although the West continues to exercise an informal empire over its former territories through its economic strength: probably a more profitable form of control than the tedious business of administration in the old imperial system. The territories formerly controlled by the nineteenth-century European Great Powers have come to be known as the 'The Third World'. In the middle of an atmosphere of rejection of the West coupled with Third World resentment at the West's continuing role in its old empires, the Christianity brought by the missionaries struggles to find a new role and a new language. Can it find a mature relationship with a past rooted in Western self-confidence and in the achievements of the Industrial Revolution?

The French Revolution

European society began the eighteenth century still clinging to the God-centred past, despite all the effects of Newtonian science and the gradual corrosion brought by rational philosophy. Queen Anne of England was still regularly called upon to 'touch' her subjects to use her God-given powers in curing the disease called scrofula or 'the King's Evil': a Holy Roman Emperor ruled from Vienna, and a 'Most Christian King' of France ruled from Versailles. By the end of the eighteenth century all this had changed; many of the traditional monarchies survived, but they had had to fight for their lives, and they could never again claim the sacred quality or the automatic respect which they had once possessed. There were new bases for power in Europe, and this was thanks to the chain of events which began in France in 1789. Things changed so much and so rapidly that already in the 1790s, Frenchmen were speaking of the pre-1789 past as the *ancien regime* – the former state of things.

The *ancien regime* of which they spoke was not exactly a medi-

eval world, but a development from it. It was dominated by a set
of monarchs who tried to make their power as complete as possible:
figures like King Frederic the Great of Prussia, the Empresses
Elizabeth and Catherine the Great of Russia, the Emperor
Leopold of Austria. They have been labelled the 'Enlightened
Despots' because they took an interest in the 'Enlightenment'
philosophy of the day, and flattered the *philosophes* into thinking
that their ideas were shaping government policy, but there was
really precious little that was enlightened about these rulers. At
best their concerns could be called enlightened selfishness: their
main preoccupation was increasing their own power and grabbing
territory, and for this, huge standing armies were necessary.
Medieval tradition, ancient systems of local law or privilege and
the confusions of government which the 'Despots' inherited were
an obstacle to their plans, making their countries inefficient and
making it difficult to collect taxes to pay for their armies.

The Despots were therefore concerned to achieve efficiency;
they had little concern to benefit the people at large if this clashed
with their own interests. Medieval institutions were left alone if
they did not get in the way; there was no change for change's sake.
However, any rival power must be crushed. If the church stood in
the government's way, the church too must be reformed and made
harmless; so Catholic monarchs brought mounting pressure on
successive Popes to dissolve the entire Jesuit Order because they
resented its loyalty to the Papacy. They finally bullied the Pope
into doing so in 1773. Religious passions had shifted so far from
the fierce confessional warfare of the Reformation century that
between 1772 and 1795 Catholic, Protestant and Orthodox Great
Powers (Austria, Prussia and Russia respectively) amicably got
together to divide up the Catholic kingdom of Poland between
them.

The eighteenth-century world was thus one of curious contrasts
between government-sponsored change and vigorous survival
from the past. The Roman Catholic Church was actually under
attack from Catholic monarchs, yet at the same time, it was full of
life and energy, with its leading clergy still patiently working away
at the huge task of carrying out the reforms mapped out two
centuries before at the Council of Trent. The paradoxes would
perhaps inevitably have been resolved, but the French Revolution
would do this in an unexpectedly brutal fashion. Few could have

predicted that France would be the seat of revolution. It was still the leading state in Europe, its language and its Enlightenment culture respected throughout the Continent. Since the French Revolution, the English have built up their own rather complacent myth about the weaknesses of pre-Revolution France, but this owes more to the brilliant presentation of Charles Dickens's novel *A Tale of Two Cities* than to historical fact. In reality, the French economy was as buoyant as the English, its divisions between nobleman and commoner, rich and poor, no worse than in England, and its established Catholic Church no more or no less in need of drastic reform than the contemporary Church of England.

The two great differences between England and France were that France had never established a proper national banking and credit system, and that it had not retained a national representative body which could co-operate with the monarchy in raising government money. Since France was very frequently engaged in major wars, this was a disastrous combination even when France was victorious, as happened when the French supported Britain's American colonists in their War of Independence from 1776 to 1783. By 1787 the French government faced bankruptcy, and it had no effective means of cutting though France's archaic revenue system to tap the greatest source of national wealth: land. If it were to impose a land tax, it realized that it would offend a huge range of vested interests from dukes to peasants. An assembly of notables called in 1787 refused to help; so did an assembly of the clergy, who had jealously guarded their ancient right to tax themselves. However, the clergy raised the whole level of the argument by pointing out that their surviving privileges were a reminder that once all taxation had been levied with the consent of the people, through a representative institution known as the States General which had somewhat resembled the surviving British Parliament.

The idea of reviving the States General met with wide enthusiasm, and if King Louis XVI and his successive ministers had been more adroit in using it, they might well have carried out substantial reform without disaster. However, Louis was not a decisive man; having assembled the States General by 1789, he could not make his mind up on vital procedural matters. In an atmosphere of expectation and with a torrent of suspicions and grievances already released by the summoning of the delegates, such hesitation proved fatal. On 17 June 1789 the 'Third Estate' (those delegates who were neither clergy nor noblemen) declared themselves to be a National Assembly and were soon joined by dissident clergy and noblemen from the First and Second Estates. Further clumsy moves from the King ensured that he never regained control of the situation, and rural France fell into turmoil. Meanwhile the Assembly declared all church property confiscated to the state, and on 26 August 1789 it passed a Declaration of the Rights of Man, owing much to the American Declaration of Independence thirteen years before. It is worth noting what a break with the past this was: a declaration of rights and not of duties. This was perhaps the high-water-mark of eighteenth-century optimism; it took half a decade of the horrors of war and revolution before a declaration of duties came as well (1795).

Even at this stage it was likely that France would develop a monarchy under a constitution, like a tidier version of the English system, but it was the religious question which pushed events a stage further. The National Assembly was as determined to reform the church as it was to reform everything else; its plan was to create a national church like that in England, but Catholic in doctrine and without the abuses of the Anglican structures. In this so-called 'Civil Constitution of the Clergy', passed in 1790, the Pope was to have no power, and would merely be accorded respect. Much of this reflected traditional French attitudes of independence towards Rome, but the fact that the Assembly paid no attention to what the Pope might think of the changes horrified many of the clergy who had gone along with everything that had happened so far. The French church was split between those who would accept the Civil Constitution and those who rejected it, the second group being much strengthened when the Pope specifically condemned the new package in 1791. The King, a devout Catholic, was increasingly identified with the opponents of the Civil Constitution, and when he failed in an attempt to flee the country in 1791, he was deprived of all power.

It was more or less inevitable, as events swept them on, that the Assembly should declare war on the traditional European Powers, beginning in 1792 with the bulwark of the old system, the Holy Roman Emperor. The idea of peaceful coexistence between different political systems hardly existed. However, war had a terrible effect on the Revolution. In 1792–3, spurred on by provincial royalist rebellions, the state began large-scale executions of its aristocratic and clerical enemies, trivial in numbers by modern standards of terror, but horrifying at the time, particularly since they included nearly all available members of the French royal family; in the process, Europe's first single-party dictatorship in the name of the people had emerged. What was especially new about this regime (contrasting, for instance, with the sixteenth-century horrors of the Anabaptists in Münster) was that its most extreme leaders regarded any form of Christian faith as a relic of the old world which they were out to destroy.

The Revolution which had begun with a sincere attempt to improve the church now sought to replace it with a synthetic religion constructed out of classical mythology and symbolism mixed up with the eighteenth century's celebration of human reason: the Christian calendar of years and months was abolished, monasteries closed, churches desecrated. Much of this outburst was imposed by government and bureaucratic decree; but much welled out of ordinary people, striking out at anything which spoke to them of past authority. Although the campaign of active de-Christianization completely petered out by the end of the decade, the Revolution had served long-term notice that Christianity would be seen as an enemy of the new world. In the short term, the campaign had wrecked the experiment of the Constitutional Church, an ally of the Revolution which was caught miserably between the de-Christianizers and those who were fighting the Revolution.

Napoleon and the Concordat

As the war dragged on, the French people became increasingly disillusioned with their masters; the church had been shattered apparently to no purpose, and since it had a virtual monopoly on caring for the poor and helpless before the Revolution, it was the weakest of the people who had suffered most by the destruction of church institutions. Perhaps inevitably, the most successful of the Revolution's generals, the Corsican Napoleon Bonaparte, gained more and more public support, in contrast with the revolutionary government's waning popularity. It would have taken a man with no ambition to resist this temptation, and Napoleon did not; he staged a *coup d'état* in 1799, and successive plebiscites, only partially rigged, gave overwhelming majorities to his assumption first of the Republican title of First Consul and later of Emperor of the French. Right up to the final collapse of his extraordinary military conquests in 1813–14, Napoleon continued to enjoy widespread support throughout France.

An astute politician as well as a brilliant general, Napoleon attached great importance to religion. This was not because he cared about it personally, but because he saw that other people cared about it a great deal. The Republic had made the mistake of attacking the church; now if he was to unite France, he would have to come to an understanding with this institution which so controlled human emotions. This would not merely be useful in France, but also throughout the large areas of Catholic Europe which his conquests brought under French rule. If he was to find an agreement to cover all these territories, he needed to deal not simply with the crippled and resentful French church; inevitably he would have to approach the Pope. Accordingly in 1801, negotiations between Napoleon and Pope Pius VII resulted in the signing of an agreement known as a Concordat which would be the model for many similar agreements between the Papacy and a variety of world governments during the nineteenth and twentieth centuries.

This Concordat was not just important for its content, which extensively reorganized the French church, but for its effect on the Pope's position. The eighteenth century had been a low point in papal fortunes, with European monarchs using or ignoring the Papacy as they pleased; the Revolution seemed to be continuing this process when revolutionary armies arrested Pius VI and watched him die in a French exile in 1799. Now the new Pope was negotiating terms for the whole French church, which had once prided itself on its independence. The new structure of appointments and hierarchy among the clergy gave the Pope much more power, a move which many lower clergy welcomed since it was likely to curb the powers of their immediate superiors the bishops. Yet the bishops themselves had reason to welcome papal power; they had been badly frightened by the power and anti-clericalism of the Revolutionary state.

The new position of the Pope was symbolized when in 1802 he agreed to be present at the coronation ceremony for Napoleon as Emperor in the Cathedral of *Notre Dame de Paris*: a curious reconciliation of the traditional church with the new people's state as Napoleon placed on his own head the crown which the people's armies had won for him. Popular enthusiasm for the Pope on this visit to Paris surprised everyone; it was the beginning of a new affection for the person of the Pope which would be of great importance in further strengthening the position of the Papacy within the church during the nineteenth and twentieth centuries. This popular mood was only strengthened when Napoleon and the Pope quarrelled about the future of papal territories in Italy, and the Emperor imprisoned Pius for years on end; significantly, even in Protestant England, centuries-old prejudices were weakened by human sympathy.

Fallout of Revolution: nationalism, liberalism, socialism

In 1815 a combination of the Revolution's enemies among the great powers of Europe finally defeated Napoleon and restored the monarchy of the Bourbon family to France; yet the past could never be restored. Throughout Europe, people had been given visions of new possibilities, particularly the possibility of governing their own lives. The French revolutionaries' slogan of 'liberty, equality, fraternity' would not be forgotten. The French National Assembly created a citizen army, whose members were the state, and who therefore had a right to a direct say in it. This implied a new type of politics, different from the traditional view of political representation seen for instance in British parliamentary life, where wealth, privilege, talent or the possession of property were the main qualifications for having a say in the nation's affairs. Nationalism might thus imitate the French example in looking to the rule of the people; it might also react against the memory of the French, for many of the territories which the French Revolution's armies overran gained a full sense of national unity throught their resentment at this foreign intervention. Belgium, Italy and Germany all built up national identities during the nine-teenth century on this basis, overturning ancient political struc-tures in the process. Their rhetoric of national resistance provided a model for the twentieth-century struggles of non-European colonial peoples against European colonial governments.

Alongside nationalism, the French Revolution produced the politics of liberalism. Although this was a creed of revolution, it was largely the revolution of a new élite against an old. The French

Revolution combined with the growing effects of the Industrial Revolution in challenging aristocracies and monarchies which for hundreds of years had based their wealth and power on farming. Even in the pre-Industrial Revolution France of 1789, the main impulse to overthrow the *ancien regime* came from groups which lay outside the landed élite: lawyers, journalists, people involved in commerce, workers in the skilled trades of the cities – what is very clumsily but almost unavoidably called the middle class. The Industrial Revolution greatly increased this group in numbers and wealth. In nineteenth-century Europe, in the more decorous politics of England just as in the turbulence of many Continental states, it was middle class groups who now sought to gain political institutions which would give them an appropriate say in national affairs: to share power with the landed aristocracy, and to gain the right to express their opinions as they wished. This was the politics of liberalism.

Often liberals saw the church as an ally of the aristocracy, especially when churchmen were so affected by their sufferings in the Revolution that they threw their weight against any idea of change. Liberals were anxious to destroy the church's remaining social privileges, particularly because it tried to influence the minds of the young in schools; control of education became one of the great political battle-grounds of nineteenth-century Europe. Liberalism was therefore a word to send shivers down the spines of conservative churchmen and aristocrats throughout nineteenth-century Europe, but there was a far more fundamental challenge to the structures of European government which also took its roots in the ideas of 1789.

If the liberals had used the rhetoric of liberty and equality, new groups calling themselves socialists also began to speak of the third element of the revolutionary slogan, fraternity: the brotherhood of all people against the oppression of existing human organizations. Once more growing out of the optimism of eighteenth-century views of the human condition, socialists could assert that people are naturally good, and that without the distortions of inequality or poverty, they will naturally behave to one another as brothers.

The obvious injustices of factory conditions at their worst were a spur from the Industrial Revolution to add to the ideas of the French Revolution. Early socialists tended to react against industrial society and to assume that the only way of achieving their aims would be to reject the world of factories; during the early decades of the nineteenth century, their main efforts were channelled into setting up new and agriculturally-based communities which would not be tainted by industrial misery, often placed in the New World where there was available land and no existing conditions of social inequality. Such efforts usually ended in failure; they could easily be dismissed as romantic and backward-looking. Not surprisingly, the hard-pressed governments of early nineteenth-century Europe felt that such groups were less of a threat to their survival than the more radical forms of liberalism.

It took a new generation of theorists to transform socialism: in France, Louis Blanc advocated a state-run socialism, in a state which would be run by the people. Friedrich Engels used his links with English industry to construct an accurate description of the wrongs of English society, going on to identify the cause and the solution in class conflict. Above all, the work of Karl Marx supplied a more rigorous system and a philosophy both of the past and of the future to socialist ideas and rhetoric. Moreover, as early as 1844, Marx was writing of the need to abolish religion, since it was a distraction from the task of freeing the people from their burdens.

This is not the place to describe either Marxism or its effect on the nineteenth- and twentieth-century world: it is enough to say that while the Western church in most of its branches has had considerable success in absorbing the rhetoric of liberty, equality and human rights as expressed in the tradition of nineteenth- and twentieth-century liberalism, it still faces very serious confrontations with many forms of socialism. The conflict is especially bitter with those regimes which claim that their politics and policies are based on the philosophy of Marx. The evidence of Christian survival in Communist Russia or of its new vigour among the Christian minority in China suggests that Christianity will find an accepted place in these cultures as it did within the hostile world of Roman paganism: yet that prompts the question as to whether it will repeat the early Christians' success in becoming a dominant force. The great difference is that Western Christendom, the world of Constantine, has itself produced revolutions of the mind which make the task infinitely more difficult and perhaps undesirable. It is these revolutions which we examine in our last two chapters.

Chronology for Chapter Sixteen

Chapter Sixteen

Revolutions of the Mind
(1800 to 1900)

We have surveyed the social and the political revolution which began in the eighteenth century and whose full consequences were seen during the nineteenth; we have also seen how these movements gave rise to new ways of looking at society and politics in the form of liberalism and socialism. There were, however, further transformations in the way that Western Europe viewed itself and its faith which developed alongside these revolutions, and which themselves deserve the description revolutionary. These were the outworkings of the great seventeenth- and eighteenth-century changes in science and philosophy which we have already examined in Chapter Fourteen. They can be summarized under three headings: the continuing effect of Kant's thought, the development of science, and the impact of new ways of looking at the Bible.

The legacy of Kant

Once something has been said, it can never be unsaid. It was impossible for anyone who thought about theology and philosophy not to sense the effect of Kant's restructuring of Western thought, although the effect might be indirect and gradual, and might inspire horror rather than excitement. The chief developments from Kant's principles predictably occurred in his own world of northern European Lutheranism. Kant's ideas could be claimed either to destroy Christianity or to state it anew: for the German university lecturer Friedrich Schleiermacher, they were the basis for a new and positive way of looking at the Protestant tradition.

Schleiermacher took up Kant's notion of individual conscience, the consciousness that there are paths of morality which we are forced to follow to be true to ourselves, and said that this was equally true of the consciousness of religion. Consciousness, in other words, was not just a cold perception of what must be done, but was a warm sense of what was holy and dependable and what should be loved: a sense of God.

Schleiermacher's ideas were particularly significant because almost for the first time in the Western Protestant tradition, they put a positive value on the other great world faiths which had been entering European consciousness since the Iberian conquests of the sixteenth century. Catholic theology had always been more ready than Protestant to talk of reason alongside revelation as one of the ways in which human beings come to know God; therefore it was easier for some Catholic theologians to see virtue in the belief-systems of other religions than it was for those who followed the emphasis of the Protestant reformers on the unique revealed truth of the Christian scriptures. Now Schleiermacher could say that the consciousness of God lay at the foundation of all religions: that there was in each an element of revelation. The unique gift of Christianity was the person of Jesus, who represented the most perfect consciousness of God that there could be. Sin was the opposite end of the spectrum: an infinite distance in consciousness from God. Here was a theology which emphasized the generosity and the tolerance of the faith. It would be the basis of the liberal version of the Protestant tradition which would be increasingly dominant in Protestant churches until challenged by a new appeal to the tradition of the Reformers in the twentieth century.

With Georg Wilhelm Friedrich Hegel we see another German academic using Kant's ideas in a very different way. Although Hegel remained an orthodox Lutheran all his life, and his ideas influenced many theologians and biblical scholars during the nineteenth century, he was never drawn by the personal emotion which made Schleiermacher treasure and build on the devotion of German Pietism. He was concerned to build a system of knowledge and of being which would dwarf the achievements of Aristotle in logic and go beyond the scepticism of Kant. Although, like Kant, he took the human consciousness as his starting-point, he denied that anything was beyond the mind's knowledge. For Hegel, our consciousness is a progress towards absolute knowledge of the Absolute, the Spirit which can be identified with the Christian God. All things are therefore in a state of progress, or becoming, a process which is achieved by the dialectic principle: a *thesis* is followed or met by an *antithesis*, and the reaction between the two in turn produces a *synthesis* which reaches a higher level than either. Such syntheses at their higher resolutions can only be understood by a philosophical élite, so all religions are a mediation of these higher truths to those who are less able to perceive them; therefore we have another way of appreciating the merits of all world faiths which contrasts with the approach of Schleiermacher.

Hegel insisted that among all the religions which gave an image of truth, Christianity was the most perfect because its truths corresponded exactly with the truths set forth in his philosophical system. However, many who admired Hegel's thought rejected Christianity altogether. For instance, quite early in his career, Karl Marx came to see the idea of God merely as a human picture, which was as much a token currency with a power to be manipulated for good or evil as was a coinage of money; yet for Marx, the image of Hegel's dialectical process, rolling majestically and unavoidably along to produce the structures and societies of the material world, remained a central reality when he rejected anything that the old German professor would have recognized as religious truth.

To many who reflected on their life and destiny during the nineteenth century, Hegel was like a remote and awe-inspiring father; the only way in which they could achieve adulthood was to rebel against him. This is seen at its most dramatic and far-reaching in the writings of the Danish philosopher Søren Kierkegaard. When Kierkegaard was a university student, the thought of Hegel saturated the university teaching in his country, but it was not simple student rebellion which led him to reject the monumental systems of the great man. Kierkegaard's personal history was full of frustration and tragedy; the mould was set in the unhappiness of a childhood dominated by a father whose profound sense of guilt harked back to the memory of his poverty-stricken youth, when he had solemnly cursed God, and to his hasty second marriage to his pregnant housekeeper, Søren's mother. This background of anguish eventually forced Søren to disaster in his rejection of the one great love of his life, his fiancée Regina Olsen, a catastrophe which left him wondering for the rest of his life whether he had thrown away his one chance of escaping into happiness.

These personal miseries are inseparable from the direction of Kierkegaard's thought. His experience focussed him on the inner life of the individual; he saw Hegel's pursuit of the Absolute as a betrayal of the individual. To this formation of the individual and of human dignity in the face of all tragedy, Kierkegaard brought a profound and intensely personal version of Christian faith, a faith beyond dogma and system. Sin was not an impersonal part of a Hegelian process, it was a dark half of human existence, a stark alternative to the path which led to Christ. In the conflict between sin and Christ, there could be no compromises, no comfort: so Kierkegaard came to feel a profound loathing and contempt for the established Lutheran Church of his day, and caused a sensation in staid Denmark by his bitter attacks on the church and one of its most respected leaders. Many thought that he had gone mad, and it is not surprising that this curious figure, writing in one of Europe's lesser languages, did not have a speedy impact in the nineteenth century. In the troubles of our own time, his passionate focus on the sufferings and the loneliness of a God-Man on the cross have taken on a new significance for Western Christianity.

To see how far post-Kantian European thought had travelled from the world of Aquinas, Ockham, Luther and Calvin, one need only look at the writings of Friedrich Nietzsche. The son of a Lutheran pastor, Nietzsche experienced his moment of revelation like Paul, Augustine and Luther before him: but for him, this moment – in August 1881 – was an exhilarating sense of the meaninglessness and absurdity of human existence. He felt that if we can accept this, we will achieve freedom, and can truly affirm the world of our being. For this to happen, it is necessary for the God outside to die. Nietzsche saw Christ as a figure who denied the world: he was an example to be avoided, not to be followed. In this, Nietzsche was perhaps reflecting a Protestant Christianity which had emphasized its separation from the world and which had made Christ a purely spiritual figure, less than a man in being fully a God. Perhaps he was teaching the church a lesson which it needed to learn. Yet for him, and for many twentieth-century Europeans who have only the vaguest idea how to spell his name, God was dead.

Science in the nineteenth century: Darwin

Long before Nietzsche made his astonished and liberating discovery of God's death, the physics pioneered by Sir Isaac Newton had been slowly sucking the world dry of divine life and turning it into a well-regulated machine built of easily-defined matter, in which disputes about fact could be decided as far as was necessary for practical purposes by experiments. The matter-of-factness of this universe, its divorce of matter from spirit, went on worrying scientists who felt a commitment to religion; it is no coincidence that many eminent explorers of the world of physics and chemistry were affected by the late-nineteenth-century craze for spiritualism. This was a movement which seemed able to restore the connection between the material and the spiritual by 'séances' which closely resembled the method of the scientific experiment. It was a comforting reconciliation after a painful separation.

However, the one basis of the Newtonian system which had appeared to safeguard God's position was its place for him as creator. This would change in the nineteenth century. Throughout the eighteenth century, nothing seemed to suggest that any of the discoveries of science denied the biblical idea of a benevolent maker of the Universe. Indeed, the mood of intelligent Christians in the eighteenth century was symbolized by the immense popularity in England of a book by the Cambridge mathematician and theologian William Paley, the *View of the Evidences of Christianity* (1794); this was the book which used the image of 'God the watchmaker', and its argument for God's existence was based on the evidences of design in creation.

With this background, the enthusiasm for geology which developed especially in England at the end of the eighteenth century seemed a buttress and not a threat to theology, and it was not an accident that many leading geologists of the period were devout and orthodox Anglican clergy. Even when they found rocks of such antiquity that the traditional date of the biblical creation in 4004 BC was obviously wrong, this was no problem for their faith; the Creation stories of Genesis were merely speaking figuratively of the timespans involved in God's plan. As extinct fossil species were recognized, this was an additional proof of God's providence. All earthly things have a tendency to decay, as the inevitable consequence of the Fall described in Genesis, and God had provided for their replacement by creating new species with which to delight his earthly subjects.

This picture was abruptly challenged by the work of a pious naturalist and prospective clergyman called Charles Darwin, observing natural phenomena on the remote Pacific islands of the Galapagos in 1835. Darwin noted how remarkably different the species of animal and plant life were here from anywhere else, and at first he marvelled at the insight which this gave into what God's creation had originally been like. However, in 1837 while he was reflecting on what he had seen, a wholly new idea came to him: perhaps these new species were not a relic of some primitive Eden, but were instead the end-product of an immensely long chain of development in total isolation from the rest of the world.

Over the next two years, he worked from this perception to produce a theory of evolution which totally contradicted the comforting world-view of Paley's book (previously among his most treasured authorities). The only way in which his data could make sense was to suppose that species battled for survival, and that evolution came when one slight adaptation of a species proved more successful than another in this battle: the process which he named 'natural selection'. God did not enter into the process, and there was nothing benevolent about the Providence which watched over it. At a stroke, Darwin had overturned reason as the handmaid of Christian revelation. Hegel had made the world of being and of ideas into a continuous struggle: now the struggle, mindless, endless and utterly selfish, held the natural world in its grip.

Between the publication of his ideas in *The Origin of Species* in 1859 and his later major book *The Descent of Man* in 1871, Darwin retreated from his insistence on natural selection; subsequent work on genetics stemming from the work of the Austrian monk Gregor Mendel shows that he should have stuck to his earlier insight. However, he remained unmoved in his central contention that humankind was not a special creation of God but was part of the chain of evolution, and there has been no serious scientific challenge to this position since. He was not the first person to talk of evolution; in 1844 the Scottish publisher and amateur geologist Robert Chambers had presented the idea in his *Vestiges of the Natural History of Creation*, in many ways a rather silly and credulous book.

It was easier to rebut Chambers than it was Darwin; from the

1860s, the idea of evolution gained wide acceptance throughout the educated public of the Western world. It fitted the Hegelian scheme of an evolutionary universe, and it chimed in with the optimistic belief in progress which was a natural doctrine for the vigorous and expansive society of the Industrial Revolution. Nor did it necessarily strike churchmen with dismay; many liberal theologians began constructing a new natural theology which saw evolution as a gradual unfolding of God's providential plan. By the end of the nineteenth century the Anglican Communion was headed by an Archbishop of Canterbury, Frederick Temple, who in earlier years had lectured in Oxford on the relation between religion and science with the assumption that evolution was basic truth. Nevertheless, for many sensitive people, Darwin's discoveries had irretrievably shaken the basis of revealed religion. Darwin himself seems to have lost any sense that there was any purpose in the universe, though he did so gently and undramatically; he seems to have felt that in the conflict between evolution and the biblical account of creation, it was all or nothing. The biblical account represented a false view of science, which must mean that everything else it contained was equally false, however beautiful the ideas of the New Testament might be. An article in *The Times* of 1864 spoke of the conflict between science and religion, and from then on, the idea was firmly fixed in the public mind that such a conflict existed. Some who felt that science had won the struggle were driven to explore the religions of the East; a curious construct of religious belief called 'Theosophy' (from its emphasis on the search for divine wisdom) gained an enthusiastic middle-class following during the 1890s. A few were driven by nineteenth-century seriousness to reject God in an almost religious way, founding atheist or humanist associations with Sunday Schools and even hymnbooks just like contemporary churches: one of their meeting-places was beautified by a stained glass window depicting Bernard Shaw.

Biblical criticism

Perhaps more fundamentally challenging to the authority of the Christian churches than the discoveries of nineteenth-century science was the work done in reassessing the text of the Christian scriptures. This reassessment was probably bound to come in an age which so valued the scientific fact, but its roots are really traceable to a parallel but distinct revolution in the way history was written and how historical evidence was weighed up: the growth of the liberal Western tradition which we examined in Chapter One. It had been the humanists of the early Renaissance who had started looking at texts to check their accuracy; we have seen how they included the Bible in this activity (above, Chapter Ten). An accurate text is a basic need as evidence in historical enquiry, but then it is a natural further step to start asking questions about this text. What were the intentions lying behind it? What were the assumptions which made it describe events in one way and not in another? Such questions were basic to the liberal Western mode of historical enquiry, which might describe itself as 'scientific' in the sense which Francis Bacon's successors as scientists up to the present day would understand the term.

Such scientific history was particularly developed by a group of seventeenth-century French Benedictine monks who gathered in a reformed version of the order known as the Congregation of St Maur. They extended their research from the familiar material of narrative historical sources like chronicles to official and legal documents; they would look at each document without sentiment or regard for its sacred character. It was inevitable that such attitudes should eventually affect the study of the Bible, and in the late eighteenth century this began happening in German universities; the trend was much encouraged by the great influence of Hegel's evolutionary approach to human affairs. Since Hegel saw the Christian God as an image of the Absolute Spirit, the stories about God in the Bible must also be images of greater truths which lay behind them. They could be described as myths, and that put them in the same league as the myths of other great world religions.

This attitude was given wide publicity by a young Lutheran pastor and lecturer at the University of Tübingen, David Friedrich Strauss. Strauss applied his enthusiasm for Hegel's symbolic approach to Christianity to writing a large-scale work on *The Life of Jesus Critically Examined* (usually known by its shortened German title *Leben Jesu*). The Jesus portrayed in the book was a great Jewish teacher, whose followers had retold the story of his life in the best way that they knew by borrowing a series of themes from the stories of the Old Testament and fitting their hero's life into them. There was no conscious deception involved, but the whole of the New Testament narratives were works of theological symbolism rather than of historic fact. The row which these views inspired was immense; Strauss's career was ruined, and he himself gradually moved further and further from Christianity in his disillusionment. For many, he had destroyed faith. Friedrich Engels was started on his long journey away from Lutheran Christianity by his feverish enthusiasm for the Hegelianism of the *Leben Jesu*.

Tübingen's transforming role in biblical scholarship did not stop with Strauss; Ferdinand Christian Baur took the treatment of the Bible as an historical document to the point where he argued that the whole New Testament was a product of violent conflicts between the Judaizing attitudes of Peter and the older disciples and the Gentile mission strategy of Paul; his approach long dominated the Tübingen style of biblical scholarship, feeding into the liberal Protestant tradition. The Roman Catholic world was affected as well; Joseph Ernest Renan was a pious young Breton destined for the priesthood who found that the combination of his reading in German biblical scholarship and his contempt for the superficial religion which he met with in Paris drove him completely beyond Christian faith; in 1863 he produced a *Life of Jesus* which utterly denied that this Jewish teacher had any divine character. The effect of the book was immense, and still has its echoes in statements like 'I believe that Jesus was just a good man'.

Alongside this complete rejection of the supernatural claims of Christianity, biblical scholars went on working on the New Testament texts in an attempt to identify a 'historical Jesus', a figure in whom the church could believe despite the huge gap which separated the thought-forms and assumptions of the first Christians from those of the nineteenth century. Right at the end of the period, the German theologian and medical missionary Albert Schweitzer wrote a work called *The Quest of the Historical Jesus* (1906), which argued that this preoccupation of liberal scholarship was misguided. The historical Christ which he saw in the Gospels was a figure who believed that the end of the world was coming immediately, and he had gone on to offer up his life in Jerusalem to hasten on the process. His career had therefore been built round a mistake; if there was a historical Jesus to be found in the Gospels, he was a figure of failure and tragedy who could only speak of failure and tragedy to the modern world. It was a vision of

Christianity which ran alongside the hopelessness and tragedy which the writings of Kierkegaard had expressed: a faith infinitely remote both from the old Christianity of dogmatic systems and from the rationalizing Christianity of the nineteenth-century liberals.

Reactions to revolution

I have now traced the many different ways in which the nineteenth century confronted the church with an entirely new situation; a challenge to its established position in society, to its alliance with the power of the state, to its authority to pronounce on the basis of its sacred writings, to the very way in which it worked out its thinking. How would it react? There is no doubt that the nineteenth century was an age of intense anxiety, not just for the institutional church. Although the Industrial Revolution had made Western Europe the temporary master of the world, and had endowed it with immense energy and hope for the future, this optimism was clouded by the shock of the French Revolution, with continuing bitter conflicts between those who honoured it and those who deplored it: shock, too, at the dramatic transformations which society was undergoing as a result of industrial change.

One symptom of this anxiety was a neurotic concern to find stability by protecting the family unit, which led to an obsession with sexuality and its control; for instance, the evils of masturbation produced a moral panic which was wholly new, and which was backed as much by the medical profession as by the church. At the same time, the emergence of reliable methods of birth control produced widespread fears that the family unit was under attack, and there were a series of sensational legal cases which represented an unsuccessful attempt to suppress artificial contraception. It was not surprising that at the end of the nineteenth century the Viennese psychiatrist Sigmund Freud should come to identify the sexual drive as the most important force lying behind human behaviour; nineteenth-century neurosis about the subject had long implied that this was so.

Although the church played a prominent part in this new emphasis on sexual regulation, it also tried to reassert its old authority in a variety of ways, going back to old certainties. To illustrate the wide scope of this reaction, we can consider three phenomena in three very different parts of Western Christendom: the growing centralization and conservatism of the Roman Catholic Church, the Catholic revival in the Anglican communion and the growth of Fundamentalism in the United States.

Roman Catholicism and Vatican I

In Chapter Fifteen we saw how the French Concordat of 1801 began the process of restoring papal fortunes from their low point; throughout the nineteenth century, the Papacy went on consolidating its position within the Roman Catholic Church. It was a concern for its position which stopped the Papacy becoming an automatic supporter of a return to the past when Napoleon was finally defeated in 1815: the great Catholic powers of eighteenth-century Europe had often humiliated the Pope, and it was not surprising that early-nineteenth-century Popes did not want to go back to that age. In some parts of the world, Roman Catholicism might actually gain from the spread of liberal ideas, particularly in Protestant northern Europe or in America, where the liberal belief in equality of all citizens worked to remove traditional laws discriminating against Roman Catholics.

There was therefore some reason for liberals to hope that the Papacy might look favourably on them in conflicts with conservatives, especially in the sequence of revolutions which broke out in widely separated parts of Europe in 1830 and 1848. In either case, however, these hopes were to be disappointed. A movement of liberal Catholics, which had emerged in France after a second revolution in 1830 had overthrown the restored Bourbon dynasty, was coldly rebuffed and condemned by Pope Gregory XVI in 1832, and its leader left the church. In 1848 and the years after, new hopes for an understanding between Roman Catholicism and liberalism were dashed because of the problem of the Papal States. These were the territories which the Papacy had built up in the early Middle Ages to preserve its independence of secular rulers; for a thousand years, the Popes had taken it for granted that the maintenance of the States was vital for the good of the Papacy and hence for the church as a whole, although in actual fact, ownership of the States had often made the Pope act like any other secular ruler defending his interests.

The French Revolution had swept away all other similar ecclesi-

astically governed territories in Europe, and apart from the Papal
States, they had not been restored in 1815. The States thus stood
out as an oddity from the past, and they also stood in the way of
the increasing desire of Italians to turn the motley collection of
regimes in their peninsula into a single nation. It would be this
clash which aligned the Papacy firmly on the side of conservatism;
rebellion in the Papal States had prompted the Pope's snub to the
Liberal Catholics in 1832. The story was repeated after 1848. In
1846 a Pope had been elected as Pius IX who astonished Europe
by the strength of his goodwill towards liberalism. When revolutions broke out all over Italy in 1848, he still lent his support to the
movement, setting up parliamentary institutions in his territories,
but when liberal nationalist armies overran the Papal States, and
when revolutionaries killed his Prime Minister and forced Pius to
flee from Rome, his liberal inclinations were replaced by a horrified loathing of what they had done. Over the next few years a
consolidated kingdom of Italy directed by Count Cavour, the chief
minister of the royal house of Savoy, nibbled away piecemeal at
the Papal States, justifying its military takeovers at each stage with
an appeal to liberal principles. Pius, in understandable fury, issued
a series of statements condemning liberalism, collecting them all
up into a *Syllabus of Errors* in 1864. This document culminated in
a statement that it was an error to say that the Pope 'can and
should reconcile himself to liberalism and modern civilization'.

It was tragic that the complications of Italian politics should
have brought the leader of the Roman Catholic Church apparently
to set himself against the forces of democratic progress in the
Western world. All over Europe liberals were horrified, and some
liberal Catholics left the church. However, among other Catholics
there was a very different mood. Pius, who was personally a
delightful and lovable man, attracted great popularity, which increased the prestige of the Papacy still further; this was an encouragement of the centralization process which the concordat had
begun. In 1850 Pius yielded to the increasingly fervent popular
devotion to the Blessed Virgin Mary, which coincided with his own
Marian enthusiasm, to issue a definition of the Doctrine of Mary's
Immaculate Conception. Definition of doctrine was always a rare
occurrence; this established the precedent that the Pope could do
it on his own initiative.

In 1870, in the same year as Italian troops seized the opportunity to enter Rome and bring to an end the last remnant of the Pope's temporal power, a General Council of the Roman church brought the Pope's spiritual authority to its highest level ever. Pius convened the Vatican Council (now generally known as Vatican I) to define the nature of the church and the nature of doctrine, so shaken by the Enlightenment and the French Revolution. The first act of the Council was to affirm the whole package of doctrine defined three centuries before at the Council of Trent, but then it got on to the question of the Infallibility of the Papacy in teaching revealed truth. There had been increasing pressure on Rome from devout laity and some bishops to get a clear declaration of this infallibility, and now this pressure resulted in the Council solemnly declaring the infallibility of doctrinal definitions pronounced by the Pope, although with careful safeguards which disappointed the more extreme supporters of the idea. There was considerable opposition from some bishops, but Pius's personal popularity overcame their objections, and most of them left Rome rather than be seen to be voting against his wishes.

Papal authority was now supreme in the church, and it was used to make the Roman Catholic hierarchy a consistent opponent of social and ideological change. Pius's successor Leo XIII saw that Pius's clash with liberalism had gone too far, and did his best to moderate it, but he initiated a drive against 'Modernism' in the church which destroyed any chance of Roman Catholicism taking a positive attitude to new ideas in biblical and theological scholarship until well into the twentieth century. Similarly, in his encyclical (circular letter) beginning *Rerum novarum* (1891), he took great care to set forth the problems which industrial society posed for the church, but he made no effort to come to terms with the ideas of Socialism or to encourage Catholics to find any common ground with it. A further encyclical of 1896, *Apostolicae Curae*, condemned the ordinations of Anglican clergy as null and void, underlining the stark claim of the Roman Catholic Church to be the only authentic representative of Christianity in the Western world.

The Catholic Revival in Anglicanism

Apostolicae Curae came as an unexpected and crushing end to conversations between a group of Anglicans and Roman Catholics about the possibility of recognition of Anglican Orders by Rome. At the beginning of the nineteenth century, such conversations would not have been possible nor considered necessary in the Church of England, but in the intervening period, an extraordinary theological revolution had occurred within the Anglican Communion; it had rediscovered its Catholic heritage alongside its legacy from the Protestant Reformation. As we have seen, the High Church party in the Church of England had languished during the eighteenth century, and its most remarkable representative, John Wesley, had taken his religious revival in a rather different direction. The most lively force in eighteenth-century Anglicanism seemed to be the Evangelical movement which ran alongside Wesley's Methodism, yet by the early nineteenth century, Evangelicalism was losing its momentum as it gained acceptance within the church. When a new departure came, it was as a result of a combination of remnants of the old High Church group with Evangelicals who had lost faith in their movement's capacity for spiritual dynamism.

The new movement was triggered off by a group of Oxford academics; hence its name of 'the Oxford Movement'. These men were worried for the future of the Church of England; the High Churchmen among them looked back to the seventeenth-century past, seeing there a perfect union between church and state in England. Now this union was becoming a lost dream. In 1828 the government abolished restrictions on Protestant Dissenters holding public office in England and Wales; in the following year, virtually all state discrimination against Roman Catholics was removed. What did this say about the position of the Established Church? Worse was to come. The electoral transformation brought about by the Reform Act of 1832 produced a reforming government determined to tackle the many structural faults of the Anglican establishment. It was one of these reforming measures, an eminently sensible proposal to reduce the absurd number of Anglican bishoprics in Ireland, which aroused the wrath of a High Church clergyman named John Keble. In 1833 he preached a sermon to the Oxford assize judges with the alarming title of 'National Apostasy'; he saw the Irish proposal as a deliberate attack on the church by the state, breaking the unity which they had formerly enjoyed. This would be the end of the Church of England.

The dramatic long-term effect produced by this unlikely beginning was proof that there was a widespread sense of anxiety among Anglican clergy produced by increasing nonconformist success and the ineffectiveness of the Established Church's ramshackle institutions in responding to the challenges of the nineteenth century. Keble and his associates discussed the various problems of the church in a series of pamphlets which they called *Tracts for the Times against Popery and Dissent* (hence the movement's alternative name of 'Tractarianism'). Goaded by the government's apparent lack of sympathy for the church, the Tractarians began emphasizing that the church had a life of its own independent of the state, and that this life was dependent on its claim to be the true representative of Catholic Christianity in England. Once more the Anglican Church's Catholic structure was reasserting itself against its Elizabethan Protestant theology. The Tracts aroused both immense interest and much hostility among the educated public; widespread fears that this was really a conspiracy to reintroduce Roman Catholicism into England were fuelled when in the decade after 1845, several Tractarian leaders (interestingly, nearly all former Evangelicals rather than old High Churchmen) suffered a crisis of confidence and defected to the Roman Church.

After this apparent disaster, the fortunes of the Catholic revival began improving, mainly thanks to a parallel Anglican impulse to rediscover the Catholic past which had its roots in the University of Cambridge. Here a group of undergraduates founded a society to study how medieval English churches had been designed and used; they called it the Cambridge Camden Society, and as it became more widely based, it was renamed the Ecclesiological Society. The Tractarians had mainly been concerned with theological problems; they had done little to change the style of worship in Anglican churches, which was then usually a very unimaginative and colourless presentation of the Book of Common Prayer. The work of the Ecclesiological Society persuaded a large number of energetic young clergymen that liturgy should be transformed largely along medieval lines; the old High Church emphasis on the central importance of the eucharist in spiritual life should be expressed in outward show and in beautiful churches which were either medieval buildings restored or new structures taking their inspiration from them. A further initiative reintroduced monastic life to the Church of England: first communities of women and later, rather lesser numbers of men.

This new clerical energy aroused widespread astonishment and great controversy within the Church of England. The movement's activists were abusively nicknamed 'Ritualists'; there were sometimes riots at their services, and later in the century, Evangelical opposition to them produced unsuccessful attempts to curb their activities by law. However, what saved the ritualists and the survivors of the Oxford Movement was their undoubted energy and love for their parish flocks; they made a point of working in the new industrial slums, where although their elaborate services baffled the poor, their pastoral care won them much affection and success. Many of the changes which they introduced in worship gradually spread very widely through the Anglican Communion, and beyond into the Free Churches; much of the renewed emphasis on the eucharist within Protestantism throughout the Western world can be traced to the pioneering influence of these 'Anglo-Catholics'.

The Catholic revival began as a backward-looking movement and it continued to treasure the past, but it also developed an interesting capacity to come to terms with the new biblical scholarship. This was not so in the early days. German biblical work took a long time to have an effect in England, partly because few Englishmen could be bothered to read German; however, by the 1850s a group of English clergy and academics nicknamed 'Broad Churchmen' were convinced of the value in the new approaches to biblical criticism and the work of modern science. In 1860 some of them got together to produce a book called *Essays and Reviews*. Evangelicals and the early Tractarians forgot their own quarrels to unite in a storm of abuse against the authors; this was one of the first in a series of periodic bloodlettings in the Anglican Church over liberal theology which has continued to the present day. However, three decades later, a number of younger Anglo-Catholics felt that their Catholic theology was capable of using the new approaches and coming to terms with them; in 1889 they in turn produced a collection of essays whose title *Lux Mundi* proclaimed their conviction that the Light of the World was to be seen in new insights on the Bible and the scientific world as much as in traditional doctrine. Older leaders of the Catholic revival were scandalized, but an association between liberal theology and Catholic inclinations within Anglicanism has persisted.

Not all the impulse to accepting the new ideas was Anglo-Catholic, however. 'Broad Church' views remained an important strand within Anglicanism, distinct from the Catholic revival, while a very significant influence in making biblical criticism acceptable within the English Free Churches came from a very different and unexpected direction. Arthur Samuel Peake, a layman within the Primitive Methodist Connexion, was one of the greatest biblical scholars of his day, but his roots within Primitive Methodism and the fervent conviction of his preaching was enough to convince many doubtful Free Churchmen that it was possible to adopt the new critical methods and still to remain a biblical Christian. *Peake's Commentary* brought moderate biblical criticism into the centre of English church life.

Fundamentalism

If Roman Catholicism and Anglo-Catholicism both emphasized the past in their different ways, the same thing happened in the very different world of American Protestantism. In origin, this was a reaction to the growth of theological liberalism within the mainstream Protestant denominations; from the 1870s a series of conferences, headed by those at Niagara-on-the-Lake, Ontario, reinforced the mood of resistance to the impact of Darwinism and of the Tübingen approach to the Bible. The movement was given particular appeal by the adaptation of the old American revivalist mode by Ira Sankey and Dwight L. Moody, whose impact was felt as much in Britain as in America. Those involved were much influenced by a 'dispensationalist' style of theology, which like Joachim of Fiore long before, saw all history as divided up into a series of periods or 'dispensations' which were about to be summed up in a second coming of Christ. Generally these trends were seen within existing denominations, for conservatives sought to win them away from liberal views rather than to break away from them.

'Fundamentalism' was a name derived from twelve volumes of essays issued by a combination of British and American conservative writers between 1910 and 1915 entitled *The Fundamentals*. Central to these essays, which like the Oxford Movement's *Tracts for the Times*, were of varying quality and importance, was an emphasis on five main points: the verbal inerrancy of scripture, the divinity of Jesus Christ, the virgin birth, a version of the atonement theory stressing penal substitution, and the resurrection and coming-again of Christ in the physical body. Having thus stated the case, fundamentalists created organizations to promote it: in 1919 the World's Christian Fundamentals Organization was founded, expanding through its use of mass rallies from a mainly Baptist base to affect most Protestant churches, particularly those in the southern American States.

There were some remarkable figures in the Fundamentalist leadership, particularly William Jennings Bryan, a Presbyterian layman, three times a candidate for the Presidency of the United States and for a time a Secretary of State in the administration of his fellow-Presbyterian President Woodrow Wilson. It was Bryan who was involved in the most celebrated clash between liberal and fundamentalist American Protestantism when in 1925 he led the prosecution of John Scopes, a young high school teacher in Tennessee, for teaching Darwinian evolutionary theory. Since the States of Mississipi, Florida, Arkansas and Tennessee itself had all been sufficiently influenced by the fundamentalist movement to pass laws forbidding such teaching, Scopes's conviction was probably inevitable, but the case brought intense public interest and did the fundamentalist cause more harm than good; it was a hollow victory. The 1930s brought an end to the conservative Protestant attempt to suppress the consumption of alcohol in the United States by the legislation of Prohibition, and between them, these two setbacks forced fundamentalism into the wings of American religious life for several decades.

Tradition and conflict

The churches of Western Christendom met the various revolutions which confronted them in the nineteenth century by reaffirming traditional doctrine; they were also diverted from the seriousness of these revolutions by the undoubted success which they were experiencing. Their numbers were increasing, especially in the overseas mission field. Much of their energy, too, was absorbed in internal conflicts: conflicts about their attitude to Darwinian science and biblical criticism, conflicts about the nature of the church. Such struggles were probably necessary as the church came to terms with societies which no longer automatically wanted it established, but they also obscured the fact that there were other items on the agenda.

The example of England is instructive. In the Church of England, Anglican discontents produced the Catholic revival, which began by wanting to return to the old settled relationship between church and state, but which painfully regained the insight that the church could exist as a body on its own, relying on its sacred character rather than on its links with the crown to give it identity. However, the building-up of Catholic Anglicanism produced a reaction of extreme hostility from the older-established Evangelical party which absorbed a major part of Evangelical energies well into the twentieth century; the Evangelicals did not succeed in quelling their opponents, and their failure to do so marginalized their own place in Anglican life until as late as the 1960s. The Anglican Catholic revival also scandalized the nineteenth-century Free Churches, and ended any chance of a reunion of any part of the Methodist Connexions with the established English Church. Conflict between the Established Church and the Free Churches was a constant feature of nineteenth-century religious life. Meanwhile, the various Methodist bodies were working out the ambiguous legacy of the work of John Wesley, trying to find the structures which would best fulfil their wish to bring salvation to England; their disagreements went on producing new denominations throughout the nineteenth century, from the Primitive Methodists to the Salvation Army.

Nineteenth-century churches thus present a paradoxical picture of intense energy and structural change combined with an ineffective response to the greatest changes which the world around the church had undergone during its nineteen centuries of life. In the middle of their debates about ritualism, church establishment, Darwin and German biblical critics, English churches said little about socialism and the movements which industrial society had produced. The Primitive Methodists were better than most English Protestant denominations in working within the new industrial institutions of trade unionism; small groups of Anglicans tried to apply an understanding of socialism to their faith. Overall, the impact was not great. It was only when their internal disagreements began to cool, and their structural success began to falter, that the Western churches were forced to consider the new situation which they found around them.

Chronology for Chapter Seventeen

1861–5	Civil War in United States of America
1905	In decree on Catholic Action, Pope Pius X recommends frequent communion
1906	Pentecostal revival, Los Angeles
1909	First mass production of cheap car (Ford's Model T) begins
1910	World Missionary Conference, Edinburgh
1912	Rudolf Bultmann begins teaching career
1917	Russian Revolution begins
1919	Karl Barth, *Commentary on Romans* is published
1922	Mussolini and Fascist party gain power, Italy
1924	Paul Tillich begins University teaching career
1925	First 'Life and Work' Conference, Stockholm
1927	First 'Faith and Order' Conference, Amsterdam
1929	Concordat between Vatican and Mussolini
1932	Union of most British Methodist denominations
1933	Hitler and Nazi party gain power, Germany; concentration camps set up
1938	First large-scale aerial bombing of civilians, Guernica (Spanish Civil War)
1945	Atomic bombs dropped on Hiroshima and Nagasaki
1947	Church of South India formed
1948	First World Council of Churches assembly, Amsterdam
1949	Mainland China controlled by Communists
1950	Pope Pius XII defines Doctrine of the Assumption
1958	John XXIII becomes Pope
1962	First session of Second Vatican Council
1963	Paul VI becomes Pope
1967	Most laws against homosexuality repealed, England and Wales
1968	Papal encyclical '*Humanae vitae*' sparks Roman Catholic controversy
1978	John Paul II becomes Pope
1986	Roman Catholic Church backs overthrow of President Marcos of the Philippines

Chapter Seventeen

Constantine's Church Crumbles (twentieth century)

It is likely that you will be more familiar with the events of twentieth-century history in Western Europe than with earlier periods, so there is no need to retell the story of this century in detail. All I will do is remind you of some of the most significant events, and draw out their importance and their roots in the past: how they relate to the industrial, political and ideological revolutions which we have examined in the last two chapters.

First, the Industrial Revolution of steam, textiles and iron led to a second industrial revolution based on the power of the internal combustion engine; from the mid nineteenth century, oil, from being a comparatively minor source of heat and light, took on a central role in the world economy. The fact that so many easily available oil-fields were to be found in the Islamic world of the Near East brought a new importance to the region, and it was a major factor in restoring the power and self-confidence of Islam. Now, after the oil crisis of the 1970s, we are entering an age of exploration in alternative sources of energy; the next revolution now taking place is based on information technology and the development of artificial intelligence, which means that the old industrial Western states are beginning to share their economic and political muscle with Asian leaders in the field like Japan and South Korea. The internal combustion engine brought Westerners the possibility of comparatively cheap private transport, which created the prospect of unprecedented personal mobility and leisure. Alongside this, a frightening problem of unemployment has also emerged. If Westerners insist on committing their present levels of time to paid work in order to maintain their standard of living, there is simply not enough work to go round in the West.

The first Industrial Revolution also serviced the military machines created by world powers in the nineteenth century. The Civil War of 1861–5 fought between the southern and northern States of the USA was the first major war which was decisively influenced by the new achievements of engineering and transport; in the First World War (1914–18), this mechanization was applied to the killing of unprecedented numbers of active combatants, and in the Second (1939–45), the development of aerial bombing extended the process to civilian populations. The end of that war was hastened by the dropping of the first two nuclear bombs on Japan, marking the point where human technology had finally developed the capacity to wipe out advanced forms of life on the planet. Although up to the date of writing this book, the shock of those first two bombs has prevented anyone using their destructive potential in any further wars, so-called 'conventional' wars have continued to stretch non-nuclear military technology to extremes of viciousness and destructiveness in every year since 1945.

Why has the twentieth century been so marked by warfare? Is it simply that mankind now has the weaponry to fight wars in ways which a minority always wished to fight? A more satisfactory explanation is that the West has not yet recovered from the forces of disruption which the French Revolution released. First liberals fought with conservatives, and the new nation-states fought with each other; then in 1917–21 the force of Marxist or Communist socialism gained an unexpected victory in Europe's most backward great power, the Russian Empire, against the predictions of the founding fathers of Marxism. The First World War so exhausted the Russian state machine of the Tsars as to make revolution a possibility, and then the inspired leadership of Lenin turned that revolution towards the foundation of a totalitarian state professing Marxism as its official ideology. War with the Japanese and its extension into the Second World War had the same effect on the Chinese state, which had in any case been in confusion since the mid-nineteenth-century interference of Europeans; from 1949, China like Russia has been dominated by an officially Marxist state with a proclaimed hostility to organized religion of any sort. Religion was (and is) seen as a competitor to totalitarian state systems demanding the absolute allegiance of their subjects. After

1945, much of Eastern Europe was organized by Russia into client states professing the same Marxist ideology to act as a security barrier against further invasion from the West.

The Communist success of 1917, accompanied by the collapse of the Great Power governments defeated in the First World War, led to the development of another group of anti-religious totalitarian ideologies in Europe: Fascism and Nazism. These exploited a sense of humiliation, rootlessness and despair which can be traced in the long term to the anxieties of Industrial Revolution society and of the post-1789 upheavals, and in the short term to First World War defeats and subsequent economic chaos. Traditional conservatism could respond to Fascism's pose as a defence against the spread of Russian Communism. Attempts to dress up Fascism as a coherent system of thought like Marxism could not eventually hide the fact that its central appeal was to fear, greed, and the hatred of other people; however, its military defeat in 1945 seems permanently to have broken the undoubted fascination which Hitler, Mussolini and their imitators were able to exercise over the minds of millions of ordinary Europeans. The Fascists and Nazis were able to neutralize most active opposition from the churches within the territories which they controlled, and ultimately it was the intention of Adolf Hitler to remove any possibility of Christian interference with his plans, by destroying Christianity altogether.

The horrors of Hitler's regime, particularly the revelation of the insane sadism which it directed against the entire Jewish race, came as a deep shock to Western Christianity. Despite Hitler's basic hostility to the churches, it was easy to see the way in which traditional Christian attitudes to Judaism had created this monster. Christians were also uncomfortably aware that despite much heroism from Catholic and Protestant alike in resisting Nazi evil, many Christians had remained passive, and some had actually supported the regime and its ideology. Shame at this legacy was one factor in producing new Christian attempts to understand and make amends to the Jewish faith, and in turn to produce a new thoughtfulness about how Christianity might relate to other great world faiths.

A further consequence of the Industrial Revolution was the invention of reliable mechanical methods of birth control, together with major advances in medical techniques which could make abortion into a routine matter. The effect of the wide availability of contraception has been to dissassociate sexual activity from the procreation of children, and in turn to put a question-mark over the necessary connection between sex and marriage. Sex becomes an expression of relationship, in effect, part of the Western cult of leisure, rather than the property of the marriage bond. Such a change in the role of marriage has had several consequences. Traditional Christian-associated models of marriage have in practice if not in theory given a subordinate place to women in relation to men: now this has been challenged in every department of Western society. Western Europe's horror of homosexual activity, which developed after the eleventh- and twelfth-century Reformation, has lessened, and tolerant attitudes to homosexual relationships have become widespread. However much some sections of the Christian church may deplore these developments, it is difficult to imagine any radical reversal in them. It is also interesting that the totalitarian ideologies of Marxism and Fascism view this sexual revolution with as much suspicion as do societies based on traditionalist Christianity; quite possibly it will prove the most far-reaching of all the revolutions which we have considered, for it affects the very basis of human behaviour.

The church in the new world

None of the developments so far described, it will be noted, owes much to the initiative of the church; it has stood on the margin of the most sweeping changes of human history. Christendom was constructed comparatively quickly in the two centuries after Constantine I's alliance with the church, and despite the shock of the barbarian takeover of the Western Roman Empire, it went on to its greatest success in the united Western church of the Middle Ages. That was a time when the church stood at the centre of change in a society which was on the brink of becoming the major force in the world; so as we told the story of our 'two Western Reformations', we were in effect forced into describing the whole of European development. Now, after the intellectual changes which have been at work since the seventeenth century, the church has steadily moved to the edge of Western priorities and concerns; from being a department of the state and the guardian of all people from the cradle to the grave, Christianity has become a choice of the individual, one among a whole range of activities which give people their identity and which provide meaning for their lives. There is much survival from the older world, especially in the form of traditional religious institutions which witness to continuity in society; yet it is worth noting that in the two areas where the traditional institutions of a church-state link are at their strongest, in England and Scandinavia, formal religious practice runs at a lower level than in any other industrialized society.

Christian life and practice has not fully taken account of the new situation in which it finds itself. To do so, it will have to abandon memories of centuries in which it was able to control a largely agriculturally-based society. Such a total transformation is not impossible, for it has happened before in the history of the church. Christianity's first roots were in a peasant culture on the fringe of the Roman Empire. For five hundred years after these first decades, it made quite a successful effort to adapt itself to a classical civilization whose base was in urban commercial centres. However, after the fall of the Western Empire, most of its ministry was redirected to societies where farming mattered most, and where towns were secondary to the power of land-based aristocracies which justified their power by reference to the Christian God. The church still hangs on to many assumptions from this agricultural world. Its liturgical calendar, traditionally very elaborate in many branches of the church, reflects the rhythms of the farming year, and in all its branches, its language is still that of the pre-Industrial and pre-French Revolution world. It still speaks of Jesus Christ as Lord, King and Good Shepherd: words which conjure up ideas of hierarchy, male domination and a society of farmers. Folk-memory still gives these words a meaning in the ears of twentieth-century Western children; but when will the memory fade? How long can our Christian language go on living on borrowed time? No doubt this analysis sounds negative and gloomy; it need only be if we fall into the medieval trap of thinking that there can never be change for the better in the church and in society. In all sorts of ways, the church has been moving and changing amid the horrors and excitements of the twentieth-century world, and after we have surveyed these movements, we may be better able to assess possibilities in the future.

Church movements (1): ecumenism

All the historic bitternesses which we have seen develop over
nineteen centuries came to seem less relevant once Western
Christianity moved out of its European homeland and started
trying to convince non-Europeans of its value. It became increasingly difficult to explain to a sceptical Hindu why religious bodies
which talked constantly of the oneness of the church and of the
love of Christ should remain at permanent loggerheads over
whether a bishop or a presbytery should govern Christ's church.
The first initiatives in ecumenism therefore came from the mission
field. As early as 1855 a 'General Conference of Bengal Protestant
Missionaries' met at Calcutta, and in 1879, at a conference at
Bangalore at which for the first time fourteen Indian Christian
workers were in attendance, the prospect of a 'Church of Christ in
India' was discussed. Similar conferences in other parts of the
mission field were held during the nineteenth century, but the
results were oddly parallel to the contemporary activity of colonial
governments, defining 'spheres of influence' so that Protestant
denominations or missionary societies within churches were not
in competition with each other; there was little say for non-
Europeans at these events.

The World Missionary Conference held at Edinburgh in 1910
was in a different league from these local conferences. Apart from
the scale of the enterprise, this meeting set up a Continuation
Committee; at first this was very limited in its scope, but it only
took until 1921 to become the International Missionary Council,
which in turn produced various regional councils. However, a
further result of Edinburgh was to extend the concerns for Christian
co-operation beyond the mission-field and back to the heartland
of Western Christian disagreements. One of the delegates at
Edinburgh was the bishop of the American Episcopal Church in
the Philippines, Charles Brent, who became convinced that the
next initiative must be a body which could explore the Faith and
Order professed by Christians. It took much planning by the
Episcopalians, particularly because of the disruption of the First
World War; overtures to the Pope were politely but firmly re-
jected. Nevertheless the first Faith and Order Conference met at
Lausanne in 1927.

Parallel with this initiative was a move to relate the faith of the church to society round it. The inspiration here was Lutheran, the idea of Archbishop Nathan Söderblom, the Primate of Sweden, who wanted the churches to forget their differences in facing up to the problems which the revolutions of the previous three centuries had brought to their world. The first 'Life and Work' Conference to discuss these issues was held at Stockholm in 1925; increasingly the establishments of the various mainstream Protestant churches took an interest in what was happening, and sent official delegations along to subsequent meetings. There began to be considerable personal overlap between these various bodies, so that Dr J.H. Oldham, one of the leading figures behind the Edinburgh Conference's Continuation Committee, was also heavily involved in 'Life and Work', while Söderblom's friend the future Archbishop of Canterbury William Temple was active in both 'Faith and Order' and 'Life and Work'. The establishment of mature churches with indigenous clergy in the wider world, together with the obvious problems of Western Christianity in its European homeland, made it increasingly unreal to talk of a distinction between 'home' and the 'overseas mission field'. It was natural to begin thinking of combining the existing bodies into a single organization which would be composed of representatives of the various churches, not just of the missionary societies or of individual churchmen of goodwill.

The Second World War delayed progress as had the First, but in 1948 the first assembly of the World Council of Churches (WCC) was held in Amsterdam. The main initiative lay still with churches in the Anglican and liberal Protestant traditions, and there were difficulties in extending the process either to the whole family of the Western church or beyond into Eastern Orthodoxy. The problems were illustrated by the delay in incorporating the International Missionary Council into the WCC, a move which was not accomplished until 1961: Orthodox churches were suspicious of the overtones of the word mission, given the history of Western encroachment on their flocks, and many Evangelical Protestants were suspicious of what the WCC might do to hamper their own vision of what mission meant. The acceptance of an amalgamation, which was strongly urged by the 'younger' churches, was a major statement that the Christian world together was responsible for proclaiming a single message to the world. Only the Roman Catholic community remained aloof from this move, and during the 1960s, the mood within Rome began to change, as we shall see; although the Roman Catholic Church still has only observer status within the WCC, its attitude to the activities of other Christian bodies has radically changed.

Another aspect of the drive towards ecumenism in twentieth-century Christianity has been the urge to create visible unity among churches. The first steps came within denominational families which had been split by arguments over strategy and church government during the eighteenth and nineteenth centuries; even in the homelands where these disputes had taken place, it was easy to see that a general agreement had ended the bitterness which the splits had created and that the time was ripe to come together again. So American Presbyterians ended the division which reactions to the eighteenth-century Great Awakenings had created among them; British Methodism and Scots Presbyterianism formed unions which carried along the vast majority of their memberships. Alongside this, various Protestant churches came together in unions in the area of the West's nineteenth-century expansion, such as Presbyterians and Congregationalists in South India (1908). In the Far East, the Japanese forced Protestants into union in their own country and in the lands which they conquered so that they would have a single body to deal with; a similar union was brought about by the unfriendliness of the government in Communist China after 1949.

The most difficult task was to bridge the chasm in church government which had separated episcopal from non-episcopal churches at the Reformation. So far the only major unions to achieve success have been in the Indian sub-continent, starting with the Church of South India in 1947, after years of careful planning. Most other schemes, for instance in west Africa, Canada or Australia, have failed to achieve their full potential through opposition from a sizable group among the heirs of the Catholic revival in the Anglican Communion, who have been concerned to safeguard the particular version of the apostolic succession which had survived in the Church of England at the sixteenth-century Reformation. In English talks between Anglicans and the Free Churches, those who held such views joined with Evangelicals who felt that too much weight was being given to episcopal ordination, to produce a series of Anglican defeats for schemes of unity throughout the 1960s, 1970s and 1980s.

Evangelical participation in these defeats reflected a widespread feeling among Evangelicals throughout the world that ecumenism of the sort promoted by the WCC was not what they wanted; they were looking for a consensus of doctrine on Protestant Reformation lines which would transcend denominational boundaries and make them irrelevant. In this, they could point to a tradition of Evangelical interdenominational co-operation which stretched back to the confusion of eighteenth-century English religion and to the activity of the American Great Awakenings; the work of the Evangelical Alliance since 1846 provided the model for what they wanted to see.

Church movements (2): Vatican II

Anglo-Catholic opposition to schemes of unity of the South India type has been fuelled by their increasing hopes of an understanding between the Anglican and Roman Catholic communions which would lead to visible reunion. Such hopes have been possible because of a great change in the spirit of Roman Catholicism, the same change which has made a radical difference for the better in the relations between Rome and the WCC. This came about quite abruptly as a result of a second Vatican Council (Vatican II) promoted by the Papacy itself. Before the event there was little indication that there would be any change from the uncompromising exclusive stance adopted by the Roman Catholic Church at Vatican I. The only new direction which came in the early twentieth century was to modify some of the excesses of clericalism which the Council of Trent had left untouched within the Roman communion, by restoring a vision of the eucharist as an offering by the whole people of God. This impulse, which had started in the Belgian Roman Catholic Church at the turn of the century, expressed itself in new experiments in the planning of church buildings, gathering the congregation in a more intimate relationship with the eucharistic table; in 1905 Pope Pius X, a keen liturgist, issued a decree recommending all Roman Catholics to receive communion daily if possible, thus reversing a trend which since the early Middle Ages had made the laity mere spectators at most masses. Otherwise official pronouncements of Rome only reinforced the aggressive stance of Vatican I, while in 1950 the pressure of Marian devotion led Pope Pius XII to use the papal power of infallible definition in defining the doctrine of the bodily Assumption of the Virgin Mary into Heaven. This was not a move calculated to ease Protestant prejudices against Rome.

The abrupt change of climate came when Pius XII was succeeded by the Patriarch of Venice, who took the title John XXIII. Undoubtedly John was elected because he was seen as a safe man: elderly, but with a distinguished record as a scholar and papal diplomat. However, he immediately set about a vigorous programme of action; he created twenty-three new Cardinals as a first step in greatly widening the international character of this key group within the Roman hierarchy. The most decisive departure was to call a new council for the whole church to meet at the Vatican; it was not a move that anyone expected, and the Pope claimed that the idea had come to him in a sudden inspiration of the Holy Spirit. He defined its agenda as the renewal of the church; in doctrine, discipline and organization. The Council met in four successive sessions between 1962 and 1965, although John himself died after the first session.

The most striking gesture made by the assembled bishops in the first session was to make their own choice of members for the key commissions to carry out detailed work for the Council; they rejected the prepared list, and thus declared their independence of direction from the Roman Curia (that is, the papal Court and its senior ecclesiastical bureaucracy). Although few more positive decisions were taken before Pope John's death, the second Session continued after the election of Pope Paul VI to make important statements about the place of bishops in the church, a question which the Council of Trent had done its best to avoid answering. The bishops made it clear that they regarded themselves as a 'college', that is, a body, not a mere collection of individuals to be directed by the Pope; they also created the conditions for a revival of the diaconate as a separate order of ministry, not just a probationary stage towards the priesthood. This recalled the practice of the early church and the continuing practice of the Eastern Churches. By contrast, their statements on the 'Instruments of Social Communication' were curiously unimaginative, and serve as a reminder that one should not oversimplify to suggest a uniform pattern of radical insights in the Council.

The third session did some important work in opening up the prospects for a non-imperialist ecumenism with other Christian bodies. There were three documents of significance here: the Dogmatic Constitution of the Church, the Decree on Ecumenism and the Decree on the Eastern Catholic Churches. The fourth session was mainly concerned with reordering the church in various ways: setting the shape of the new synod which would help the Pope to govern the church; considering new directions for religious orders, religious education and the role of the laity.

After the close of the Council, Paul VI set up various commissions to carry out his pledge of maintaining the direction set by John XXIII. His time as Pope was crucial in establishing the work of Vatican II beyond the point where it could ever be effectively reversed, and this despite his own quite clearly ambiguous attitude to the explosion of change which the Council had unleashed. On the one hand, the commissions which he established produced quite uncompromisingly radical reforms, the most obvious of which was the establishment of the liturgy in the ordinary languages of the faithful, some four hundred years after the Protestant Reformation had done so. On the other hand, the policies for which Paul was personally responsible showed a marked conservatism: his encyclical *Mysterium Fidei* (1965), for instance, was a restatement of traditional Roman eucharistic doctrine, and his Declaration on Sexual Ethics (1973) equally made no concessions to changing views on sexuality in the secular world.

It was in the same field of sexuality that Paul met with a spectacular defeat; in 1968 he went ahead, ignoring the work of a papal commission, to issue a complete condemnation of birth control in the encyclical *Humanae Vitae*, and he was astonished and deeply hurt when this caused an outcry among the Catholic laity of the Western world. The encyclical is now widely ignored (except, ironically, in those underdeveloped countries where the massive growth of population presents a critical economic and social problem); this is itself a step of great consequence in the renewal of the Roman Catholic Church. For the first time the laity have in substantial numbers rejected the Papacy's assumption that it can legislate for their lives without proper consultation. It remains to be seen whether the remarkable personal popularity achieved by Pope John Paul II will be enough to give him the backing for his strategy of halting or reversing the most radical work of Vatican II.

One of the most interesting features of post-Vatican II Roman Catholicism is that it seems finally to have abandoned its hankering after the *ancien regime*. Very frequently during the early twentieth century, the Roman Catholic hierarchy was to be found lining up against forces of democracy or of the left; this stance was reinforced by the Communist takeover of Russia and the general fear in inter-war Europe that Communism would spread west. The Italian church hierarchy found it easier to do a deal with Mussolini's Fascist regime over the lost Papal States than it had done with earlier parliamentary Italian governments; in Spain, the church supported the establishment of General Franco's dictatorship against the coalition of left-wing anti-clerical forces which had dominated the previous democratic republic. In inter-war France, the Catholic authorities were mostly aligned with the increasingly hopeless royalist movement. During the Second World War, the clear moral need to resist Nazism helped to change the church's mood, and after the war it ended its suspicion of democratic politics in southern Europe to support specifically Christian-based political parties which would act as a bulwark against Communist advance.

However, after Vatican II, Catholicism discovered a new alignment with popular movements which actively confront repressive regimes of both traditional right and left. In some cases, this confrontation does link with traditional politics: in Poland, the church has been the only alternative focus of national identity to the institutions of the Communist state, and it has acted both as a stimulus to resistance to centralizing Communism and as a restraining force on popular activism against the government. In the Philippines, the church's hierarchy and lower clergy both played a large part in the overthrow of the corrupt pseudo-democratic regime of President Marcos, whereas in South America, some bishops and theologians have been committed to a much more thoroughgoing attack on institutions which they see, as denying human rights and justice to ordinary people. The Papacy's attitude to this change has been ambiguous; while the Polish Pope has been at the heart of his own people's search for basic human rights, he has done his best to curb the 'liberation theology' of South America, where (in contrast to the Polish situation) the pressure of events has caused theologians to question the authority structures of the church as well as those of the secular state.

Church movements (3): responses to Kant

One of the features of new explorations in theology during the twentieth century has been the rich variety of attempts to find a positive response to the directions taken in European thought after Kant. The first response, during the nineteenth century, had been that of liberal Protestantism which took its inspiration from the contrasting sources of Hegel and Schleiermacher; but the liberals' approach, already challenged by Albert Schweitzer, seemed to have very little to say to the terrible irrationalities of the First World War. This can be seen in the career and thought of a former liberal theologian, Swiss-born but German-trained, Karl Barth. Barth's liberalism disintegrated during his years as a pastor in neutral Switzerland, on the very edge of the war on the Western Front. His sense of frustration and anguish at the situation led him to read Kierkegaard, and he found that he could identify with this rejection of Hegelian rationality and see war-torn Europe as revealing the paradox of human existence, a fallen life powerless before the majesty of a God far beyond the arguments of philosophy.

This insight lay behind his *Commentary on Romans* (1919), for the epistle was as central to his spiritual pilgrimage as it had been for Augustine or Luther; this was a bold and bleak declaration that the Epistle was speaking directly to the twentieth century, yet it was also an uncompromising reaffirmation of the principles set forth by the Protestant reformers of the sixteenth century. This is the question posed by Barth's work: should he be classed as a conservative or a radical theologian? Even though one has to take into account the fact that he was great enough to admit to changing his mind in several respects, he retained the central belief that the liberals had taken a major wrong turning in seeking to find an understanding with the directions taken by secular thought; for him all human achievements, however impressive, are irredeemably shot through with sin.

Barth might be seen as the Calvin of the twentieth century, although his attitude to universal salvation or damnation was much less clear-cut than Calvin's. Like Calvin, he was prepared to nerve the church to take political action in the world; perception of human evil did not lead him into passive pessimism, but into uncompromising action in the Confessing Church which took its stand against Hitler's attempt to take over the German Protestant churches. Yet he never retreated from the critical study of the Bible which was one of the intellectual achievements of the nine-teenth century church. The phrase which has come to describe his style of theology expresses the fact that it can never be seen as a simple return to a past orthodoxy; it is a neo-orthodoxy, some-thing which has its own life and its own future.

Other leading German theologians of Barth's generation took different directions in their theological exploration. In contrast to Barth, Paul Tillich was prepared to use the tools of philosophy in constructing theology; in his eyes, it was a necessity for responsible theologians to use the philosophical insights of the modern world in approaching Jesus Christ, for the theological quest was only part of the human quest for meaning. This was an attempt to come to terms with lay thought, an attempt which Barth did not begin to make and did not seek to make. Rudolf Bultmann, like Tillich, wanted to present the gospel in terms of the preoccupations of twentieth-century minds. Applying this to his lifetime's study of the New Testament, this meant developing a radical scepticism about the form of the biblical narratives. They needed to be 'demythologized': stripping them of the assumptions of the writers, who had been locked into a world-view which had virtually no contact with the way in which modern people could perceive the universe. The Bible must be freed from the 'reason' which had ordered its narrative in particular ways, so that modern Christians could use their faith as freely as possible to perceive the message of Jesus. At the centre of this faith, as in the classic Lutheran tra-dition, remained the fact of Christ on the cross.

Church movements (4): Pentecostalism and the Charismatic Movement

One of the most significant forces in Western Christianity is the growth of religious movements emphasizing the role of the Holy Spirit in the development of the faith: significant chiefly because in their Third World form, they offer the prospect of a new adapt-ation of the Western Christian tradition as radical as the trans-formation from rural to industrial Europe last century. The roots of the movements are to be found in the ferment of piety in the eighteenth century in which John Wesley played a leading role; he emphasized the doctrine of personal holiness, which could be found both in the Catholic and in the English Puritan spiritual traditions on which he drew so widely. This doctrine spread beyond the various Methodist bodies to feed into 'Holiness' movements which became of great importance in the religion of the black communities emerging out of slavery in the nineteenth-century United States; and it is there that the roots of Pentecostalism are to be found.

The Holiness movements also lay behind the spirituality of leaders like Dwight L. Moody who were prominent in the development of Evangelical Fundamentalism (see Chapter Sixteen), but the Pentecostal phenomenon was to move in another direction. Emphasizing 'Baptism in the Spirit', and giving a leading role to speaking in tongues in the fashion recorded by Acts, it broke all the conventions of American religion (whether Evangelical or not) by ignoring the race barrier; when the first great Pentecostal revival occurred in Los Angeles in 1906, blacks and whites played an equal role side by side. As the movement grew and a more formal structure emerged, this became less true, but by then the appeal of Pentecostalism in the Third World had become established.

This is not to say that Pentecostal churches did not develop a significant presence in Europe; here too, they fulfilled a need within Protestantism for a way of worshipping God which was not so dependent on the rather conceptual, word-based structures which the churches of the sixteenth-century Reformation had developed in their practice. Speaking in tongues was only part of the picture, and indeed many branches of Pentecostalism have been concerned to play down the phenomenon; equally important were singing, dancing and an appeal to the appreciation of colour and form. As in the Catholic revival of nineteenth-century Anglicanism, although without a similar commitment to exploring tradition, the appeal lay in broadening the response of the whole person in worship away from intellectual constructions.

With this central emphasis on worship, the early Pentecostals were reluctant to institutionalize their success through organizations; but their numerical growth, together with their strong commitment to founding communities of believers, made it inevitable that organizations should develop. The chief institutional forms in England became the Elim Foursquare Gospel Alliance

(1915) and the Assemblies of God (1924). The predominant
expression of these bodies became old-style Evangelicalism with
the addition of all the doctrines which centred on the idea of
Baptism in the Spirit. Yet the Pentecostal phenomenon did not
end there; rather like the eighteenth-century Evangelical Revival,
it established both an independent presence and also a lively base
within traditional denominations, and some of its leaders, for
instance the English Anglican clergyman Alexander Boddy, remained loyal to their old denomination. While it was the independent Pentecostal bodies which showed the most dramatic development in the first half of the century, from the 1960s growth in what
came to be known as the 'Charismatic Movement' began on a large
scale in the older denominations. Growth was particularly rapid in
the most unexpected place: the Roman Catholic Church, simultaneously being affected by 'revolution from the top' in the Second
Vatican Council.

A movement of such liveliness was bound to cause tensions
within established structures, as the example of similar movements
of energy from the second-century Montanists onwards has shown
us by now. There was a tendency of Charismatic groups in denominations to set up their own organizations to help their sense of
fellowship and to promote their insights, which would often lead to
clashes with existing centres of authority; also, charismatics
were often impatient of institutions which separated them from
like-minded Christians in other denominations, and practised
their own forms of enthusiastic ecumenism which alarmed more
cautious churchpeople. Very often, charismatic groups in their
turn produced separation from existing church structures, particularly when they met lack of sympathy from congregations and
from church leaders. This produced the phenomenon of 'house
churches', loosely organized chains of communities which have
often expanded so quickly in a short space of time that they have
had to buy church buildings which are beyond the declining needs
of established denominations. Frequently a feature of their meetings distinguishing them from traditional evangelicalism and indeed from the older Pentecostal groups is the absence of a 'Gospel
sermon', which they see as restricting to their worship of God as
the constricting forms of traditional liturgies.

The Charismatic Movement and its House Church offshoots are
largely products of the affluent West. Figures for their growth

produced in 1980 put their membership at some eleven million, and the white Pentecostal family at twenty-one million, but both these were dwarfed by the estimated eighty-two million members of 'non-white indigenous' churches concentrated overwhelmingly in the Third World. Nearly always one can find links in the histories of these churches with the early Pentecostalists, but now they are one of the chief agents in the quest for a Christian spirituality which is distinct from the Western traditions represented by the older churches built up in the Third World during the colonial era.

Frequently Third World leaders have criticized the indigenous churches for diverting people from the desperate poverty and injustice which afflicts so many Third World countries; it remains to be seen whether they can respond positively to this criticism. Nevertheless, their delight in celebration in worship reflects once more the move away from the word-based culture of Western religion, and shows a new attempt to find what is best in the past of other world cultures. In terms of sheer numbers, they will probably soon become the chief representative of the Western Christian tradition in the world, and they may well be able to draw other churches of Western origins in the Third World into a common fellowship stronger than any links with 'parent' churches. When this new stage in Western Christianity's history makes a nonsense of the terms 'West' and 'East', a new world of ecumenism may open up beyond the hesitant steps of the twentieth century. Constantine's church has disappeared.

Conclusion

'May you live in *interesting* times' is often alleged to be an old Chinese curse. Whether or not the Chinese ever used this expressive phrase, the Christian church was especially cursed with 'interesting times' in the twentieth century. Yet the large scale movements which we have described in Chapter Seventeen do not suggest that the church has lost its ancient capacity for radical adaptation in the face of radical change. The Western church faces a world where the West has irrecoverably lost the advantages that it had been building up over other world cultures since the fifteenth century. As a reflection of this process, the numerical strength and dynamic growth of 'Western' Christendom is now in what in previous chapters has been called the Third World, but what is nowadays significantly known more often as the Majority World. This may well mean that the synthesis of doctrine which we have seen built up in the early church, culminating in the work of the Council of Chalcedon, is due for a basic revision, not merely at the hands of a few European theologians, but through the very different cultural experience of other continents.

This may not be as disastrous as might at first sight appear. The Christian message and the Greek world-view derived from Plato and Aristotle were never easy bedfellows, yet there was little alternative for the church in the classical world but to try and unite them. Nevertheless, how could such a world-view ever make sense of the monstrous paradoxes which lie at the heart of the Christian proclamation: a single supreme God who is also three, a God who becomes human and who dies in failure on a cross, thereby destroying death? The early church made a noble effort to understand these claims, but even in the subtleties of its most advanced theological disputes like the Monophysite controversy, it could never claim to have 'solved' them. Instead, even the early church's constructions of creeds had behind them the aggressive cry of one of the West's earliest theologians, Tertullian: 'I believe because it is impossible to believe!'

If the magnificent synthesis of Greek and Christian thought which Orthodox, Catholic and Protestant have inherited from the early church failed to make the faith anything but paradoxical, the disintegration of that synthesis in the wake of the seventeenth- and eighteenth-century revolutions is perhaps more a sign of hope than a case of mourning. Now the church enters a new world where ancient divisions come to seem less relevant, and where the distracting preoccupations which Constantine's Christendom bequeathed to Christianity are being put to one side. Now the church can face the world around it in a new way; maybe it will always find that there must be more than one way of meeting the world. Sociologists of religion commonly distinguished between three main types of religious organization: the sect, which tries to keep itself separate from the world, the denomination, which finds an accommodation with the world, and the church, which seeks to take over the world's life. Frequently in Christian history these types have been in conflict; a new broader ecumenism may be able to range them alongside each other in a mutual recognition of their complementary value.

In the 1960s sociologists also centred their discussion of religion on the concept of secularization. There are many ways of seeing the meaning of this word: it has been described as 'the disenchantment of the world', the gradual ebbing away of the quality of the sacred in existence. The word's inventor, G.J. Holyoake, defined it as 'the doctrine that morality should be based on regard to the well-being of mankind in the present life, to the exclusion of all considerations drawn from belief in God or a future state'. Much of what we have seen in the previous four chapters confirmed the existence of this secularizing process. Given the linear sense of time so common in the West, and nineteenth-century ideas of progress so encouraged by Hegelian thought, it was natural to suppose that the secularization process would gather momentum and that religion would wither away in the face of it.

Now that expectation has been decisively checked. From the 1970s and 1980s, religious belief and practice, not simply within Christianity, have flourished in many forms. Much of this growth has been in various forms of fundamentalism, self-conscious revivals of traditional religion, even though the traditionalism is often merely one version or partial understanding of the past. In the United States, conservative evangelical Protestantism recovered from its symbolic defeats in the 1920s and 1930s to become part of a mood of renewed national self-confidence (or self-assertion): a process curiously similar in timescale has taken place in fundamentalist forms of Islam, first most obviously in the Iranian Revolution of 1979, but later throughout the Islamic world. The election of a Polish Pope in 1978 began a discreet movement in the Roman Catholic Church away from the spirit of the Second Vatican Council and resulted in the proclamation of an unashamedly centralising form of traditionalism: it remains to be seen whether this represents the future of Roman Catholicism. Russian Orthodoxy and indeed Russian religious practice in general experienced a huge growth after the implosion of the atheist Soviet State. Alongside the great expansion of 'mainstream' Third World Christianity, many cults more or less related to Christianity, such as Sun Myung Moon's Unification Church, and others in a loose conglomeration of 'New Age' attitudes or consciousness, have made an impact on the West; what is especially striking is that their influence seems to have been greatest among some of the best-educated and well-to-do young people of Western society. Only Europe, together with the most European of former British colonies, Canada, Australia and New Zealand, seem to continue as examples of the 'secularization' model, while the rest of the world appears to be in a different mood.

If religion has flourished, materialism has faltered. The most avowedly material of all political systems, that of Soviet Russia and its unwilling satellites, collapsed in intellectual as well as financial bankruptcy. The progress of science and humanism, proceeding from the time of Francis Bacon in increasing isolation from the ethical and moral concerns which theology might have brought to it, has now been challenged not merely by the catastrophe of the nuclear bomb, but by worldwide alarm at the effects of industrial and technological pollution. From the 1970s, concern for the physical environment became a major political issue; mainstream politicians were forced to take seriously a much wider view of the way in which the planet should be treated. This indicates a new awareness of universal values, which is some answer to the fears of many nineteenth-century free-thinkers that a decline in religious practice would lead to a general collapse in morality. The way in which ordinary people of all beliefs and none have been mobilized in an effort to remedy the crisis of agriculture in Africa is impressive evidence of a new seriousness, a popular commitment to consideration for others, which the Christian churches can only welcome. They should not begrudge those outside the Christian fold a share of ethical concern.

We have many reasons to be anxious for our society and for the world, but as we have seen in this survey of Christian history, there have been plenty of ages of anxiety before. We may rightly fear that the civilization fathered by the Christian West may destroy our planet in the near future, but Christians have no need to fear the inevitable changes which will come to the church if our world survives. For all the immense complexity of the two-thousand-year Christian story which we have followed, we need to remember just how young an institution the Christian church is in the whole human story. Twenty-first-century Christians stand in the first youth of their community, a few faltering steps away from Paul, Constantine, Gregory VII, Luther, Descartes; they should expect this youth to go on producing new varieties of Christian experience as strange, tragic, joyful and unexpected as anything in the past.

For Further Reading

Introductory works

E. Cameron, *Interpreting Christian History: the Challenge of the Churches' Past,* Blackwell, 2005

J. Comby (with D. MacCulloch), *How to Read Church History* vol. 1, SCM, 1985, and vol. 2, SCM, 1989

F. L. Cross and E. A. Livingstone (eds.), *The Oxford Dictionary of the Christian Church,* Fourth Edition, Oxford University Press, 2005

Sheridan W. Gilley and W. J. Sheils, *A History of Religion in Britain: Practice and Belief from Pre-Roman Times to the Present,* Blackwell, 1994

Adrian Hastings (ed.), *A World History of Christianity,* Cassell, 1999

R. Harries and H. Mayr-Harting (eds), *Christianity: Two Thousand Years,* Oxford University Press, 2001

Jonathan Hill, *A History of Christian Thought,* Lion Hudson, 2003

Hans Küng, *Christianity: Its Essence and History,* SCM, 1995

Norman P. Tanner, *The Councils of the Church: A Short History,* Crossroad, 2001

Rowan Williams, *Why Study the Past? The Quest for the Historical Church,* Darton, Longman & Todd, 2005

Part I: The Building of a Culture

Peter Brown, *The Rise of Western Christendom: Triumph and Diversity 200-1000,* Blackwell, 2003

Norbert Brox, *A History of the Early Church,* SCM, 1994

Henry Chadwick, *The Early Church,* Penguin, 1967

G. R. Evans, *The First Christian Theologians: An Introduction to Theology in the Early Church,* Blackwell, 2004

R. Fletcher, *The Conversion of Europe,* Fontana, 1997 [USA, *The Barbarian conversion: from paganism to Christianity,* Holt & Co, 1999]

W. H. C. Frend, *The Rise of Christianity,* Darton, Longman and Todd, 1984

Stuart G. Hall, *Doctrine and Practice in the Early Church,* SPCK, 1991

Ian Hazlett (ed.), *Early Christianity: Origins and Evolution to AD 600,* SPCK, 1991

J. N. D. Kelly, *Early Christian Doctrines*, Continuum, 2000

Christoph Markschies, *Between Two Worlds: Structures of Early Christianity*, SCM, 1999

J. Stevenson, *A New Eusebius*, SPCK revised edition by W. H. C. Frend, 1987

J. Stevenson, *Creeds, Councils and* Controversy, SPCK, revised edition by W. H. C. Frend, 1989

Frances Young, *From Nicaea to Chalcedon: A guide to the literature and its background*, SCM, 1997

Frances Young, *The Making of the Creeds*, SCM, 1991

G. R. Evans (ed.), *The Medieval Theologians*, Blackwell, 2001

Isnard Wilhelm Frank, *A History of the Medieval* Church, SCM, 1995

Judith Herrin, *The Formation of Christendom*, Fontana Press, 1989

F. Donald Logan, *A History of the Church in the Middle Ages,* Routledge, 2002

Joseph Lynch, *The Medieval Church*, Longman, 1992

R. W. Southern, *Western Society and the Church in the Middle Ages*, Penguin, 1970

Part II; Through Two Western Reformations 1000–1700

D. Bagchi and D. Steinmetz (eds), *The Cambridge Companion to Reformation Theology*, Cambridge University Press, 2004

John Bossy, *Christianity in the West 1400–1700*, Oxford University Press, 1985

Euan Cameron, *The European* Reformation, Oxford University Press, 1991

Eamon Duffy, *The Stripping of the Altars: Traditional Religion in England c. 1400– c. 1580*, Yale University Press, 1992

Christopher Haigh, *English Reformations*, Oxford University Press, 1993

Alister McGrath, *Reformation Thought: An Introduction*, Blackwell, Revised third edition, 1999

Carter Lindberg, *The European Reformations*, Blackwell, 1995

Carter Lindberg (ed.), *The Reformation Theologians: An Introduction to Theology in the Early Modern Period*, Blackwell, 2001

Diarmaid MacCulloch, *Thomas Cranmer: A Life*, Yale University Press, 1998

Diarmaid MacCulloch, *The Later Reformation in England 1547–1603*, Palgrave, 2000

Diarmaid MacCulloch, *Reformation. Europe's House Divided*, Penguin, 2004 [USA: The Reformation: a History]

Peter Marshall, *Reformation England 1480–1642*, London, 2003

S. Ozment, *The Age of Reform 1250–1550*, Yale University Press, 1980

Graham Tomlin, *Luther and his World*, Lion, 2002

Part III: New Worlds

A. Anderson, *An introduction to Pentecostalism: global charismatic Christianity*, Cambridge University Press, 2004

Nicholas Atkin and Frank Tallett. *Priests, Prelates and People: A History of European Catholicism since 1750*. Oxford University Press, 2003

D. W. Bebbington, *Evangelicalism in Modern Britain*, Routledge, 1993

Callum Brown, *The Death of Christian Britain: Understanding Secularisation 1800–2000,* Routledge, 2001

O. Chadwick, *The Victorian Church*, 2 vols, SCM, 1966, 1971

Harvey Cox, *Fire from Heaven: The Rise of Pentecostal Spirituality and the Reshaping of Religion in the Twenty-First Century,* Da Capo Press, 1996

Adrian Hastings, *A History of English Christianity 1920–2000*, SCM, third edition, 2001

David Hempton, *Methodism: Empire of the Spirit*, Yale University Press, 2005

Philip Kennedy, *A modern introduction to Theology: new questions for old beliefs*, IB Tauris, 2006

Mark Noll, *A History of Christianity in the United States and Canada*, Eerdmans, 1992

Henry Rack, *Reasonable Enthusiast: John Wesley and the Rise of Methodism*, Epworth, third edition 2002

B. M. G. Reardon, *Religious Thought in the Victorian Age*, Longman, 1980

Barrie Tabraham, *The Making of Methodism*, Epworth, second revised edition, 2006

John Munsey Turner, *John Wesley and the Evangelical Revival*, Epworth, 2002

B. Sundkler and C. Steed, *A History of the Church in Africa*, Cambridge University Press, 2002

G. Wacker, *Heaven below: early Pentecostals and American culture,* Harvard University Press, 2001

B. G. Worrall, *The Making of the Modern Church*, SPCK, 1988

Index

All dates given are AD unless otherwise stated. Dignitaries such as kings and bishops are indexed by their personal name alphabetically through the index, with cross-references from the source of their dignities. The only exceptions, which are grouped together under their dignity without cross-reference, are Popes, Roman Emperors and Roman Empresses. For these three groups, dates are given in the form: date of birth; regnal dates. For all other people, dates of birth and death only are given. For further regnal dates, readers should consult *The Oxford Dictionary of the Christian Church* and the *Dictionary of National Biography*. Occasionally a date may occur in other references in order to clarify which event they refer to: e.g. Lateran Council II (1139).

Seleucia, Council of, 86
Seleucid Empire, 34, 41; Kings, *see* Antiochus III and IV
Semi-Arians, 92
Seminaries, 195
Senate, Roman, 28–9, 32
Separatists, 208, 210, 213
Septuagint, 32, 35–6, 49–50, 68; *see also* Bible; Hebrew Scriptures
Servetus, Michael (1511–53), 162, 175–6
Sexuality, 66, 108, 112, 128, 266, 280, 287; *see also* contraception; homosexuality; marriage
Seymour, Edward, Duke of Somerset (?1506–52), 178
Sicily, 18, 111
Simeon, kinsman of the Lord (first century), 39
Simeon Stylites (*c*.390–459), 86, 101
Simeon, Charles (1759–1836), 218, 230
Singapore, 238
Sinope, 48
Slavery, 20, 44, 186, 218, 230–1, 291
Smyrna, 61, 72
Socialism, 238, 254–5, 269, 275
Society of Jesus, *see* Jesuit Order
Society for the Propagation of the Gospel, 227
Sociology, 296
Socrates (*c*.469–399 BC), 14, 18, 23
Söderblom, Nathan, Archbishop of Uppsala (1866–1931), 283
Solon of Athens (early sixth century BC), 14, 20
Somerset, Duke of, *see* Seymour
Sophocles (*c*.496–406/5 BC), 14, 25
South Africa, 247
South America, 184–6, 199, 243, 288
South India, Church of, 276, 284–5
Southern, Richard (1912–), 120, 130
Spain, 76, 97, 114, 117, 122, 124, 130, 182–8, 203, 205, 276; church in, 164, 192, 288; Kings of, *see* Ferdinand V; Philip II; overseas empire 182–8, 196, 198–200, 212, 243, 245; Queens of, *see* Isabella
Spanish Succession, War of, 200, 204
Sparta, 20, 22
Spener, Philipp Jakob (1635–1705), 218, 232–3
Speyer, Diet of, 169
Spiritual Franciscans, 124, 140, 144, 148, 150, 152
Spiritualism, 261; *see also* Séances
Sri Lanka (Ceylon), 246

States General in France, 238, 249–50
Stefan Bathory, King of Poland (1532–86), 182, 194
Stockholm, 276
Stoicism, 60, 80
Strasbourg, 174, 218, 232
Strauss, David Friedrich (1808–74), 256, 264–5
Subordinationism, 69
Sudan, 244
Suetonius Tranquillus (*c*.70–), 74
Sulpicius Severus (*c*. 360–*c*.420), 102
Summa Theologiae, 124, 142
Sun-worship, 79, 88–9, 98
Switzerland, 172–6, 180, 289
Syllabus of Errors, 256, 268
Syria, 52, 84, 94–5, 101

Tacitus, Cornelius (*c*.55–120), 30
Tatian (*c*.160), 42, 50
Templars (Knights Templar), 131
Temple, Frederick, Archbishop of Canterbury (1821–1902), 256, 263
Temple, William, Archbishop of Canterbury (1881–1944), 283
Tertullian (*c*.160–*c*.225), 42, 57, 59, 62–3, 295
Tetrarchy, 87, 89
Tetzel, Johann (*c*.1465–1519), 162, 167–8
Teutonic Order, 124, 132
Thales of Miletos (early sixth century BC), 14, 23
Theatre, 21
Theodoric the Ostrogoth (*c*.455–526), 104, 114
Theodotus (second century), 42, 64
Theosophy, 263
Theotokos, 94
Thessalonica, 97
Third World, 247, 290–1, 293, 295, 296
Thirty Years War, 200–4, 212, 223
Thomas Aquinas (*c*.1225–74), 124, 141–2, 144, 150–1, 234, 260
Thomas Becket (1118?–70), 133
Thomas à Kempis (*c*.1380–1471), 144, 159
Thomism, 142, 154
Thucydides (late fifth century BC), 6, 22–3, 25
Tillich, Paul (1886–1965), 276, 290
Tiridates III, King of Armenia (238–314), 84
Tithe, 130
Tokugawa family, 182, 198
Toledo, Archbishop of, *see* Ximenes